The Road To Ruin, And Back

by
Steven Garvey

Foreword

Road Transport, whatever guise or box you may put it into, be it haulage, traction, distribution or the "modern" concept, logistics, is I'd say, not recognised for what it really is. To put it plainly, without any of the above you would not have anything. Everything goes by road at some point or another. "put everything back on the railways" is a popular cry, so is "reopen the canals and send goods that way", but those options, whilst paving the way for industry in the old days, are just not viable in todays fast moving societies. You must consider that the railways, whilst under construction, were supplied with all of the paraphernalia required, and it was all brought by horse and cart before the inception of lorries in most of the cases.

Goods taken by rail used to sit in railway sidings before being shunted to where they could be unloaded, usually, ironically, onto lorries for distribution !. The canals, however many there may be, are remote from many areas and canal travel is far too slow to cope with the demands of the "just in time" deliveries that many supermarket and distribution centres run nowadays. Even then from the canal basins and wharves the goods would still have to be transported once again by road, unless the factories and distribution centres were right there on the canal-side.

The average person I am saddened to say, does not like lorries. To them they are a hinderance, slow moving lumps, holding car and light van drivers up on their journeys. Some people are frightened by their size, scared to pass them on motorways and the like. What is unavoidably obvious, if people would just think about it, is that they and the drivers who are negotiating the roads of Britain, kept away from their families and homes by a trade that demands that they sleep in their lorries for a few nights, all the working week, or even weeks on end, do keep us all moving and supplied.

During the daytime and at night whilst people sleep, in all weathers, goods are being transported all over the UK which will find their way onto breakfast tables, stock the shelves of chemist shops, supermarkets, paper shops, engineering companies, power stations, pubs and hotels, as well as the parcel someone ordered the previous evening for next day delivery, and in fact, all the different types of things we need to lead our normal lives.

I myself, over the years, have carried many and various types of cargo. From small tins of peas, carrots, beans and all forms of canned foods and drinks, I've delivered jams, Christmas puddings, cake mixes, in fact any foodstuffs and soft drinks that can be found on the shelves of supermarkets and shops. I've carried beers, wines and spirits too. I have collected and delivered farm vehicles, tractors and the like, and plant, such as a twenty ton bulldozer.

I've delivered stone, slate, sand, cement, bricks and blocks, factory machinery, all white goods such as washing machines etc., clothing and nappies, ships engines, flooring and roofing supplies. Timber, Christmas trees, steel (coils, plate, tubes, girders, pilings, scaffolding and ingots) have all been carried on vehicles driven by myself. Sea containers too (twenty, thirty, and forty feet long)

I have delivered bales of cloth, wool and rubber. I've hauled racehorse fences and marquee equipment, garden fences and sheds. I also, along with a "second man" (mate) have delivered high loads, wide loads and long loads. I've hauled portakabins, army, navy and air force supply equipment, trailers, jet skis, full sized go karts, cars, vans. Full loads of empty glass and plastic jars and bottles. Paints, lacquers and varnishes have all been on vehicles I've driven.

I've transported newsprint, reams and sheafs of paper and paper pulp. After training, I've carried hazardous chemicals and gasses, drums of oil, fridge goods and almost everything else you can think of, barring petrol and livestock. A general haulage driver, or at least most of them, will carry everything imaginable that will fit (or almost fit) onto their vehicle, it's more varied than most people could ever imagine.

This collection of stories I've compiled is my way of trying to highlight the ups and downs of driving lorries, starting from my life as a child and then as a sort of transport industry apprentice in my youth until my time as an HGV articulated lorry driver, and up until my retirement. As I'll explain later, the lorry drivers are often treated in Great Britain very badly, they are also treated kindly by some others which will also be covered in this book. All long distance lorry drivers have stories to tell, good, funny and bad. All of them with families, have to contend with, most of the time, not being with their wives and children on their birthdays, the anniversaries, bonfire and halloween nights and of course their own birthday. I was not present when my Dad passed away, which will be talked about later in this book.

Without sounding condescending, you have to be a special breed of person to be a long distance lorry driver, it has to be in your blood. It can be a very lonely occupation where you're left to your own devices, where you, and you alone have to think on your feet and act in accordance with the situation at hand. It requires total concentration to do the job safely, driving for long periods at a time on busy motorways and roads. It's definitely not "sat on your arse all day doing nothing". It involves early starts, late finishes and long hours in all kinds of weather, all a part of the job of a long distance lorry driver.

I have been honest in my recollections although I may not have been able to the remember all of the peoples names or the exact times in the stories, or the exact wording that people have used, it is however the way I remember it all.

Introduction.

My name is Steven Garvey, I was born in Liverpool on a snowy winters morning in December 1953. From being as young as I can remember I always had a love of lorries. My Dad, along with many other jobs he had undertaken, drove one when I was just about old enough to know what they were.

Whilst we were still living in Liverpool I can remember that on occasions he would take me with him if he was going somewhere local. On one trip, and I must have only been around six years old, he took me with him to Preston docks, when we got there he told me not to get out of the cab and to stay seated and not move around in the cab, he promised me that he would buy me a toy if I did as I was told. That was music to my ears but I still sat there scared stiff whilst the lorry was being loaded with bales of cloth. These bales were big and heavy and were lowered onto the lorry by a crane with a hoist and when they landed on the deck of it they did so with a thud and rocked the whole vehicle quite violently, it was a dangerous job for my Dad, he had to keep an eye on the bales that were being lowered as it was known for them to come adrift from their "grabs" (sharp pointed lengths of steel that gripped the bales on either side) and drop. If one of those bales landed on you it would cause serious injury or even death.

All I can remember is every so often the cab I was sat in would shudder and rock from side to side which frankly put the fear of God into me, but I sat in my seat with the thought of a toy as a "thanks for doing what you're told" in my mind. My Dad was true to his word and after he'd loaded, on the way back to Liverpool, he stopped and bought me a Dinky fork lift truck which actually worked, when you turned a little handle the forks went up and down, I was made up !

One other lorry incident in Liverpool I vaguely recall was when my Dad came home for his lunch one day, I must have been very young but I remember climbing onto the back of his lorry and from there I opened his cab door and clambered in. I sat in the drivers seat and pretended to drive, pulling the steering wheel left and right as if I was steering. The lorry my Dad drove at that time had a ratchet hand brake near the door which you pulled up several times to set the brakes, There was a little

1

button and release handle you pressed in to release them which I must have knocked whilst I was "driving Daddies lorry". The street we lived on had a very slight incline and yes..... as you may have already guessed, the lorry began rolling, ever so slowly but... it was rolling, I was having a great time ! I was driving ! Now there was no way I could reach the pedals so I couldn't have stopped it that way, and I didn't understand about the handbrake, so as the lorry picked up a little speed I began to panic. The next thing I recall was the drivers door being thrown open and my Dad running alongside trying to get in, he must have thought better of that idea and he began yanking at the handbrake ratcheting it up and down, that worked as it wasn't moving very fast and the lorry stopped. I did not get a toy that day ! I got a clip round the ear and sent to my room for a few hours. I suppose my Dad must have thought I needed some sort of punishment even though I was too young to realise what could have happened. The next time I saw him he sat me on his knee and apologised and gave me a lecture about doing things without his permission. I still don't know (or remember if he'd told me) how he knew the lorry had moved away from our front door but I'm certainly grateful that he did !

I suppose from that day I was destined to drive lorries and that hunger to do so never left me. We stayed in Liverpool until I was around eight and a half, it was around then that my parents bought a fruit and veg shop on Hyde Road in Gorton Manchester, and we all (Mum, Dad and my two younger siblings at that time, Anne and Peter) moved there. Hyde Road was and still is a very busy trunk road out of Manchester, it is part of the A57 which runs in its entirety from Liverpool to Lincoln. The shop was on the Manchester bound side of the road and the opposite lane went towards Sheffield. I recall many hauliers who operated tipper lorries which passed our shop regularly to and from Yorkshire carrying coal. There was a Belisha beacon zebra crossing just offset from our shop window and one wet day I remember being in the shop bothering my Mum for an apple or something when somebody must have stepped onto the crossing and all I remember is the screech of brakes as a tipper lorry heading towards Sheffield hurtled whilst skidding towards our shop window, it mounted the kerb but stopped just short of our window, I reckon my Mum may have needed clean underwear after that episode and I was pretty shaken up too.

I used to go to my parents bedroom at the front of the premises and look down onto Hyde Road and watch with glee the lorries trundling up and down the highway, I was only eight and a half but I could tell you all the makes of them, ERF, Foden, AEC, Scammell, Atkinson, Commer, Bedford, Seddon, Dennis, Guy, Dodge, Leyland and many more. I would draw pictures of lorries on any bit of paper I could. I did a painting at my secondary school when in my first year of an artic' negotiating a tight turn in a town setting that was put on display in the the art classroom (I never did get that painting back !) Lorries, even then, were a passion for me. The shop didn't work out for reasons unknown to me and we sold up and moved a couple of miles away to a big three storey house in Levenshulme.

Dad had told us we were going back to Liverpool and at first I kicked off and sulked because we hadn't. I was asked to go and look out of what would be my bedroom which was in the attic, its windows were at the back of the house, it looked out onto a haulage yard right behind us. I was in my element, watching the comings and goings of their lorries I knew in my mind that I wanted to, and would, drive a lorry someday, little did I know of the many joys and the heartaches that would happen to me on my chosen path.

Chapter One.

The nutter, the thief and a fair cop' ?

I did not get on well at secondary school, I didn't like it and it didn't like me. I'd passed my eleven plus but failed grammar school level, the next levels were technical and then secondary modern, I fell into the technical school level. I attended Ardwick Technical High School, the first year was ok and I was streamed into an "A" class. It went down hill from there, my favourite subjects being art, geography and English language and literature. I was good at those but I just couldn't grasp the methods in maths and science that they tried to teach me. I could get to the answers my own "round the houses" way but was always marked down for doing so. I started skipping lessons, out of frustration, with my school friend Eric. We'd wander round Manchester city centre, dodging police officers and anyone who we thought might be a corporation "wag" (truant) officer, occasionally though we would go to a cafe in Levenshulme and ask a guy who was the uncle of one of our friends if we could spend the day with him in his tipper lorry. He used to collect Derbyshire stone from the quarries around Buxton and deliver it to sites around the Manchester area. He drove a Dodge ten ton rigid and we used to love travelling around with him. In the end I was off school more than I was in it, so it was no surprise that when I found a job and asked if I could leave school early, they were probably glad to see the back end of me, and happily for them, and me, they let me go.

My first job was for Express Dairies who were based at Lloyd Road in Levenshulme. I started as a shop lad (the drivers called us "nippers") and my job was to go with a driver delivering milk and all the paraphernalia that milkmen sold to shops rather than households. I was happy with this job as it involved lorries. We used to start early in the mornings at 05.00 and usually finish around 13.00.

We had a Commer Karrier Bantam unit which towed a thirty foot semi low step down trailer. The sides and rear of the trailer had lengths of chain which were there as some sort of load securing, in my opinion they were useless. There was an axle with small twin wheels about four foot from the rear of the trailer.

4

I remember one winters morning a relief driver who had a reputation as a bit of a "head case" took me out (my regular driver was off on holiday) he turned up at the dairy with his pet Alsatian dog which he put in the cab and told me to sit on the back for the day. I was young and fit and didn't particularly like the idea of sharing the cab with a big dog so I wasn't bothered about doing it.

As the day progressed we had shifted nearly all of the full milk crates and replaced them with empty bottle crates, as normal, we had started stacking from the rear of the trailer, they were about a foot from the roof with the front two rows stepped down lower and reaching about two thirds of the way towards the step, we were coming to the last shop on our round and I recall this driver going rather faster than he should have. I was sat on the step facing the empties, I don't know what he was playing at but he drove at speed almost to the shop and then slammed on his brakes. All I remember is looking up and seeing this wall of crates containing empty bottles as if in slow motion tipping down towards me, I covered my head with my hands and curled up as best I could as the crates and their empty bottles fell onto and around me. Many of them fell off onto the street and the pavement, all I could hear was smashing glass.

After it had all stopped I pushed away the crates around me and clambered backwards onto the swan neck where there was a small plastic window which gave a view through to the small rear window on the unit, I could see the driver writing in his delivery book, he finished writing and got out of the cab, as cool as you like he said "did something fall off ?" I was astounded. Luckily I didn't have any cuts but I was bruised. People on the street came out as did the shopkeeper, presumably to check if we were alright and that his delivery was intact, which it was, so we took his order in and he lent us two brushes, the driver then said "I suppose we'd better clean it all up".

It took us a long time and there was more broken glass than unbroken, It took an age to do it and we didn't finish 'till 14.30 that day. I don't know what the driver said to the bosses back at the dairy but nothing more was said to me about the incident. After that I asked the dairy supervisor not to put me with him, other lads would swap with me, well a change is as good as a rest !

On another occasion I was out with my usual driver Sid, we were about half way through the delivery round. It was a hot summers day and I was in the cab with the driver but we had another new lad with us whom we were "showing the ropes" of the job to, he was on the trailer which he didn't mind as it was summer and it was hot. When we reached a certain shop in Moss Side, Sid told me I was to help him take what was a fairly large order into the shop, there were differing types of milk and quite a lot of trays of plain yoghurts, he asked the other lad, a burly Scottish one at that, to stay with the lorry out of sight and see if anyone came out of the shop and stole anything off the trailer (he had noticed that goods had gone missing a few times previously whilst we had been in the shop) The lad hid himself behind some crates and waited whilst we went into the shop, we delivered the goods and finished our business and said goodbye, then went back to the lorry.

The Scot was sat on the swan neck lighting up a cigarette, my driver asked him if anything had happened and he told us that after we'd gone into the shop a lad he presumed was the owners son had crept out of the back gate and sidled up to the lorry, he grabbed a tray of yoghurts and was just about to lift it off the the trailer when the Scot leapt out from behind his hiding place and whacked the thief's arm with an empty plastic crate, the thief let go of the case and yelped before running off to the rear of the shop and disappearing.

I burst out laughing and so did the Scot, Sid though, was not too happy about what the lad had done to the thief and told him he had only wanted him to observe. The shop owner didn't come out so his son must have told him what had happened too, they were obviously in the wrong so they just left it. When we got back into the cab the Scottish lad stayed on the trailer and Sid set off with a big satisfied smile on his face although he didn't say anything. We never had anything go missing from there after that !

Life at the dairy was good for me, for my age, it was a fairly good paying job. It was only five days a week as all the shops we delivered to doubled up on a Friday to cope with weekend demand, you have to remember that a lot of shops in those days closed on a Sunday, supermarkets were just about rearing their ugly heads above the horizon, which, once they became prevalent, would bring seven day shopping to the public. The hours

6

were suitable to me as well, although only a youth, I could get up early and be there on time, although there were a few times hen Sid had to cover for me in the mornings at the dairy whilst loading the lorry on his own because I'd overslept. They were rare though, in the main I was reliable and got there even though I may have been a bit hazy or half asleep for the early part of the morning.

There was one occasion in the summertime when I'd finished work, I went in the works canteen and had some chips and gravy, then gone home and taken myself to bed at around 15.00. I remember waking up and seeing my little old fashioned alarm clock (which wasn't digital) which showed the time to be 4.45 I jumped out of bed, threw on my clothes and work coat, flew down the stairs and out of the house and was half way down Cromwell Grove where we lived, before I realised there was a lot of traffic about for that time of the morning, which of course was wrong ! It was 16.45 ! I'd woken up and thought I was going to be late for work, which of course, I wasn't. I believe this happened to many of the workforce in the dairy at one time or another. The joys of early starts !

I remember one lovely warm summers morning, I was walking along Stockport Road to work which was just under a mile away. I had on my Express Dairy uniform, which was a three quarter length long sleeved coat. It was blue and made of a light denim type of material, there was the Express Dairy Logo on the front top pocket.

I was ambling up the road when I heard a car engine behind me, it was 04.40 and in those times there wasn't much traffic about at that time of the day. It was a police "panda" car (where the panda nickname name came from I don't know) anyway he slowed right down and kind of kerb crawled a few yards behind me as I walked along. Suddenly he revved up, put on his blue flashing light and speeded up to just in front of me, he jumped out of the car and shouted for me to stop and stay where I was, which I immediately did. He came over to me and said "what are you up to at this time of the morning ?" I replied that I was on my way to work. "Work ? Who starts work this early ?" He said. I replied that I worked at Express Dairies and pointed to the logo on my overall. He was a young bobby and looking back he had probably not been doing the job for very long. He said "anybody can get hold of a coat like that, we've had reports of somebody robbing premises in this area, have you got anything on you ?" At this point he walked closer to me and told me to assume the search position, I had nothing on me but a packet of fags, a book of matches and a few bob with which to buy my breakfast with. He searched me thoroughly, even patting down my legs and then said with no apology "well it's obviously not you, get on your way" he walked off to his car and drove off.

I continued on, a little shaken by the whole episode. There was a garage forecourt just before Lloyd Road and as I passed it I spotted the panda car parked, partially hidden behind another car, I continued on my way and turned left into Lloyd Road where the dairy was about a hundred yards up it on the right. As I turned to cross the road to go into the yard I looked to my right to see the car, plus bobby, observing me entering the premises. I understand the police have a very difficult job to do, and they have to deal with some dead legs but I think his attitude was totally uncalled for, I can only assume that he must have thought I had a dishonest face !!

I enjoyed my time at the dairy, for my age I was paid quite well and I was out in the elements, be it cold, rainy or sunny. Whatever the weather we always made the deliveries to the shops with very few problems and my job involved transporting goods, which is what I'd always wanted to do.

Chapter Two.

Living, working, loving, you never stop learning.

Whilst working at the dairy I had several mates who did too, one of them, Alan, had aspirations similar to me and had always wanted to drive articulated lorries, so one day after work he asked me did I know the whereabouts of Geoffrey Reyner Transport which was in Droylsden. I did know, because before I ever had a job I used to buy all day bus tickets at the weekends and plan a route which took in haulage companies. I'd cover a certain area at a time with the aid of a telephone book from which I would glean all the addresses of the companies I wanted to visit, I then, with the aid of an A to Z map book, would go and see all these depots around Manchester when most of the fleets were parked up at weekends.

I know that seems a bit geeky but I was obsessed with all things concerning lorries and road transport. Anyway one day we both went off to Reyner's on our time off from the dairy as Alan had got a job interview to be a yard lad there. I remember getting off the bus and walking towards the depot and we both saw this lad, he was weighing us up intently, he had very short hair for the time and he had a parka coat on which was full of lorry related badges (I too began collecting them and wish I still had them now !) He said to us suspiciously "what do you two want ?" Alan replied that he was there for an interview and the lad told us it would be with the yard foreman George, he pointed the way to Georges office, we thanked him and made our way to the warehouse office. The lads name we later found out was John, and I've some tales centred around him to share with you later.

The upshot of the story is Alan got the job. I too asked if there were any openings for me and George replied that one of the yard lads was taking his HGV test in a couple of weeks and that if he passed it then there would be a job for me too. It was only about three weeks later that Alan got in touch and told me to go and see George, and after doing so I put my notice in at the dairy and started there as a yard lad a week later.

The job involved the loading and unloading of lorries, or transhipping as we called it. I learned very quickly how to drive and safely use a fork lift truck under Georges expert guidance. He had been a lorry driver and was one of Reyners earliest members of staff. He had vast experience of all things related to the job including handling hormonal teenagers !

Through George I learnt the correct way to load, sheet and rope a vehicle, which I may have driven, once again under his watchful eye, to the warehouse from another part of the depot. Although he was the main tutor to us yard lads (there were four of us) others chipped in too, there was Bill who was at one time a night trunk driver and had become the deputy under George. Some of the drivers helped us learn too, those who were not always in a hurry to get away, but would spend time with us putting things right when we'd not done it to their standard. I look back and am so appreciative of their attention and I tip my hat to them all.

I did around eighteen months as a yard lad. Near the end of my time there I could be trusted to go as passenger in an artic' with a driver to Robertsons Jam works in Droylsden, he'd drop the trailer and leave me there whilst the trailer got loaded and I'd sheet, rope and fly sheet it. The driver would then return and drop another empty trailer, pick up the loaded one and take it away leaving me to do the same procedure with it. This could happen three or four times in a day and I'd go back with the last driver with the final load. I never had any complaints about how the trailer had been loaded or sheeted from any of the drivers who collected the loaded trailers which were to be taken to de-livery points all over the UK.

There were several occasions when I would be picked up by a driver and we'd go to a fertiliser factory at Burscough Bridge in Lancashire. The driver had loaded twenty tons of one hun-dredweight bags of raw fertiliser the previous day at Maldon in Essex and this factory in Burscough Bridge would process the raw stuff into small pellets and re-bag it. We'd arrive there around 09.00 and begin to handball the load off, once empty we'd have a tea break and then reload with some processed pel-leted one hundredweight bags, so it worked out that the driver and myself had handled twenty tons each. Once loaded we would sheet and rope the load then that particular driver would go and leave me there until another of our lorries turned up and we would then repeat the process once again. This meant that when we had finished I had personally handled forty tons in total. I would then go back with the driver to be dropped off at home, or if it was early enough, back to the yard. I remember that I used to stink to high heaven, as you can imagine fertilizer isn't quite what you would call a pleasant smell, my Mum used to make me go straight into the bath when I got home, I can't understand why !!

Talking of stinking to high heaven reminded me of when I and my best mate Eric (who was known as Dangle, he had followed me to Reyners after leaving the same dairy where I'd previously been) were sent to one of Reyners warehouses in Openshaw. We were to unload eighteen tons of bagged potash out of twenty foot containers onto pallets for storage in the warehouse. There were an awful lot of containers to unload over many weeks and we were offered five bob (25p) bonus each for every container we unloaded as a sweetener. We relished this and we really worked hard to do as many as possible in a day. On most days we'd unload four containers between 08.00 and 17.00. with a half hour lunch break in between. Don't forget we were only sixteen but we were as fit as fiddles, and £1.00 a day each was a great incentive to graft rather than mess around like a lot of teens would do. We did have our moments though..

One day Dangle and I had finished our chippy lunches and we decided to play a prank on the foreman there, his name was Johnny Travis, a lovely fella who had at one time been a ten ton rigid driver, he always wore what looked like a coal mans hat which was tipped at an angle to one side of his head and he never had a Woodbine cigarette out of his mouth, he'd smoke around sixty a day. Well on this particular lunch time we got a length of rope and whilst he was having a lunch time nap in a small wooden 6'x 4' shed which doubled as his office, we very quietly, whilst crouching down, put the loop end of the rope over the door handle and then fed it round the shed a few times. I then got on the gas fork lift truck. I fitted two fork extensions which we used for oversized pallets and reaching across vehicle beds, then I positioned the truck behind and under the shed, Dangle then passed the remaining length of rope behind the lifting mast of the fork lift a few times and I tied it off with a towing hitch to secure it. Johnny hadn't heard a thing, but he must have had the shock of his life when I began to lift the

11

shed....with poor Johnny inside it, off the ground to about four feet in the air !. He wasn't pleased, "you little bastards ! put me down now, I'm gonna batter the pair of you and I'll sack you both ! fucking put me down !" and all the blasphemies he could muster, but we didn't hear...... we were in stitches laughing.

I eventually put the shed down and we undid the towing hitch and unwound the rope from behind the lifting mast then we kind of shook the ropes to loosen them....from a reasonably safe distance might I add, we then ran away and climbed like chimps onto the pallets of potash bags which were stacked three high where we hid out of sight. Johnny managed to rattle the door enough to fully free himself from the shed and came out to look for us and presumably leather us. He was too long in the tooth to climb up the pallets and we could hear him walking round muttering obscenities and every now and then he'd shout something like "come down you little arseholes, your days are numbered, I'm gonna give you a good hiding when I get my hands on you".

By this time we were getting a little worried that we'd gone too far and we were both pleased when the next container turned up at the door and Johnny had to go and book it in. He shouted "right playtimes over get down here there's work to be done" we looked at each other and though no words were spoken we knew we had to climb down and face the music, we'd had a good laugh and would accept whatever was coming. We gingerly made our way to where Johnny was guiding the driver as he reversed the rear of the container into the warehouse open door. Johnny turned round and saw us stood there like two frightened mice, he walked over and a smile slowly emanated from his mouth and he said quite sternly "don't ever do anything like that again lads, it might have seemed funny to you but it wasn't for me" he kind of gave us both a half hearted kick on the backside each and told us "now get this bloody container unloaded" which we did, but we were still laughing all through the process.

I always had the deepest respect for Johnny after that and remember him dearly.

I also used to go out with drivers as a "mate" or second man as they were known, I'd help manually handball full loads of fruit or veg' off at Manchester and Liverpool wholesale markets and warehouses. There was one driver who used to take me who turned out to be a right lazy bastard, I remember the first time I went with him, we were delivering crates of oranges to this cellar warehouse in the central area of Liverpool.

The driver who's name was Jack E. said, after he'd parked up outside and given his paperwork to the warehouse operatives, "you start taking the ropes and sheets off lad, I'm just going to fill in my log book, I'll be with you in a bit". Well that "bit" lasted 'till I'd unroped and unsheeted the load and wrapped them all up, and... until I had taken every single box of oranges off the forty foot trailer on my own. I remember when I reached the head board looking through the little glass window on the rear of the cab and seeing Jack fast asleep across the engine cowling with his trilby hat across his face.

I did have a moment of fun one day with Jack though, We'd gone to Liverpool fruit market and for some reason I can't recall my mate Alan was also with us, when Jack went to hand in the paperwork I noticed that the twenty ton load of bagged carrots we were delivering had shifted at the back near side end of the trailer and were leaning out about a foot. Jack had noticed it too and he told me and Alan to get on top of the load whilst he gently untied all the ropes. We kneeled down and spread out what little weight we had and gingerly pulled all the ropes over to the off side of the trailer.

Once they were off we once again very carefully pulled the front sheet up onto the top of the load and gently wrapped it up. It was now time to take off the rear sheet, Jack was barking orders at us to stand on the the bags of carrots where the front sheet had been and pull the sheet up very gently towards the front of the trailer, he stood on the floor trying to take the weight of the leaning carrots and as the sheet slowly edged towards the front of the trailer...... yes you've guessed it, the leaning carrots fell off the side of the trailer, and knocking him to the ground in the process, almost covered Jack up.

Alan and I nearly fell off the load we were laughing that much ! All you could see of Jack was his head poking out of a pile of string bagged carrots, his trilby hat was at a very jaunty angle on the top of his head and I can still see his frothing mouth and his bulgy eyes as he was shouting for us to get down to free him and "stop bloody laughing !" We and some of the market guys soon dug him out, he was unharmed and was helped onto a chair and given a cup of tea with only his pride hurt. Alan and I ended up unloading the whole trailer but we would have done that even if he hadn't had his mishap.

It was an enjoyable morning after that and we laughed through most of it.

I also remember one morning when I had to walk to Belle Vue from my home because Jack E. always refused to drive down from there to Levenshulme which was about a mile and a half in distance. Other drivers had no problem with picking me up at home as I lived on the main road connecting Belle Vue and Stockport Road in Levenshulme but Jack wouldn't do it. Anyway this particular morning we were due to go to Liverpool fruit market, he'd arranged to meet me at 05.45 which meant I had to walk to Belle Vue as the buses didn't run that early. I remember it was cold and raining quite heavily on a dark winters morning. I left home at about 04.45 to give myself plenty of time to walk it.

I arrived at the pick up point at Belle Vue in a milk float which was on its way to begin its rounds in West Gorton. The milkman had picked me up about quarter of a mile from Belle Vue, he had took pity on me traipsing up a very rainy Mount Road with my thumb out, hoping to cadge a lift. As I got out at Belle Vue he told me it was 05.25. I was soaked to the skin. I only had my two piece overall set of jacket and trousers on. I sought out a doorway to shelter in and waited for Jack, who was known to be late on many occasions.

I waited there, popping out to the roadside every now and then looking for the lorry coming down the road but there was no sign of Jack. After quite a while I asked a passing postman what time it was, he told me it was 06.35. I'd been there over an hour. I gave it ten more minutes in case I'd got the pick up time wrong and at around 06.45 I walked down the road to the bus terminus at Belle Vue greyhound dog track and got on a bus (which were by now running) home.

My Mum was up when I walked into the house and she went berserk when she heard what had happened. I got undressed and went and had a bath. Mum dried my clothes out by the fire and told me that I wasn't to go to work that day and that I should phone the yard and explain what had occurred.

14

I rang George my foreman at 09.00 and I asked what had happened to Jack, he replied that Jack.. bless him…. had rung Reyners when he got to Liverpool and told them I hadn't turned up at the pick up point ! I told George chapter and verse what had actually happened, I was fuming, the lazy lying bastard had actually blamed me. I informed George that I didn't intend on coming into work that day or maybe ever again at which point George calmed me down, he said that he believed me and asked me to come into work after lunch time, which I did. I got paid for the day with overtime for the early start and I informed George and the traffic office that I never wanted to second mate Jack again.

He had obviously been late that morning and he'd gone straight to Liverpool without me to save some time. The slime ball wouldn't look me in the eye after that and I heard he told other drivers that I was a lazy little c… Well they and I knew who was the lazy one out of the two us, and it wasn't me !

I've had many pranks pulled on me whilst working in the yard in Droylsden. One particular day I had to visit the toilet for a "sit down" for want of a better phrase. The toilets were at the rear of the main office building near the canteen, you had to pass the garage and the vehicle wash to get there.

I was sat on the toilet contemplating the way of the world when all of a sudden I was showered with a bucket load of filthy water from the gullies of the vehicle wash, which was launched over the top of the toilet door, all I heard was a maniacal laugh and somebody making a quick exit. I was absolutely soaked but I knew instinctively who was the perpetrator. Do you recall I mentioned a lad named John, the one who had shown my mate Alan and myself the way to Georges office, well it was him, I'll call him John S. I finished what I'd gone in to do and exited the toilet to find an audience who had been prepped by John S on what had happened.

I scanned the laughing crowd but he was nowhere to be seen, then I heard the same manic laugh and looked up to see him running along the top of the garage roof waving his hands like a monkey.

He was always up to tricks like that, you had to have eyes in the back of your head when he was around. I remember him once tying one of the lads bike to the warehouse roof beams, he and the bike had been raised on a pallet by someone on a fork-lift up to the beam, he then he roped the bike to the beam, the pallet was then lowered with John S on it.

When the owner of the bike who we called "peachy" came to collect it from the warehouse at lunchtime, that is what he was greeted with. He went bonkers, asking everyone who'd done it, although there was really only one person who would do stunts like that, John S. He wasn't there when"peachy" was asking who was responsible, however after a few minutes John S did turn up, and after being threatened with being reported to management, he laughingly apologised and offered to lift him up to retrieve the said bike. You can guess what happened next… John S did lift him up on a pallet, again with the aid of the forklift truck, and then once at roof beam height he switched off the engine and left the poor lad up there stranded on the pallet in mid air ! He was up there for about 10 minutes, which must have felt like an eternity to the lad before George and Bill came in and lowered him down. John S got a half hearted roasting off George for that episode.

As I mentioned earlier, the vehicle wash was near the canteen and one day a fella named Ray was in the canteen having a brew. John S walked in and asked Ray if he wanted half a sandwich which he hadn't found tasty enough for himself. Ray was a big eater and eagerly replied "yeah if you don't want it, thanks". John S handed him a white plastic bag with one of those prepacked triangular sandwich boxes with half a butty in it. Ray had a quick look and proceeded to devour it.

John S waited 'till Ray had eaten half of it before bursting out laughing. It transpired that the sandwich had been discarded and left on the floor of the wash by the garage wall three days earlier by somebody. John S had noticed it on the first day but left it there until he saw Ray going into the canteen, so he picked it up and cleaned up the white plastic bag a little before offering it to Ray. He did take it in good humour though and he also ate the whole of the butty. As I said, he was a right handful John S. and although I was to be on the receiving end of many of his pranks we grew up to remain good friends.

Another character at Reyners was a guy named Ralph Toone, or "Pop" as he was known. He was the near retirement father of another lad who worked there named Brian, more about him later. Pop drove a ten ton Seddon rigid. He was quite a heavy smoker and was known for cadging cigarettes. When I was working in the yard, he'd sometimes come to the warehouse to do some transhipping and he'd always say something like "lend us a fag son" which I would if I had any, knowing I wouldn't get it back, but that was how it was with Pop. He'd take the ciggie and leave me to load (and usually sheet and rope) it for him whilst he went and sat in the office chewing the fat with the yard foreman. None of the yard lads minded helping him in that way as he was always very grateful when someone did.

I once went as a second man with a bloke named Joe B. he and Pop both had wide loads which were for delivery to Southampton docks. I remember on the return journey home on a Saturday when I ended up coming back with Pop for some reason. We had pulled into Keele services on the M6 for a brew and something to eat and also because he wanted to find me a lift into Manchester with some other driver.

He lived at Knutsford, so didn't want to travel into and then out of Manchester which is around nineteen miles each way after dropping me off in order to get back to Knutsford. We were in the drivers cafe which at the time was upstairs in the building which straddled over the motorway, linking both sides of the services. I got myself sausages on toast and Pop followed me very closely but didn't get any food. We ordered a mug of tea each and sat down. Pop then pulled two stolen cooked sausages from his greatcoat pocket (which he nearly always wore when it was chilly or wet). He then proceeded to de-fluff them saying "I'm not paying the prices they charge here son" he then scoffed them.

He cadged a fag from a driver he vaguely knew, then asked a Reliance Tanker driver, who was going into Trafford Park, if he could give me a lift to the bus terminus at Southern Cemetery, where I could then get a bus home. The driver said that would be OK, so after finishing our drinks we went our separate ways.

I suppose a lot of people reading this may think he was a bit of a liberty taker but he wasn't, it's how he was, he could be very persuasive yet charming, I thought the world of him and always gave him the respect he (as far as I'm concerned) deserved.

When Pops retirement date was looming all the lads and staff at Reyners had a collection for him. With the proceeds, the

17

guy who organised it all, bought him, on behalf of everybody, a really expensive clock, not very imaginative I know, he also organised a lads only leaving party in Droylsden which Pop attended. There were a lot of drivers, office, garage and yard staff who turned up for that party and when the clock had been given to him, one of the organisers also gave him a plastic bag. Unbeknown to Pop, with what money was left after buying the clock, they'd bought him 200 cigarettes. He took the bag and peered inside, he had a rummage around it and then said "thank you all" there was a slight pause before he added "you could have bought me some fucking matches as well you tight bastards !" The place erupted in laughter, the cigarette cadger had us all in stitches. When we all quietened down, Pop gave what was a humorous and yet moving speech. That night was the last time I ever saw him, but I'll never forget him.

Sea shipping containers (or "boxes"as they are commonly known) for storage and refurbishment purposes is a lucrative business, and Reyners were one of the companies who realised this in it's earlier days. They had a lot of land in the Droylsden depot which surrounded Royal Mill, an old cotton mill, which Reyners owned, but leased out to a toy manufacturing company. They used what was known as the "back yard" to park their empty trailers, in order to make space they moved them to another part of the yard, and the back yard was then where the first of many empty containers were put for storage.

They used a medium sized forklift with extended forks to lift them off the lorries, which in itself, was quite precarious, as the right balance had to be found on the forty foot boxes which did not all have designated slots for the forks, although these were prevalent on most twenty foot boxes. The ground was also very rough with potholes and ridges and I witnessed a few containers sliding off the forks due to this.

A decision was quickly made to construct a frame which would sit over the top of the forty footers, it was securely fastened to the lifting mast of the forklift and had twist locks on each corner of the frame to fit into and lock onto the boxes top lifting lugs. This was all well and good, but as it was to be constructed by Reyners engineers it did not have any hydraulics to turn the twist locks. This is where we, the yard lads, got involved, and you must understand there was nothing like health and safety enforcement in those days.

I can remember being given a hammer and then climbing a ladder up to the roof of the box as it sat on a lorry with the lifting frame in place on top of it. I would then go to each of the four corner lugs and hammer the twist locks into their locking position. I'd then descend the ladder after which the container was lifted off the lorry and put into its position once it had been checked over. I'd then go back up the ladder and reverse the operation so the frame could be lifted clear and be moved away.

As time went on the climbing up and down the ladder took up too much time, so we yard lads made the rash decision to sit on the frame as it was lifted up and put into place on the container roof, we'd then hammer all the twist locks into position and then sit down between the framing on top of the box whilst it was lifted off the lorry, lowered to the floor for checking and then taken to where it was to be stored. Now this could have been at floor level or on top of another container.

The containers come in two heights, the most common being eight feet six inches, there is also a less common nine feet six inches which were classed as over-height. As stated, if the box was stacked on top of another it meant being lifted up to a height of around twenty feet. Remember how I told you the ground was rough ? Well that caused a lot of swaying as the forty foot box lurched in and over pot holes.

I used to be on the top of this mass of swaying metal, clinging on for dear life as it was moved either off the lorry or into position for stacking, which at that time was two high. I was still there as the frame was lifted to around twenty feet in the air before it was moved forward, usually swaying quite precariously, into position for lowering onto the box below it, and it usually took a few shunts and adjustments to get it perfect, which it had to be for stability, only then could I let go of my steel like grip on the frame to get up and undo the twist locks with the hammer. I would then sit on the frame whilst it was raised and reversed away from the stack, still swaying and lurching, before being lowered to the floor.

This practice was done in all weathers by the way, rain, snow and wind. Obviously this was not a safe practice and the powers that be quickly realised it, so another frame was quickly constructed, which was again securely fastened to the lifting frame on the forklift, only this one was made to fit into the top and bottom lugs on one side of the box, which meant that it was lifted from one side or the other of the box, not from the top and it involved no twist locking as the frame had a hook on each corner which when lifted, hooked in behind the lugs, enabling a safe lift. It also cut out the need for me to take a spare pair of undies to work with me when I was on container duty !!.... (I didn't really !!)

This also meant that we yard lads didn't have to go on top of the boxes anymore. There wasn't a problem with the twenty foot boxes as they had fork lift slots. The storage business picked up and the back yard was soon full with stacks of boxes three high, so after some restructuring, they moved all of the trailer parking to other areas in the yard, which gave Reyners even more space to store them. They then began to store them in an area of the main yard too.

The container people in charge had learnt the lesson of rough ground handling, so they scraped the area flat before laying concrete sections over it, making the whole operation a safer and more stable one. After many years, and with the purchase of a large, built for purpose container lifting stacker truck, and a fully functioning workshop in which to carry out any repairs the boxes may have required, the business boomed so much so that they opened another extra yard for storing them, and they remained a profitable line of business for the Reyner company until it moved from Droylsden in 2005.

Each yard lad took turns at going on handball loads or being a "second man" on wide, high or long loads, or all of them together sometimes. My first wide load experience was with a guy called Bert Wilson. I'd only been at Reyner's about a week when George said to me one Wednesday afternoon "Scouse (which was his nickname for me) pack a bag with some overnight gear for tomorrow morning, you're going on a wide load with Bert to Grangemouth docks." "Where's that ?" I asked. He told me it was in Scotland somewhere roughly between Glasgow and Edinburgh and that I could be away for two nights.

I was made up, I went into the main office and got two nights expenses which at the time was, if I remember correctly,

7 shillings and 6 pence (7s/6d). I was told that Bert would collect me from my house at 07.00. Bert was a great man, he drove a Seddon unit with a Rolls Royce Eagle diesel engine that used to purr, it was a lovely machine.

The next morning he picked me up from home in his unit and we went to Mirlees Diesel Engineering in Hazel Grove where he had unhitched his already loaded trailer the night before. I arrived there to see an eighteen ton case containing an average sized ships engine which was thirteen foot wide, it stood about eight feet in height and its length was around thirty feet. Bert had put four chains around the case securing it onto the trailer and it was ready to go.

We hitched up and waited for a pre arranged police escort to come and take us out of the premises and through suburban Manchester to the M6 at Haydock. From there we had Lancashire Constabulary who escorted us North on the M6 which at that stage was not open all the way up to Penrith, we had to come off the M6 at the Carnforth spur and we were then routed, escorted by Cumbrian police, through Kendal and up and over Shap Fell on the A6 in order to rejoin the M6 at Penrith.

I'll never forget that feeling, I had made it….. I was on my way to being a driver. Bert had had a laugh at me as we'd approached Kendal because I'd combed my hair and stuck my elbow out of the open window, "never mind poncing yourself up for the birds" he laughed "keep your eyes on the road, the lamp posts and whatever's on the pavements on your side" I did as I was told diligently, I loved every second of it as we wound our way through Kendals narrow streets and river bridges escorted by police motorbikes.

Surprisingly to me, we made it all the way to Grangemouth that day, we arrived in the early evening and Bert left the whole rig on the dockside where we would be unloaded the next day. We stayed in the seamen's mission which was somewhere near the docks and we each had a little room with a chair a sink and a bed in it.

We went out and had a couple of pints that night, even though I wasn't old enough to legally drink, topped off with a fish and chips supper after which I slept soundly until my travel alarm woke me up at 07.00.

We got back to the lorry at around 08.00 whereupon we removed the chains off the load, then a tall ladder was brought to the side of the load and, with Bert steadying it, I was told to climb up and onto the case. A dockside heavy lift crane then lowered a weight spreading frame which had six chains attached, these had shackles on so that they could be spread over and down onto the case.

I remember there was a freezing wind blowing and and how cold the chains and shackles were. I affixed the shackles to the pre made lifting points on the case, I had to shorten the ones in the middle of the case, I then clambered back down the ladder, which was no easy feat as my hands were numb with the cold. The ladder was removed and the crane then lifted the case just off the trailer, Bert then slowly pulled away from under the case until the whole rig was clear of it. He got our delivery notes signed and we drove over to near the dock gates where Bert found a phone and rang Reyners to see if we had a return load to pick up. They must have thought we wouldn't have been unloaded so quickly and had not got anything lined up.

We went and found a cafe and had some breakfast and then rang them again. They hadn't found anything and it was a Friday so after about two hours of sitting around we were told to head home empty. Bert dropped me off at the yard that night and thanked me for helping him. I'd enjoyed the trip and the only downside was that I had to give back one nights expenses which I hadn't needed.

As yard lads we went on many wide, high and long loads to many places, another one I recall was my first visit to the London area. I was with a driver called Keith Hunt, an old hand who had vast experience with abnormal loads having worked at Edward Beck heavy haulage in Reddish, Stockport.

I was to mate him with a wide load to Kent, there was also a second carbon copy load which another driver called Sam Fellowes was taking, and he was mated by Alan, both loads were going to the same place.

We picked up the loaded trailers early in the morning, which were single thirteen foot six inches wide pieces of steel ducting from a fabrication works in Miles Plating, Manchester. Under police escort we all eventually made it to a big lay-by near the Beacon transport cafe on the A1 at Bignells Corner in Hertfordshire. We stayed in digs there overnight and the next day we

22

waited for our escort which would take us through London (no M25 then !)

For some reason unknown to me, which was probably because there were two vehicles, we were told that we weren't to be taken through in the daytime and would instead be escorted through in the evening.

That evening six police motorcycles turned up at the lay-by at around 18.30. The leading officer asked to see our movement orders and after checking all was OK he asked Keith if he'd "like to donate to the police tea fund" now Keith as I said was experienced in all things related to abnormal loads and, despite Sam moaning about it, gave the officer ten shillings. He knew they would look after us and anyway Keith would get it back from Reyner's as expenses. The lead officer said "right lads, how fast can your lorries go ?" Keith replied that we could go up to sixty mph, The officer said "right follow me, stay together and keep up, don't slow down or stop because we'll have everything stopped for you". He wasn't joking ! We set off for our journey through London to our destination at Northfleet in Kent at 19.00 in convoy fashion and we headed south towards the capital.

It was like we were royalty ! Traffic at every junction was stopped for us, we drove through red lights, travelled along the centre of the roads, and around some roundabouts on the wrong side ! We never stopped, down Archway Road and Holloway Road and then winding through to Aldgate. I remember going over Tower Bridge at quite a pace with no other traffic on it but us, then out through south London onto the A2 and then eventually on to a wharf at Northfleet, where a factory was being extended, and that's where we parked overnight to be unloaded the next day.

I can't recall exactly how long it took us, and don't forget, we had come through with wide loads, but I do remember we had booked into a pub for the night near the wharf and we got there in time to book in, wash and change, have a bar snack and a few beers, well before closing, which was at that time 22.30. I think you'll agree that was well worth the ten bob (50p).!!

On another occasion I was a mate with Sam (who I mentioned in the previous tale). We were taking a similar sized piece of ducting down to Northfleet from Manchester and as

23

usual we'd been routed off the M6 at the A5 running south through Cannock, Tamworth, Atherstone and on to Hinkley where we were, under police motorbike escort, diverted through the town to avoid the low bridge on the A5 there.

It was in winter, it was early evening, and it had already gone dark. We were going up a road and the escort had all through traffic stopped but we came upon a car which was parked on my side of the road and made it a very tight situation to cope with. The copper had stopped and tried to find the driver of the car, he even went into a pub a few yards on the right past the car but had no luck, he asked us if we thought we could pass by it. Sam replied that he thought we would be able to, so we began to proceed slowly through the gap left for us.

The car, as I said, was on my side so I got out to guide him and left my door window open so I could communicate with Sam, the bobby had gone to the rear of the lorry to placate waiting drivers behind us. Sam edged forward and I kept my eyes on the overhanging load which was very close to the parked car, I shouted and waved to Sam that all was OK and to keep edging forward. He carried on and then there was the sudden sound of metal upon metal scraping noise followed by something crashing noisily to the ground.

Sam stopped and shouted to me "what the fuck have we hit on your side ?" I replied that all was good on my side and Sam got out to see what had happened. It transpired that as we were passing the car Sam had failed to notice a pub sign high up on the wall, the kind that hang out on brackets, and a lug or joint on the metalwork of the load had caught it which brought it and some brickwork crashing down. The escort copper was soon with us and after speaking with the pub landlord we were told that we did not need to worry about it as he would sort things out. So after a relatively short time we continued on our way.

On one trip I was mating a guy called Pete Treacy, we were taking a fifteen foot wide by one foot six inches high heater element to Port Talbot in South Wales. We'd had a good run down from Trafford Park in Manchester and had been left by our police escort in a lay-by near the Usk turn-off, south of Monmouth on the A449, to await our next escort. The police escort duly arrived, just one, on a motorcycle and after all the usual checks he said much the same as the London bobbies had, keep going, don't stop and that he would have our path cleared. He took us off the A449 onto the Usk road as per our movement order and we did as he said following him diligently.

He took us into Usk and I got out as Pete negotiated the river bridge there, I kept my eye on the load on my side and guided him as it passed ever so close to the bridge parapets whilst the police bike had everything stopped and clear for us to proceed across to the other side.

When we cleared the bridge the escort had a word with Pete saying "as I said just keep going, you may lose sight of me but I'll be stopping everything until you've cleared past them, I'll wait for you further along the route" He set off and we followed him out of Usk and into the countryside. I recall that on the narrow lanes we were skimming the tops of the hedgerows at some points.

All was going well as we motored along although I was a bit nervous about us driving fairly quickly around bendy country lanes and then it happened.......we rounded a bend and came face to face with a ten tonner box van hurtling towards us, Pete took evasive action, swerving to the left whilst braking, we narrowly missed a telegraph pole, the hedges and whatever happened to be behind them on my side were being sliced by the load.

The oncoming vehicle did not stop in time and the load on Pete's side hit the offside mirror and then the front offside corner of its box and sliced through and along the side of the box van body like a knife through butter, spilling its load out onto the road. The load was...wait for it...ladies sanitary towels ! There was not a lot of spillage to be honest, it must have been less than half full, but there were quite a lot of split boxes.

Pete got out and ran back to the driver of the box van who was still sat in his cab, he was white with shock but had no obvious injuries and he eventually got out of the van. After a few minutes or so, the police motorcycle came back, he got off his bike and walked over to the driver of the van and angrily said "what are you playing at ? I told you to stay put where I stopped you and not to move 'till this lorry had passed you, it's a simple instruction and you've disobeyed it, well now you can pick up this mess and I'm booking you for it" the box van driver had obviously seen and heard the officers instructions, but as we were on a time lag behind him he must have assumed we'd either turned off or stopped, so he foolishly carried on.

We were there quite some time whilst everything was sorted out and more police arrived at the scene. We checked our load which was still secure and intact, although scraped of its paint on the collision side and looking like we had taken on camouflage on my side !. We eventually got untangled from the van and the hedgerows and continued safely on our way to Port Talbot without any further scares.

Reyners did many abnormal loads and on one I had been a second man to a fella named Jimmy S. He and I had unloaded one in the London area and our back load was from the Olympia Exhibition Centre near Hammersmith Road in London, we were to collect an exhibition stand that should have been dismantled and ready to load.

We arrived at Olympia mid afternoon and found ourselves in absolute carnage, there was gridlock all around the centre, nothing was moving very far and we eventually pulled up and parked in the middle of the road outside the place with nowhere else to go. We were a few vehicles behind one of Reyners other lorries who had also come to load what we were loading as it required two vehicles.

The other truck was driven by Bob Harman, a huge hulk of a man weighing around twenty three stone. He was so heavy that he had a piece of 4 x 4 timber wedged underneath the seat of his Seddon unit to support him. He'd been there around twenty minutes and had found out where our loading door was. Bob told us we were not near enough to the door to get inside and that he had been waiting along with everybody else for traffic to move. He asked us to go with him so he could show us where we needed to be in case we were split up. We left the lorries where they were and went inside, once we knew where to go we returned to our vehicles.

As we approached where they were "parked", in the middle of the road as there was nowhere else to go, Bob spotted a youngish police officer opening his cab door, he approached the officer, who by this time, had climbed into his cab and asked him what he was doing. "I'm moving this it's in the way" said the bobby. Bob replied "well as you can see officer there's nowhere to go apart from about 15 feet from where it is, any-

26

way jump out and I'll move it for you now" The bobby by now was trying to start the lorry, "look officer, if you'll just get out I'll move it, it's my responsibility not yours" said Bob. The officer got a bit shirty at that and told Bob to get out of the way, Bob didn't move and opened the cab door "look, I won't ask again, please get out of my lorry now !" The officer then seemed to lose his senses and jumped out shouting at Bob as he approached him, grabbing at his clothing in a menacing way, Bob tried to step back but the bobby was shouting and manhandling him, I still can't believe what happened next !

Bob stopped backing away and punched the bobby once in the face, he went down like a sack of spuds, out for the count. Jimmy and I then witnessed police officers quickly arriving at the scene as if out of nowhere and they arrested Bob. I may add that not one of the officers touched him and he gave himself up without any further scuffles, he then walked away under his own steam to a waiting police van parked somewhere out of sight. He shouted "look after my lorry Jimmy, see if you can get it loaded for me, where are you staying tonight ? Shepherds Bush ?" Jimmy shouted "yes" to which Bob replied "I'll see you there" and then he was gone. Jimmy made a statement to another officer telling him everything that had occurred and then we were left alone.

I stayed with Bobs lorry and moved it forward whenever I could until we eventually reached the door where we could drive in to load. We took both vehicles inside the building and Jimmy loaded our lorry first. We then loaded Bobs and secured the load ready for him. We explained to the lads who were loading the lorries what had happened, and asked if Bobs lorry could be left inside until he, hopefully, returned later that evening to retrieve it. They said that wouldn't be a problem so we phoned Reyners and put them in the picture.

We did meet up with Bob later that evening, we were parked at Shepherds Bush lorry park and staying in digs not far from there. We were in a boozer near the lorry park when Bob walked in. He had been charged with assaulting a police officer and had been bailed so he'd phoned Reyners who had informed him where his lorry was and he'd then gone back to Olympia to retrieve it. He slept in his cab that night, as he usually did, and was gone when we turned up to leave the lorry park the next morning.

As a footnote to this story I'd like to add that the court case against Bob was never heard, we understand that the officer involved had passed away in a water skiing accident whilst he was on holiday. A strange story, but it's all true. There was also a documentary on T.V. about the life of a lorry driver which involved a film crew travelling around the country with Bob, showing the watching public what life was like for him as he traversed the roads of Britain.

There was a company in Hyde near Manchester where Reyners used to load steel "dish ends". They were in essence the bowl type ends on large (and small) steel tanks, they were welded to the main body of a tank at either end giving it that rounded appearance.

I went there many times with a driver to load and deliver them but on this occasion I went with a fella called Harold Hadfield who everyone called "the gonk" to second man him with a twelve foot six inch wide dish end, it was for delivery to a company in Tipton, near West Bromwich in the West Midlands. We had a ten ton ERF rigid lorry with a flat bed, on which we stood the dish end in its upright bowl appearance. We chained the load down securely and set off after phoning the police to be told that an escort wouldn't be necessary as the load wasn't that wide and there was a driver and second man present.

We left Hyde and made our way across to the M6 and headed south. I didn't have a lot of respect for this particular driver as he always put yard lads down, saying things like we didn't know fuck all, we were all little wankers and the like. He also thought he was Gods gift to women, and he was one of those who thought he knew it all, you get the picture ?

Anyway we were going along on a sunny, clear day when he said something like "right I'm going to show you how to make this job easy lad" he reached down and behind his seat as we travelled along the M6 at around sixty miles an hour, which I thought was too fast, carrying a wide load without an escort, but according to the driver, I knew nothing.

From behind his seat he produced a small wooden handled brush, he proudly waved it in the air and said "this here is my alternative to cruise control" he then leant forward and wedged the brush between the accelerator pedal and the underside of the front dash board.

The lorry was now travelling along without him having to touch the accelerator, all he was doing was steering the vehicle. He then proceeded to lift both his legs up off the floor and swung them around resting them across the engine cowling. He said "this is how you do it son, no need for hard work when you use your brains" he then got out a cigarette and lit it, leaning back in his chair like he was on holiday or something ! To say I was nervous would be very true, he said "what are you looking so worried about ? I do this all the time, you don't know sod all you kids"

We must have travelled like that, thankfully with no incidents for about six to ten minutes, I had somewhat come to terms with the situation when, looking ahead on a long straight stretch of road I saw brake lights in the far distance, then more. I turned to the driver who was still lounging and told him. He looked too, saw them, then quickly spun his legs down and tried to dislodge the brush with his foot, which was pressing down on the accelerator at full rev's. He'd wedged it tightly and it didn't come out, he was panicking by now and leaned forward trying to grab it with one hand as he steered. The lorry was veering across the inside and middle lanes and I could hear horns beeping behind us.

Ahead I could now see three lanes of stopped traffic, he was cursing as he attempted to retrieve the brush which he eventually did, he sat up and started to brake harshly as we were now around three hundred feet away from the stopped traffic. I thought we were going to crash so I lifted my feet up and pushed them up against the passenger side dashboard ready for the impact, I was really scared. We came to a stop on the inside lane about three foot away from the rear end of another lorry.

I looked across to the driver who was white with shock, as were the knuckles on his hands which were firmly gripping the steering wheel. He said "fuck me that was close ! The bloody brush was stuck there", he looked at me and said in a light hearted manner "do you need to change your undies lad ?" I told him that I was OK but that I thought his "alternative cruise control" was a rubbish idea.

I still get shivers when I think about that day, what a dick head. Yes folks…. you're right, they are out there amongst us !

One of my last trips as a second man involved a wide load to a power station near St. Neots in the Huntingdon area of Cambridgeshire. I was with a driver named Joe, who I've already mentioned, he was an old hand at Reyners.

By this time in my career I was confident enough to try my hand at driving an artic' on the open road if somebody would ever have given me the chance. As yard lads we would regularly drop and pick up trailers for drivers, we'd also take them to the fuel pumps and fill them with diesel whilst they had a brew or sorted their paperwork etc. etc. whilst they were in the yard at Droylsden.

On this particular trip I asked Joe many times if I could "have a go" only to be rebuffed with "you're fucking joking aren't you ! we've got a wide load behind us......NO !!" Of course, I was most upset at this but to be fair we were travelling with a load fourteen feet six inches wide and twelve feet in height. It was on a semi low trailer and it had a heavy duty winch on the swan neck, which at one time was used for a cable drum contract that Reyners used to have.

We got the load delivered safely to the power station despite Joe being almost constantly bothered by me asking him to let me drive, even though I was nowhere near old enough or experienced enough to be able to do so !. After unloading, Joe phoned Reyners for our backload instructions. He was asked to make his way to where the beginning of the newly constructed, but not yet opened M6 at the Catthorpe Interchange off the M1 near Rugby was. We were to pick up a full load of empty cable drums from a site on the motorway there and return them to Blackley in Manchester.

This we did, and once loaded Joe asked the site foreman if we could travel along the M6 which, as stated earlier, was now finished but not at that time opened officially. Joe was advised that he could indeed go that way, as long as he proceeded with caution as there could still be plant and other construction paraphernalia which was waiting to be cleared or picked up so we set off on a clear sunny day northbound on the motorway.

As you may have already guessed, we had not been travelling five minutes and I began to pester Joe to let me drive. I was throwing all the ammo I could at him, "there's nobody but us on here", "you won't see any coppers on here" and the like. Eventually Joe gave in, "right, you mithering so and so, you can drive, but I'll be watching everything you do, no speeding, don't go above fifty and if I say stop, you stop, right ?" Of course I agreed. He pulled up on the slow lane and we swapped seats, the next thing I recall was me driving a loaded articulated lorry on a motorway and I'd not yet reached seventeen years of age.

If I may say so, I never put a foot wrong, Joe sat and watched me intently, but he didn't have to warn me or correct me on anything for the whole of the fairly short, but to me, very long journey. I drove a 180 Gardener ERF with a David Brown gearbox towing a forty foot semi low trailer loaded with empty cable drums along the M6 and I was absolutely in my element.

The stretch of motorway we covered ended at the Castle Bromwich turn off in the Birmingham area and that is where Joe swapped back over with this very reluctant young man, to continue the rest of our journey home. It was my first time driving an artic' on the open (but closed and empty) road, and it remains a fond memory of mine.

There are many stories I could tell you about when I was assisting (being a second man) to drivers on wide loads and handball loads but I'd probably need another book to do it. My time as a yard lad put me in good stead for when I began to drive and I learned a lot, and continued to learn, as a driver myself.

Geoffrey Reyner had a policy of training young lads "the ropes" then they would put them through their driving test with the hope that they would eventually go in for their HGV licence and become fully fledged Reyner drivers.

This happened to me, as soon as I was old enough for a provisional licence I applied, and was then given driving lessons, paid for by Reyners, by a local school of motoring. I didn't need many and I was soon put in for my test, which I passed first time. I then used to go out in the works pick up van for spares and parts for the garage, or collect small light objects from various companies which would then be transhipped onto bigger vehicles doing multi drop deliveries.

If you can recall I mentioned a lad called John S who had pointed the way to Georges office to my mate Alan and myself, well I was taking Johns place as a "spare"as he had passed his HGV class one test. Alan had taken the place of another lad, and was, as he was a year older than me, now driving a seven and a half ton flat back Leyland light goods vehicle in which he drove all around the UK making deliveries.

The idea from Reyners was a shrewd one and the little Leyland earned them good money, it was so good in fact that they ordered another one for me and then I too was off all over the place. Really the lorry was only made for local deliveries, like bread, milk and the like, it wasn't an ideal vehicle for doing long distance runs in. I used to carry a spare set of injectors which the maintenance foreman gave me, and a set of spanners and a wrench which I used to change them with, the injectors were not built for constant high revving distance runs and they used to blow and leak regularly. The cab use to stink of diesel fumes, as did I !, I'd regularly get diesel sprayed onto my clothes whilst changing an injector.

One of my first jobs was a load of used tyres, I loaded them on a Friday afternoon and they were for delivery the following Monday to a firm in the Bermondsey area of London. At the time my brother Pete was working in London, he'd left home as a young lad and found his way down there, as many did and still do. He was working in the Houses of Parliament restaurant and bar and was staying in a hostel not far away from there. I'd been in contact with him and he told me he was fed up and was thinking of leaving. With this in mind I asked the manager on the traffic desk if I could be allowed to travel down to London on the Sunday in order to visit our Pete and then deliver the tyres on the Monday. He replied that I could.

I left at around 10.30 on the Sunday and ran down there after arranging to meet Pete at Parliament Square. It seems unreal, but I did find him after going round it a few times and he clambered in. I asked him if there was anywhere I could park near the hostel but, as now, it's all double yellow lines everywhere and there wasn't a suitable place to pull up let alone to park.

I drove around for a bit and then found myself at around 19.00 outside New Scotland Yard which was only a short distance away from where Pete was staying. I recall there were road or pavement works being carried out so I reversed in between two lots of coned off areas and found myself literally parked outside the reception of the most famous police station in Britain.

Pete and I went into the reception and I told the officer there of my predicament, how I'd driven down to see my brother etc.

etc. and did he know of where I could safely park my vehicle which was loaded with tyres. The load was fully sheeted and as far as the bobby on reception would have known they could have been new tyres. He took a moment and asked us to hang on and went into an adjoining room, he emerged soon after and asked me what time I would be leaving the area the next morning to which I replied "half six". He then shocked me by saying "right, well as long as you leave at half six you can leave it where it is, it'll be safe there" You could have knocked me (and Pete) over with a feather ! You may not believe it but I swear that's how it happened, my lorry was left outside of New Scotland Yard for the night ! I still to this day find it hard to believe, but it did happen.

I stayed in the hostel that night with our kid and the next morning, as promised, myself and our Pete (whom I'd persuaded overnight to come back home with me) arrived at the police station and I went in and thanked the officer on duty, we then left and headed over to this rather seedy yard on an industrial estate where I was to unload the tyres. The guy in the yard told me to back into it and take off the ropes and sheets and then they'd unload me after having a brew, which I did.

It wasn't a big place and there were two other lads who worked there, we were offered a brew too, we leaned up against the back of the load to drink it. Not long after this a big black car, I think it was a Wolseley or something like that, was driven to the yard gates. The driver stayed inside it but out of the passenger door emerged a giant of a man in a long black overcoat carrying a briefcase, he leant back into the car to say something to the driver and as he did one of the lads who worked there told us to get into my cab and stay there until this guy had left. He seemed pretty insistent and worried so we did as he said.

The big guy walked into the yard and entered the office building, he wasn't in there more than five minutes and then he walked out, got back in the car, and it pulled away.

I got out then and asked one of the lads what all that was about. He replied with a knowing nod "have you heard of the Richardsons ?" which I hadn't, but apparently as I later found out, they were south London rivals to the Krays. The lad may have been having me over, I'll never know, and I don't know what business this man had with them, but he certainly looked a menacing sort of guy, not the sort you'd want to cross. Soon

33

after this episode we started to unload and after doing so and phoning Reyners London office for further instructions, I left there to go and do three pickups for my back load up to the North. It was certainly an eventful and quite unbelievable trip, but it's all true.

Reyners had a large workforce and amongst them were many characters. I am going to tell you a little story that relates to one of them, his name was Harry B. He drove one of the rigid ten ton four wheelers and was in his fifties when I started in the yard at Reyners, a very experienced transport man. I got along with Harry very well, we used to have a good craic, He used to call me a "spunk bubble" but it was all in good humour.

One thing Harry was known for was his effing and jeffing, he'd do it every other word, all the blasphemies he could muster came from his mouth, but he was one of the better drivers who used to take time to show me the right way to do things related to the job. He was known as effing Harry by all the workforce, even the office staff called him that because he didn't just swear at yard lads, it was everyone at the company, nobody escaped.

Once I'd got my driving licence and started to drive my four tonner I'd quite often ask him where such and such a place was, I may have known where the town or city was but Harry knew where the places I was delivering to were in those towns or cities. I met him one day in a cafe on the A5, he was heading north and I was going to London. After telling me where each of my drops were he asked me where I was going to stay that night. I told him that I'd probably stay at the Silvertown Motel in east London. He replied that as I was finishing my last drop of the day in Tulse Hill in south London I should go to some digs that he used to stay in at Stockwell, which wasn't far away from there.

He described the way there from my last drop in detail then told me to knock on the door and say that he'd sent me. I said I would and thanked him. We finished up and went our separate ways.

The day went well and I followed Harrys instructions. Once unloaded, I ended up in a square, something like Albert Square in "Eastenders" but this place was in Stockwell, I have a vague memory that the digs were called "The Albion". Anyway, I parked up and made my way to the house.

I knocked on the front door and a lady answered, She asked could she help me and I stutteringly replied "yes, I'm a lorry driver and I wonder if you have a bed for me tonight please" she looked at me with a puzzled look and asked me had I booked. Again I nervously replied "no, Harry sent me here" she frowned and asked "Harry, Harry who ?" I replied that I worked for Geoffrey Reyner and so did Harry. A look of realisation came across her face and she replied "Oh... you mean effing Harry ! Why didn't you say that in the first place, yes there's a bed for you, come in". As I said, everybody knew him as effing Harry !

Sometimes in life I have been astounded by the abominable treatment that I as a lorry driver have received on some occasions and I have also been very grateful for the kindness and understanding that, (and there's not many), people have shown to me too. This is a story of the latter. One day whilst driving the Leyland I was delivering a four ton piece of mining equipment to Blackhall Colliery in County Durham. I'd had to "load and go" that day from the Manchester area and arrived at the colliery at just after 16.00.

I found the guy who would be unloading me and he informed me that I wouldn't be unloaded that day, it would be first thing in the morning. He asked me where I was staying that night. Now at the time if I was unable to find digs in a cafe, pub or B&B, as a last resort I would sleep across the two seats in my cab in a sleeping bag on a board propped up with cushions. I explained this to him and I said that this is what I'd do if he didn't mind me staying on site. He replied in a friendly Durham accent "oh no you won't ! Give me a few minutes to sort a few things out here and then you can come to my house and stay there for tonight". I thanked him and politely said that I couldn't possibly put him in that situation and that I'd be OK in the cab. He said not to worry and that all would be fine and insisted that I went back to his house.

I was a little apprehensive about the situation but agreed, I need not have worried. After he'd done what he needed to at the colliery he climbed into my cab and asked me my name, which I reciprocated and asked him his name, which for the life of me I cant recall now, (it was at the time of writing this, 50 years ago) he was in his late middle age and he directed me to his house which was a few minutes drive from the colliery.

He asked me to follow him in and I tentatively did so. The first thing he did was shout from the front door "lass I've brought a driver home from work, he'll be staying with us tonight" A lady appeared from another room, and to my surprise she smiled, said hello to me and asked my name. I was very coy and feeling a little bit uncomfortable but she was very pleasant and set me at my ease.

I was shown to a small spare bedroom with a single bed and was told where the toilet and bathroom were. I retrieved my overnight gear from the lorry and, after washing and changing, I made my way downstairs where I was greeted by the both of them.

To say they were lovely would be an understatement, his wife had spun out whatever they were having for dinner and made me a plate up too. We sat around the table chatting afterwards, we then sat down to watch a little television. At around 18.30 I was informed that if I didn't mind I was to accompany them to the local social club for a few pints and play bingo if I wanted to. We all went out together and had a great night (although I didn't win at bingo !).

The next morning I was awoken with a gentle tap on the door and after getting ready and having a cooked breakfast of bacon and eggs, I said my farewells and thanked his wife before we boarded my lorry and made our way back to the colliery.

Those people were the salt of the earth, no edge to them whatsoever and although I offered to give the guy some money for looking after me, he wouldn't hear of it and refused me with a thank you. I would imagine that they are no longer with us but I will forever be grateful for their hospitality and friendship.

As a footnote to this story I'd like to tell you about the time when I too made someones life a little more comfortable than it would otherwise have been.

Reyners had an office and small yard with three lorries running out of it at Cradley Heath in the "black country" region of the West Midlands. One of their drivers, Bob, had loaded at the yard in Droylsden one Friday night, he was going to have something to eat and a few beers in the local "glue pot" before staying for the night in the yard. He would then be driving home on the Saturday morning.

I was talking to him in the yard canteen late that evening whilst he was pushing three tables together, end to end. I asked him what he was doing, he replied that he was setting up his bed for the night, he was then going to get his sleeping bag and a cushion from his lorry and sleep on the tables that night. He explained that it was as comfortable as his non sleeper cab lorry and that the canteen was heated, whereas his lorry wasn't.

I was astounded, I mean I've "roughed it" but sleeping on hard tables was another prospect all together. I didn't say anything but I went and used a phone in the warehouse office to ring my wife Pat, I asked her if she would mind if I brought Bob to our house, give him something to eat, and then let him sleep in a spare bedroom that we had for the night. Pat was a little apprehensive about this at first but after explaining his situation and what had happened to me several years earlier, she eventually agreed.

I went back to the canteen as Bob was returning with his sleeping gear and told him that he could come to our place to sleep. Bob, like Pat had been, was a little unsure too and explained that he'd be fine on the tables. After a little more coaxing I managed to sway him and he agreed to the idea. I left my lorry at Reyners that night and travelled back to Reddish with Bob in his lorry, I showed him where he could safely park it then we made our way to my house.

To cut a long story short Bob had a meal with us and, after having a bath and changing into casual clothes, accompanied Pat and myself to our local working mens club where we met Dave, my brother in law, we all had a good night and Bob left, not too early the next morning, a much more refreshed man than he would have been after sleeping (and maybe falling off !) tables in the depot canteen.

There's a place in the Greater Manchester area called Astley, It's on the A580 East Lancashire Road which connects Liverpool to Manchester. Reyners got regular five days a week work there with a company named Comprehensive Shipping.

They used to have car parts delivered there and they would pack them in crates and cases and distribute them to docks and ports for shipping to countries all over the world. Reyners had two of the seven and a half tonners working out of there at one time, myself and a lad named Ted (he was the son of the warehouse foreman named Johnny in Openshaw that I mentioned earlier in this book) We had to be at the warehouse in Astley at 06.30 in the mornings to load up with cases, mainly for Liverpool, Birkenhead, Preston or Hull docks, I also loaded for London docks once which I will tell you about later.

One morning I had loaded up with cases for two deliveries in Liverpool, Canada dock and Huskisson dock. I set off at around 07.30 and arrived at Canada dock at around 08.15. After waiting (which was always the story there) for an hour or so, I was sent into a shed where around two thirds of the load was taken off by the dockers. Once I had got all my paperwork sorted, I set off to my next dock. I still had for delivery there two identical cases which measured around five feet long by two feet in depth and height, each one weighing around 750 kgs. I travelled the short distance to Huskisson dock, arriving there at around 10.20

I found it was not so busy, so after booking in at the office and getting my paperwork stamped I was asked to go into a particular dock shed to unload. There was nobody in the shed when I went in so I unfastened my ropes which were securing the cases and returned to my lorry to wait for the dockers who would unload me. There wasn't a soul to be seen and the only noise I could hear was from a fork lift truck which had been left running and was parked in the middle of the shed.

My hopes were lifted as I spotted a guy walking through the large door of the shed so I got out from my vehicle and walked over to where he was. I asked him why there was nothing going on regarding the unloading of vehicles and he told me that all the dockers had gone to a union meeting, this happened fairly regularly on the docks and these meetings could go on for some time.

I explained that I only had two cases on and asked if he could take them off for me. He replied that he was not an unloader and that he worked in the dock office, he walked over to my lorry and had a look at the cases, I showed him the paperwork for them and asked could he check them, I was hoping that he would succumb to my wishes and unload me. He checked my notes and said he would sign them but he couldn't take them off, I'd have to wait for the dockers to return. After this he walked off and out of the warehouse.

I returned to my vehicle and waited.... and waited.... and waited. I wanted to get all the freight off and return to Astley after lunch, where, hopefully, I could reload for the next day and get an early finish.

At around 11.40 I thought to myself, if I didn't get them off then I'd be there till God knows when, I had come to the conclusion that the dockers would not return until after lunch time, if at all, and I didn't fancy waiting to see if they would return to work. I saw the fork lift which was still ticking over and thought "sod this, I'm going to take them off myself" I got out of my lorry and had a quick scan outside to see if anyone was about and after seeing it was clear I got onto the fork lift and proceeded to take off one of the cases. I picked out a spot where I could see other cases with the same destination which was stencilled onto my cases and decided to put them in that area. I knew how to safely handle a fork lift from my days in the yard at Reyners.

I had landed one of the cases on the floor and had just got under the second one when out of the corner of my eye I spotted the bloke who I had spoken to earlier coming through the shed doorway. When he saw me he stopped in his tracks and flustered out loudly "what the fuck are you doing lad !!?, you'll have the fucking port out on strike if anybody sees you on that, you'll have to get off it" I replied that I knew how to drive one and that I thought it would be OK as I continued to pick up the second one and manoeuvre it over to the other one on the floor.

He was walking alongside me blabbering and waving his arms in a frantic manner saying how he'd never seen anyone do what I was doing and how he could lose his job for letting me. I landed the case and reversed away from it to the point where the fork lift had been before, I got off it and walked over to him and apologised for not realising that I'd done anything wrong, adding that it was all done now and nobody needed to know anything about it. He was still effing and jeffing saying the whole port would be on strike if anyone else had seen me, he remembered that he'd signed my paperwork and told me to "fuck off sharpish before anyone sees you, you'll get me fucking sacked lad !" so with that fond farewell ringing in my ears I got back into my vehicle, left the shed and exited the dock.

I realise now what sort of problems could have arisen if I'd been caught by anybody else but the office guy, Reyners, and myself in particular, would have probably been barred from all Liverpool docks or possibly all docks everywhere. At the time I pleaded ignorance to the guy, and I got away with it. I never ever did it again though, that was a very fortunate, but one off situation for me.

One day I had unloaded at the docks in Hull with a load from Comprehensive Shipping and I was sent to back load a four ton case from an engineering works near the docks.

I loaded the case just forward of the rear axle and roped it down securely. I set off on what was a beautiful summers day to return to our depot. There was no M62 then and I was travelling along the old roads. As I neared Goole I saw two girls who were thumbing for a lift, in those days it was quite common to give a ride to hitch hikers so I pulled up and asked them where they were heading for. They told me they would like to be dropped off in the area on the west side of Knottingley. I was heading that way so I told them to hop in and off we went.

We chatted a little about where they'd been and general chit chat until we reached a junction where they wanted to be dropped off. They thanked me for the lift and got out. I set off towards Wakefield where I'd planned to stop for a brew at The Red Beck cafe east of the town.

As I said it was a really clear bright sunny day and as I climbed to the top and then over a brow of a hill I was blinded by the sun, I squinted my eyes and suddenly realised that all the traffic had stopped so I braked really hard. I came to a skidding stop literally a couple of inches off the back of a flat back lorry, my relief at stopping was short lived as I heard a sliding noise and then a heavy thud against the headboard of my lorry. Due to the harsh braking the ropes holding the four ton case had snapped and it had slid along from where it was and up to the headboard, this then caused my vehicle to lurch forward and the grill and front bumper on my lorry were pushed into the rear body and crash bar of the flat bed in front of me.

I got out as did the driver of the lorry in front and we surveyed the damage. Luckily the impact was not great so there was minimal damage to my bumper and a crease across the grill. The other lorry had no damage to speak of. The other driver told me there was no reason to swap details and as soon as the traffic began to move he drove off. I drove the fairly short distance to the Red Beck cafe and parked up, I then phoned my traffic office and informed them what had happened.

They advised me to travel back to the depot if it was safe to drive the lorry so I had a cup of tea and whilst doing so it dawned on me that I had dropped the two girls off only a relatively short distance from where I'd had the bump. It may have been a different story if they'd been in the cab, one had sat on her friends knee and the harshness of the braking I'd done to stop would no doubt have thrown at least one of them towards the windscreen. This made me swear to myself that I wouldn't ever give lifts again, which I stuck to, except on one other occasion which I will tell you about later in this book.

I mentioned earlier that on one occasion I had loaded for London docks from the shipping company in Astley, the load was for delivery to a dock on what's known as The Isle of Dogs in Londons east end.

I loaded the cases one afternoon and set off southbound. I had been instructed that I had to be at an office on Holloway Road in north London at 07.00 the following morning and meet a forwarding agent manager who was going to go with me to the dock, apparently the ship was closing on the evening when I had set off, this meant that no freight would be accepted after that time, he was hopefully going to "sweeten" somebody on the docks to get me unloaded.

I ran down to some digs at a cafe in Markyate on the A5, south of Dunstable, and stayed there for the night. I got away very early the next morning and arrived at Holloway Road, standing at the doorway to the premises at around 06.45. Bang on 07.00 a guy turned up in a suit and invited me in and upstairs to his office telling me that we'd have a cup of tea before setting off to the dock. Upon reaching his office he fished into his suit pocket and said "That's for getting up early son" as he passed me some folded bank notes. He disappeared into a kitchen type annex to brew up and I looked at what he'd given me, it was £30, that was more than half of what I could earn in a good week ! He returned with a brew and we quickly downed it before setting off for the dock.

He told me to follow him, I was a little apprehensive about this as London traffic, particularly at that time of day, didn't offer me much hope of staying behind him. He assured me he would make sure I could see him and that if we were to be split up he would wait until I caught up with him, so off we went. He

41

was true to his word and, after he got out at the dock gate to speak to the bobby on duty there, I found myself trailing behind him onto a very quiet empty dock with a big cargo ship on the quayside.

He exited his vehicle and came over to me, he asked me to stay in my lorry and wait until I was signalled to go into the shed. This I did and after around ten minutes a bloke came out of the dock shed office door and waved to me to go along to a big shed door which was being opened as he gestured for me to come. I drove down and straight into the warehouse and the door was closed behind me. I'd hardly had time to get out of my lorry when I was descended upon by around six dockers, they helped me take the ropes and sheet off my load and wrap them up ! (I'd never seen that happen anywhere up to then and I never saw it again)

Two forklifts then proceeded to unload the cases and within six or seven minutes my lorry was empty. I put my folded sheet and ropes onto the empty flat as the door was being opened and I drove my vehicle outside to tie them on. As I was doing this the guy from the forwarders came up to me and handed me my signed paperwork and said " this is what's left, you can have it, thanks for everything" and handed me another £10 ! I was flabbergasted, I'd never been unloaded so fast (and never since) He got into his car and drove away whilst I happily set off to find a cafe in which to spend some of my not so little windfall. It's amazing what doors a little "filthy lucre" can open !

On another trip to London I loaded at a place not far from Wembley stadium. The load was a three ton piece of aluminium. It was around ten foot long by four foot wide and was about two feet in depth. I securely fastened it down and sheeted it as I was instructed to do by the sender. It was to be delivered to a place called Bootle, not the one in Liverpool but on the coast in the Lake District. It was some sort of high security government military site.

I arrived there the following day just after lunch time and was greeted at the fortified perimeter gate, not by a soldier, it was a civilian, who took me into the gate house to examine my delivery documents. He asked me the usual questions such as 'do you have any cameras or photographic equipment on you or in your vehicle ?" At the time I smoked cigarettes and he asked that I hand them and any matches or lighters over to him which I did. He then told me that his colleague would travel with me in my cab and escort me to where I was to be unloaded.

During all of this I was thinking "what's all this about ? I've only got a lump of aluminium on, I'm not carrying ammunition !" I was then duly escorted to one of several hangar like buildings which had fantastic raised views out into the Irish Sea, it was made of bricks and stone and not at all like the flimsiness of an aircraft hangar. I was asked to remove my sheet and securing equipment before a large fork lift truck came and lifted the aluminium off my vehicle and took it inside the hangar doors.

The guy who had been with me then signed my delivery notes and was making his way to my cab for the lift back to the gatehouse when I asked him "you'll have to excuse my ignorance but what's all this about? Is this some sort of secret service training place or what ?" He laughed at that and then walked back to me. He pointed out to sea and said "can you see that dark coloured thing out there ?" I looked and eventually spotted something in the seas haze that I'd have normally taken for a passing ship or the like in the distance. He then said "It's a target, come with me and I'll show you" We then walked through the doors into the hangar where various sized pieces of metals and aluminium were stored, we passed through a door into another room which had controls and instrument panels which looked out through a window into a long room where there was what you'd describe as a very large artillery gun.

The other end of the building was open and the guns barrel was pointing through the opening out to sea, He told me they used the different sized metals and aluminium samples to test shells fired from the guns, it was to see whether or not they penetrated the samples and how they stood up to the shelling.

He told me they were about to test one and we all put on ear defenders, he told me I couldn't be inside the building whilst the testing was taking place. I was escorted outside to the back of the building where I could see out to sea. After a while there was a short toot on a siren followed by another longer one, soon after then there was a huge bang a followed by the sound of a screaming shell which was visible to only so far out then all I heard was a distant thud as the shell hit the target of aluminium or steel which had been previously put into position out there.

"That's what it's all about" said the escort and soon after that we were on our way back to the gatehouse. I believe that the place has been shut down for some years now but it was a great and unusual experience.

The job from Comprehensive Shipping became a monotonous one for me, it was all mainly local dock or forwarding work. Having to get up to be at Astley if I hadn't loaded the previous day had got to me. Being a young man, going to the boozer with my mates seemed more important than doing a job I didn't like much. I started to turn up late, which wasn't appreciated, rightly, by the shipping company.

I let them down one Monday morning by ringing Reyners and feigning illness. A few weeks later I did it again on a Friday. The head traffic clerk Colin, called me into Droylsden on the Saturday and gave me a verbal warning, he told me that I wasn't doing myself any favours and to buck my ideas up. It wasn't a surprise then that when I turned up an hour late one Friday at Astley, I was again called in to the depot, and to my despair Colin sacked me.

I was desolate, the job I'd always wanted was over. I went home and told my parents who both berated me for being so foolish. They said I was to get out and find another job ASAP. By this time my mate Dangle had finished at Reyners, he'd had no ambition to drive lorries and had found a job driving fork lifts at a warehouse in Trafford Park, he was paid quite a lot more there than he'd been on at Reyners. He said that they were looking for another fork lift driver, he organised an interview for me and I began working there shortly after.

The job was OK and I was working with my old mate again but I knew I would never attain an HGV licence there, so it wasn't long before I got itchy feet and began looking for a job that would help me to get what I wanted.

My old mentor at Reyners, George, had by this time unexpectedly left them, which at the time was a big shock to everyone there. He had started his own transport company which was based at Green Lane on the outskirts of Failsworth. He ran three seven and a half tonners which were mainly based at a freight forwarders in the Container base at Trafford Park, although George had started to pick up his own work too. He used to have two other lads who worked for him, his son George Junior

44

and another lad who's name was Phil. I explained my situation to him and asked did he have any work for me, I'd have done part time, anything. The upshot was he invited me to his little yard and after having a chat with him, and him telling me he wouldn't have any of the messing around I'd done at Reyners, he offered me a job, driving the little lorry that he himself used. This meant he could work full time in his office, yard and small warehouse. Obviously I was very happy with this and I assured George that my lesson had been learnt, I would not let him down.

I began working for him straight away and soon got into the swing of things. The work was all local and I was at home every night, but I didn't let him down, I was always on time and everything was going well....until...I got home from work one Friday night and my Mum handed me an envelope which had been posted by hand with no stamp through our letterbox, it was to me. I opened it and there was a Geoffrey Reyner complimentary slip inside, on it was a very short message.... "come and see me tomorrow" and it was signed by Colin B. the head traffic manager.

I did go to meet him the next day, and as I walked into the traffic office at Droylsden I could see through an open door that he was seated at his desk in a little side office. He looked up and waved me in, asked me to sit down and said "so you're working with George now I believe, how's it going ?" I replied that I was quite happy there but I knew that there wasn't much hope of me advancing to HGV status. "Well, do you think you've learnt your lesson then Steve ?" He asked. I understood what he meant and apologised for my past and assured him that I had, and how him sacking me had brought me down to earth with a proper bump. "Well apart from you letting us down we always appreciated your work Steve, you are a quick learner and we think you'd make a good driver, would you like to come back ?" he asked. I was overcome, I felt so emotional, I didn't know whether to whoop or cry. "I'd love to come back Colin thank you !" I blurted out. He asked me to do the right thing and tell George, to put in a weeks notice, and then start back in a week on Monday. I was over the moon. I thanked him profusely and got up to leave, Colin then said with a pointed finger "please don't make me regret this Steve, don't let me down" I again assured him that I wouldn't, thanked him once again and exited his office.

I was walking on air, I wandered around the depot, letting on to all the people that I knew and explained to them how I was coming "home". I was back at Reyners. I had been with my mate at Trafford Park and then George for around eleven months in all, so it was very hard telling George that I was leaving. I think he was disappointed too, he'd given me a break when I was down, and looked after me, but the pull of driving articulated lorries was too strong which I hope he understood. I had always respected George and still hold fond memories of my time with him at Reyners and at his own company.

I've had many bad experiences on my travels, some occurring whilst I was parked up on an overnight stop, and had gone in pubs, which was something that happened in those days before sleeper cabs and the associated "luxuries" that came with them, such as televisions and DVD players.

On one such night I was in Glasgow. I had parked on a rough piece of land where many other lorry drivers gravitated to near Gallowgate. I met up later with another Reyner driver whose name was Brian, a quiet, heavily set man. He had parked next to me and after having a chip supper we decided to go for a beer or two in one of the bars in Gallowgate. As we left our lorries a couple of youths called to us "mind your lorry for fifty pence Mr.?" Brian lied to them and replied "I've got an Alsatian in my cab, that'll look after it" one of the lads replied "can it put out fires Mr. ?" Brian laughed and tossed a 50p coin over to them. "Keep a good eye on it then" he said and we went on our way.

We found our way to this bar, I recall it being dimly lit, we made our way to the actual bar and there was an empty stool at and facing it. Brian sat on the stool and I stood next to him, we were waiting to be served and as the barman came over he began pouring a drink from the optics facing us, a shortish woman came up behind us and wriggled her way in between us, putting her arms around us both she said with a forced smile in a pure Glasgow accent "whetch one a yous boys es gonna buy me a drenk then ?" Being young I was dumbstruck but Brian replied "sorry love but we haven't got a lot of money" She angrily pushed Brian as she replied "well get oota ma fucking seat then !" she pushed Brian so hard that he fell off the stool nearly

46

hitting on the floor, now as I said Brian was a heavily set man and he was not happy with this, He began saying something like "what the hell are you playing at ?" By this time everyone in the bar was watching, and the barman had a bottle of beer in his raised hand which we hadn't asked for, so I could only presume it was for clobbering someone with, namely Brian or myself.

I said something to the barman like "no worries mate we're leaving" and I ushered Brian towards and out of the door. Once outside Brian wanted to go back in and carry it on, but we were strangers, well outnumbered in a rough area so common sense prevailed. We walked away and returned to our respective lorries where we stayed, rather nervously on my part, for the night.

On another occasion I was again in Glasgow, having learnt my lesson in Gallowgate I'd opted to park up at Kelvinbridge in the university area of the city, I had reckoned that would be a safer place to stay.

I went to find a bar and came upon a decent looking one. I peered in through the windows and all looked very nice, it was quite full and most of the drinkers in there looked like students and the like. I went in and got myself a pint. I couldn't find a seat so I plonked myself up against an empty space by a wall and began to people watch.

Not long after, I noticed a group of people who were standing in the middle of the room, it was a mixed group of girls and lads. One of the lads leaned in towards a girl and whispered something to her and started to laugh, she backed away from him and without warning she smashed her half pint pot, the dimpled sort with a handle, right across his forehead. She screamed at him "how fucking dare you !!" And stormed off.

This guys head was pouring in blood and things started to get a bit edgy, lads pushing and shoving each other and I thought to myself "get out of here before it kicks off Steve" so I made a swift exit. After that episode I vowed never to stay in Glasgow again. Most of the time I'd go to Hamilton or surrounding areas of the city, only having to stay in it rarely.

On another trip to Scotland I had loaded at a company in Bury. It was a piece of equipment for delivery to Hunterston Power Station in Ayrshire. It was an extremely expensive bit of kit. I was told at Bury that it was worth around one million pounds, which was, and still is, a lot of money.

It was like a tube with things like spikes protruding off the body of it. Weighing around two tons, it was about ten feet long, it was laid lengthwise horizontally in a cradle, keeping it off the floor of my vehicle in order to protect the spikes, I very carefully chained the equipment down using sheets of rubber matting so as not to damage it. I rolled my main sheet across the top of the spikes without opening it out and then covered it all loosely with a fly sheet before setting off for Scotland.

I arrived at Hunterston mid afternoon on a lovely warm sunny day and delivered the load with no problems. "What's the story there then ?" I hear you asking, well although my delivery went well, it, or one the same as it, didn't go as well for a mate of mine.

He was sent to pick up another one of them a several weeks after I had delivered mine. The drivers name was Graham, and he, like Alan and Dangle was a friend of mine from Levenshulme. We'd known each other for years. Anyway he loaded the same thing that I had from Bury, it was to go to Hunterston as mine had done, and Graham secured it in the same manner as I had.

When he got to Hunterston it was raining, it had been raining for some weeks on and off. Graham was travelling down the same road at the site as I had a few weeks previously, a diversionary makeshift site road which went down a hill and had been constructed on a raised mound, it had downward banking on either side of it.

Graham told me later that as he went slowly down he felt his lorry slightly moving as he reached the bottom of the hill and before he could do anything the road collapsed on one side of his lorry and it slid sideways before turning onto its side and then onto its roof. Graham was now upside down with his leg stuck between the steering column and the engine cowling, amazingly he was unhurt.

As he sat, still in his seat, upside down with his head up against the roof of the cab (which had been dinted by the soil underneath) he saw hot engine oil which had leaked out from the engine, coming through the cowling cover, which was dripping down towards him. He tried to open his door to get out but it was jammed shut by the partly collapsed roof so he was trapped. In what seemed a long time to Graham, but in fact was only five or so minutes, people who had seen what had happened got to him, and after checking he was OK proceeded to extract him from his cab.

The expensive piece of machinery was still in position where Graham had secured it and looked all intact. He was taken to the medical centre at the site and he ended up staying overnight there in a workers accommodation room. The lorry and load was lifted back onto its wheels the following day by a crane. The road in question was put out of use after a health and safety enquiry exonerated Graham from any blame.

I spoke to him recently about this episode, he told me that as far as he knew there was no damage to the load, and that he recalls actually driving his lorry back to Reyners once it had been checked over and any faults had been put right. An amazing but very lucky escape for him.

The lorry driving culture in the seventies involved drinking, well, not so much the drinking of beer, but the social aspect of it. Drivers, especially long distance ones, do not have their families to come home to at the end of the working day, it was either sit in your cab on your own if you were sleeping in it, sit in the tv room at the digs or go for a walk, which would inevitably end up with you stopping for a swift one in a pub if you found one.

Drivers on nights out used to gravitate to certain pubs in an area, for example at Bury St. Edmonds in Suffolk there was a bar right at the entrance to the lorry park, which at that time was in the market place in the town centre, and most drivers would go in there for a beer but mainly to meet up with some other driver they worked with, just knew, or even another driver like themselves who wanted to converse with somebody other than themselves, to have a chat with them about how their day had gone or whatever. I think that's what pubs are about, don't you ? places for social interaction, if you so want it.

The trend didn't end there though, when a driver got back to their depot on say a Friday night or a Saturday morning some drivers would go straight home, others would go for a swift one in the local "glue pot" near the depot. Some would have a couple, chat with their colleagues and then go home to their families. Others, usually the ones who lived near the pub, might stay a little longer before going. Then there were those who stayed too long before heading home. That's how it was, drinking and driving was not frowned upon as much as it is today.

The breathalyser was first used in October 1967 and it became illegal to drink and drive then, depending on how much you'd had of course. Nowadays it is virtually zero tolerance, but in those days it wasn't so.

Reyners had their "glue pot" which was The Bush in Droylsden, a two minute walk away, and it was well patronised by their drivers, quite a few who lived locally and others who had to travel to other areas to get home.

Another one which was popular after working on a Saturday morning was The Vulcan in Gorton, which was more popularly known as The Monkey because it had a stuffed monkey mounted on one corner of the bar. I can remember that Froxmer Street, which ran down the side of the pub, used to have a line of Reyners lorries all parked up alongside the factory wall of the steam engine works on a Saturday afternoon.

Reyners used to let you take your vehicle home at nights and at weekends as long as you had somewhere safe to park it. I've seen six or seven units, some hitched to trailers, four wheelers and my little Leyland parked there. We were all in The Monkey having a pint or two and discussing the things we'd been up to over the past five days, the stories I've heard of other drivers escapades would easily fill up another two maybe three books. It was just that, being sociable and having a laugh and a pint.

I remember once having a "walk round" Southampton town centre with another Reyner driver called Geoff T. I'd come out of a bar and was using a phone box outside the pub to to phone my wife Pat. I'd been in there for around five minutes when Geoff came out of the pub, pulled the phone box door open and whilst I was in mid conversation he shouted loudly "come on Steve, these girls won't wait all night for us !"

Luckily for me Pat didn't believe his jokey outburst once I'd explained what sort of guy Geoff was, he was much older than me and he knew how to press peoples buttons for a laugh. It was good old fashioned banter caused by a few beers and that sort of thing was always going on.

I was with Geoff on another occasion much later on when we had both unloaded bottled beers at a brewery in Edinburgh.

We both then reloaded with pallets of "returns", stock which had the wrong rotation labels on, or broken bottles amongst the shrink wrapped packs of twelve, things like that.

We set off homeward on a Friday afternoon and made our way south. We pulled in at a place called Biggar on the A702, around an hours drive from Edinburgh to stay for the night. At that time you could park overnight in what was the market place in the centre of the small town. We had a wash and change and then Geoff cooked up some chips for us both to eat on butties. Suitably fed we decided to go for a drink in one of the local pubs at around nine o clock that evening.

We went in around three bars, the last one being by far the busiest. We found a seat and were chatting away when Geoff suddenly got up and walked over to where two lads were playing pool. I saw him pointing towards me before he walked back over to me and said, "I've been watching those two, me and you are gonna take them on, I've bet them a fiver we'll beat them, come on" with that he headed back to the pool table. I thought to myself "bloody hell Geoff what've you got us into, I'm not that good at pool" however, I grabbed my drink and followed him over. He introduced me to the lads who I could see had had quite a bit to drink, they were okay but they were well inebriated shall we say. We played them, and not surprisingly, we got beat by them. Geoff put down his cue and said "hang on, I won't be long" before spinning round on his heels and walking quickly out of the bar.

I was as gobsmacked as the two Scottish lads, one of which said "where the fucks he gone ? He owes us a fiver" I stuttered something like "oh he won't be long don't worry" even though I was worried myself. One of them said "Im not fucking worried I just hope for your sake he comes back" It was getting very edgy, I was trying to placate these irate lads and must have been doing so for what seemed like an eternity when Geoff walked rather unsteadily in carrying three unopened packs of bottled beers. He plonked them down on the edge of the pool table and said "I haven't got a spare fiver, I need what I've got left to buy more beer but you can have this lot instead, it's worth well more than a fiver" It was a gamble he'd taken, and it paid off.

The two lads looked at each other and the bigger of the two burst out laughing, he said "you've got a fucking deal boy, ya cheeky bastard !" After that it was like we were all best friends,

51

we learnt that the bigger guy of the two was getting married the next day, the pub was so packed because he and his intended were having their respective bachelor and hen nights together in the one bar. He took us to meet her saying "I'm marrying this fucker in the morning and you two are invited".

I don't recall what time we left that bar, all I remember is waking up on the Saturday morning at around 08.00 with a banging headache. I woke Geoff up and we both wearily got ourselves ready to leave. I was half expecting the lad who'd invited us to his wedding to come round but he didn't, well not before we'd left anyway. That journey back home was a real drag, Geoff flashed me after about an hours driving and we pulled into a lay-by off the A74. He said he was going back to sleep as he was feeling so rough, I carried on home as it was already late enough by then and I didn't want to finish work on a Saturday too late.

I often think about where Geoff got those beers from, have you worked it out ??

If you think about it a lot of people go home from work and never mention what's happened to them, some will discuss what may have been a traumatic or mundane experience, but only then. Lorry drivers on the other hand would have a hard job talking to their wives or girlfriends about what happened on the A1 or wherever, they wouldn't really understand what they were hearing, they may well sit and listen, even though they haven't a clue what chaining steel vessels down meant, and that's not their fault, it's the fault of the job that drivers have to persevere with for long periods of time on their own.

Please don't think I'm condoning drinking and driving, I most certainly am not. It's just, that's how it was in those days. By the time of my retirement from driving trucks I very rarely went for a pint. Sleeper cabs brought all that to an end. You had your bed, televisions, fridges and electric ovens in the cab, one company I worked at even had microwaves installed. More importantly they had night heaters which worked off diesel and kept you toasty warm when it was cold, so there was no reason to go to the pub, and mobile phones made it easy to keep in touch with colleagues, and more importantly, your wives, kids and loved ones at home.

There is one particular memory I have of a really bad trip I once had which was tinged with kindness from a fellow trucker and a night fitter from Reyners garage.

I had loaded four one ton tanks of lager from the Harp lager brewery in Manchester the previous evening. We used to take them, among many other places, to Scottish and Newcastle brewery in Newcastle which is where I set off for at 06.00 the next morning, which was a Friday.

All went well on the early part of the journey but the weather changed and it began snowing very heavily, as I reached the Scotch Corner turnoff on the A1 near Darlington I heard a bang and I looked out of my offside mirror to see a cloud of smoke followed by the vehicle body lurching over to the off side. I had had a blow out on the rear offside outer tyre. I was virtually at the entrance to the cafe which used to be there (it's a hotel now) just off the junction at the roundabout so I drove at a very slow pace onto the car park. I found a phone box and reported the blow out and where I was to Reyners, who told me that someone would be coming out to me and to sit tight.

As I said, it was really snowing heavily by now so I went to my vehicle, started the engine, turned on the heater, and waited. A tyre company came out after around 50 minutes, the tyre fitter examined the tyre and told me that he had found damage to the inner tyre as well and that it was not safe to drive with it. He said it may have happened during the blow out or by me driving it off the roadside to the car park. I explained that I wasn't prepared to sit on the busy A1 in almost blizzard like conditions where my lorry may not have been clearly visible to other drivers and where he would have had to work, he agreed with me, and said that he would have done the same.

The problem we then had, was that he'd only brought one tyre so he would have to go back to Darlington to get another one. He jacked up my lorry and took off both of the wheels, he said he would take them both away to his depot and change the tyres there as the snow was now quite thick on the ground. He placed a supporting stand under the axle as an extra precaution and told me he'd be as quick as he could, then he left.

As I was sitting in my lorry I spotted Joe B, one of Reyners artic' drivers, whom I mentioned earlier in the book, heading south on the A1. He saw me sitting there with my lorry jacked up and gestured something with his hand but I couldn't make out what he meant before he disappeared into the snowy distance.

It must have got to lunch time and I was beginning to feel peckish and was contemplating leaving the lorry to go for something to eat. It was then that I saw Joe's lorry coming off onto the slip way to the junction towards me. He pulled onto the car park, and then came over to my lorry. I told him what had happened and he said "I saw you there and I was trying to tell you I was going to turn round at the next junction and come back to see if I could help, have you had anything to eat ?" I replied that I hadn't and he asked me to go to his lorry where he'd fix me up with something.

Now in those days most drivers used cafes for their meals, but not Joe, oh no, he was the first person I can recall who had a little prima stove and grill in his cab and he did his own meals most of the time. We got into his warm cab and he proceeded to rustle us up some beans on toast and a cup of hot tea. We chatted and it transpired that he had gone down to the next junction at Catterick and turned around to come back to me. He did not have to do that, and most drivers probably wouldn't have, but Joe was a different breed who used to look out for their workmates. After we'd both eaten I thanked him for thinking of me and Joe went on his way.

The tyre fitter came back at around 14.30 and put both the newly tyred wheels back onto my vehicle, I then set off at around 15.00 in the snow, which was still falling heavily. Later, as I was slowly going over the very slippy and icy flyover in Gateshead that drops down to the Tyne bridge, everything ground to a halt. I pulled up believe it or not behind Ray, another one of our drivers who was taking a twenty ton tank of lager to be emptied at the same brewery as I was going to. I got out, leaving the engine running, and walked carefully on the very icy surface up to his cab and got into it. The reason we had all stopped was because of the ice, some cars, near the bridge, had slid into each other.

Ray told me that he'd seen me at Scotch Corner with the tyre fitter and that he thought everything was in hand so he'd carried on. After chatting for a few minutes I returned to my lorry which as I said was directly behind Rays. I sat there and I noticed that Rays skeletal trailer holding the demountable lager tank was moving, ever so slowly, but it was moving. It had started to slide on the glass like ice to the offside towards the next lane of traffic, which, like us, were all stopped.

I got out and trod carefully along to Ray to tell him, he obviously had nowhere to go so we both got out to speak to the vehicle drivers who were stopped in the outside lane and asked them all to shunt forward and backwards as much as possible so that we could clear the area where his trailer was sliding towards. We did manage to shift everything out of the way, just as the traffic in front began to slowly move off towards the now open bridge ahead. Rays trailer had slid by this time to almost a right angle across the offside carriageway so I held the the traffic back whilst Ray very gently pulled away and straightened up the unit and trailer, I then got back into mine and proceeded to slowly follow him down the overpass hill and onto the Tyne bridge. We both made our way very gingerly to the brewery arriving there at around 17.00.

The story doesn't end there, after unloading the full tanks and reloading with four empty tanks, then having a meal at the brewery canteen I set off on my journey back home at around 18.00. Up to that time I'd done twelve hours and I faced a journey of who knew how long in really bad weather, but I didn't want to stay out overnight in case the weather got any worse possibly leaving me to struggle even more than I had.

I decided that as in those times we still used manual logbooks to record our hours of duty, which could be "adjusted" to suit me, so I was going to try to get home no matter how long it may have taken me.

I made my way back down the A1 and then onto the A64 through Leeds where I made my way to the A62. Due to inexperience and the conditions, I'd not taken into account that I had used more fuel than I would normally have done. I could do Newcastle and back on a full tank when everything ran smoothly, but things hadn't gone well at all that day and I'd noticed that I was running low on fuel. I travelled along to just west of Huddersfield outside Marsden on the A62. The snow warning sign there said that the Stanedge pass over the Pennines was open.

I pulled up outside a closed garage at around 20.45 as I had now noticed that my fuel gauge was showing nearly empty, I dared not travel any further. It had long stopped snowing by then so I left my vehicle and walked back to Marsden to find a chippy and a phone. I did get something to eat and then I had a thought "would the night staff at the garage back at Reyners come out with some fuel for me" I found a phone box and tentatively rang the garage office. I was answered after a little while by Dick who was the night foreman.

I explained my situation and Dick must have taken pity on me because after rollocking me for not getting fuel earlier in the day he said that he would come out to me with some. Droylsden is fairly near Oldham where Dick got onto the A62 and he arrived at around 22.45 with a couple of five gallon cans of diesel. We put the fuel in my tank and after receiving another bollocking off Dick we both set off homeward at around 11.15.

I eventually got home at 12.45. I was totally over my time and I shouldn't have done what I had, but the circumstances were extremely unusual, and I did not want to be stuck out on a Friday night and then possibly have trouble getting home on the following Saturday morning. To this day I remain extremely grateful for the thoughtfulness shown to me by both Joe and Dick.

Sometimes fatigue can get the better of a person, it affected me on more than one occasion, and it was the reason on this particular day. It was half way through a Thursday afternoon and I'd been up early that morning returning to the Manchester area with a backload from somewhere or other a good distance down the road. I'd got the load off and was instructed to go to an engineering factory in Stockport that afternoon and load four tons of machine parts that were in pallet cages.

The transport clerk, Charles, had told me it was a nice job for a Friday as I was to take the cages to Wrexham (here's where the fatigue kicks in) and reload with another four tons of finished product which was to be returned to the works in Stockport. I thought "that'll do for me, nice little job on a Friday, should get finished handy". So off I went to Stockport and loaded the cages.

I got back into my lorry after loading and threw the paperwork into a little pocket I had in the door, I'd look at where I was going in the morning, after all it was only Wrexham I was going to. I then went home. I had some dinner, followed by a bath and being young and foolhardy, went off to meet my mates for a few beers. The few beers turned into many and I found myself back home at around 22.00. I wasn't worried as I could have a lie in the next day as I was only going to Wrexham.

I got into my vehicle the next morning at 06.30 and set off, it was a lovely clear day and I didn't have a care in the world, I tootled along until I was in the Gresford area near Wrexham where I pulled up at a little cafe and went in for some breakfast.

On re-entering my lorry after brekkie I decided to look at my paperwork to find the address of the company I was going to. I unfolded the sheet of paper and looked at the address, suddenly I got a cold shiver followed quickly by a hot flush as I read the address, it was an engineering company all right but it was in Exeter....! Yes Exeter....in Devon. I must have had a brain freeze when Charles told me what he wanted me to do, probably down to fatigue or I must have heard him wrongly, anyway it was Exeter. My next thought was to ring Charles and tell him but I thought better of it so at around 08.15 I set off in the direction of Whitchurch where I could then head south through Wolverhampton and onto the M5 towards Devon.

The M5 then, ended below the turn off for south Wales just past the Strensham services. I flew down the A38 ! through Gloucester, Bristol, Bridgewater, Taunton and on to Exeter.

I got there at around 14.15. The guy who unloaded me said he had expected me to arrive just before lunchtime, I fobbed him off with a fib about traffic holdups which seemed to pacify him and he unloaded the cages and then reloaded me. I was only there for a half hour all told. I set off northbound on my way back home. I didn't get back home that night, the Friday traffic took its usual toll and I parked up at The Sunset Cafe on the A449 at Penkridge in between Wolverhampton and Stafford. I unloaded the return cages on the Saturday morning and finished up reloading at the yard in Droylsden. I never did tell anyone of my mistake....until now !

I only ever worked one Saturday and Sunday whilst I was driving the Leyland. I was talking to one of the transport clerks, Charles, one early Friday morning, He asked me would I do him a favour and work one, at that time Saturday mornings were worked more often than not, that was when you ran in from somewhere or if you had any little jobs that needed doing done. This job wasn't like that, Charles told me I could go home at lunchtime and then start work at around 10.30 on the Saturday. I was to go to a dry dock in Trafford Park where I'd load a four ton small boat engine. I was then to take it to another dry dock at Woolwich, in south east London. It would be unloaded overnight and I was booked in to stay at a pub five minutes from the dry dock. I'd then return the next morning and drive my empty lorry home. It all sounded great to me, a bit of an adventure for a young man, so I agreed to do it. I went home and had the afternoon off.

The next morning I went to Trafford Park and loaded the engine, which was sat in a made to fit cradle. I chained it down and set off for London at around 11.45. I arrived at the dry dock in Woolwich at 18.45 where I was asked to reverse into a shed and leave my lorry to be unloaded later that night. I took my night out bag and made my way to the pub, which I, for the life of me, can't recall its name, anyway it was across the main road nearly opposite the gate to the dry dock.

The landlady, a lively Scottish woman, greeted me and I booked in. She showed me my room and told me that by the time I'd had a wash and change, she'd have a meal ready for me downstairs in the bar. All went well and I enjoyed a hearty dinner before sampling her ales. In fact it went too well, it was a Saturday night and the pub got really busy with the beer flowing copiously. I recall that at one point I was dancing with the landlady's daughter but after that I can't remember anything.

I was awoken at 09.00 on the Sunday morning with a banging headache by the landlady, who informed me that my breakfast would be ready in a short while. I got up and made myself ready then wearily made my way downstairs, where I sheepishly sat very quietly to be told of my exploits the previous night. I hadn't caused anybody any problems, but I did have a lot to drink. At one point the landlord had stepped in and advised me not to "go up west" with a crowd of revellers who were doing just that, he was worried that I would not get back in a fit state to drive the next day, and I didn't know my way around London like the revellers did. It was he who'd shown me to bed at around 12.30 and ensured that I'd gotten bedded down safely.

I felt really embarrassed about all this and thanked them for looking out for me. They laughed and told me there hadn't been a problem. Reyners had pre paid the overnight costs, so, after thanking them once again, I made my way back to my now empty lorry and set off on the long journey northbound in a very sorry state indeed !.

Long distance drivers nowadays sleep in bunks that are fitted in the vehicle cab, they are known as sleeper cabs. Before sleeper cabs drivers would either sleep on boards across the engine cowling and the seats or more commonly, in transport "digs", cafes and private homes which offered bed and breakfast accommodation for them.

The sleeping arrangements varied from establishment to establishment, some rare ones offered private rooms, but the bulk would have dormitory style arrangements where there could be multiple beds in army hut style, or four or more beds or bunk beds spread haphazardly in one room. I've slept upstairs in a converted barn. It wasn't an ideal way to get some well deserved sleep.

Some lads snored, quite heavily too, then, worryingly to me anyway, there were the smokers, the guys who woke up at intervals during the night, sat up and lit up, it may have only been a few drags on the cigarette or the whole thing, but if you were a light sleeper as I was, multi bed rooms were not a good place to be in.

Some digs offered a wake up call, this varied, at one place, a bell would be rung from 04.00 in the morning and then every half hour after until 06.30, by which time most of the drivers were up and gone. Others may have asked you what time you wished to get up and they would either give a knock on your door if you were lucky enough to have your own room, or creep into the room and give you a gentle shake on the shoulder if you were not. Some, and there weren't many, were like home, comfortable and warm and more importantly, more private, you'd have your own sink, whereas in other places you would have to wash or shower in a multi sink room, then there were the open showers, in rows, as they are in football changing rooms.

This is what life was like for the long distance drivers up and down the UK for up to five times in a week.

Modern day artic' and rigid drivers, in the main, use either box vans, containers or curtain siders to keep the freight they carry in a dry condition. Curtain siders are made with the flat deck of the vehicle, which has a roof, rear doors and waterproof curtains which slide forwards and backwards giving access on both sides to load the vehicle.

When I began in the industry, we mostly had flat chassis bodies to put the freight on. We would then spread either one main sheet if we had a rigid two axle lorry, or two main sheets covering the length of the trailer on the articulated vehicles. We would then tie down the sheets using thin rope ties attached to the them.

Once the sheet was fastened firmly down we would then use 25 mtr. lengths of rope, tightened with a slip knot known in the trade as "a dolly knot" to hold the sheets and the load securely in place. If the freight had to be kept super dry we would then spread what was known as a fly sheet, which was not as wide as a main sheet over the whole thing and fasten that down with the thin rope ties, we'd sometimes put a rope around the front and rear of these sheets but the idea was that it would gently flap during travel and water would then blow off it.

A job which involves long hours, such as a lorry driver, can, as I've already stated, bring on fatigue, it comes with the job. Starting at 04.00 and being on duty until 19.00 isn't what the average worker does. This could be done three times in a week by a trucker, add to that two more days working thirteen hours and then possibly working a Saturday morning for four hours, totals up to seventy five hours worked.

Of course truckers take breaks during their duty, at the time of me writing this, a driver would have to take a forty five minute break away from duty after doing four and a half hours of just driving. They also have to take a thirty minute break if they drive for say three hours and spend another three on other duties such as loading and unloading, which would total six hours. The rules and regulations for HGV drivers are quite complicated and I don't think that I could explain them all to you without boring you to sleep or you losing interest.

Needless to say, I have suffered with fatigue on many occasions. Any HGV driver who says that he hasn't is, in my opinion, a liar. It can take many forms, they may, heaven forbid, fall asleep at the wheel. It has happened (and not just to lorry drivers) with many dreadful consequences. I am relieved to say that it has never happened to me. The main form of fatigue though is daydreaming, this is where you are driving almost on auto pilot and you are aware of everything going on around you but your mind is thinking of something totally out of the box, you can have short spells of this or sometimes, worryingly, longer periods. You kind of snap out of it and return to reality and you think to yourself "where am I ?" You've been in that moment between being awake, but dozy with your eyes open, and actually falling asleep. I used to lower down my windows and let fresh air into my cab, then I'd pull over when it was safe to do so, park up and then either get out of the lorry and have a walk around or climb over to the passenger seat and have a ten minute cat nap, the cat nap to me was the best solution, it always worked for me.

I had a real scare though once on the M1. I was driving northbound on a long straight stretch north of Northampton on a dark evening and I must have drifted into the "half asleep" state. I could see the other traffic on the motorway on both carriageways, I could see the main train line that ran alongside the motorway at that point, but what I saw next was frightening. Out of the embankment between the train line and the inside lane I was driving along came a bloke on a pushbike heading straight across my path. I slammed on the brakes and had almost stopped before I realised there was no cyclist and no bike ! Luckily for me there was nobody right behind me and I quickly got my head together and continued on to the next services where I stopped, had a nap and a walk round before continuing on. Fatigue can be a killer, treat it with respect and stop if you feel tired, the consequences could be fatal.

Most people don't think of lorry drivers as tradesmen, but they are. I learned what I consider my trade, from a young age, a sort of apprenticeship. I was taught by the guys who knew the transport business, but it doesn't happen in many companies nowadays.

I mentioned earlier that Reyners had a policy of taking on youths, learning them the "ropes", putting them in for their car driving tests and then, when they became of age, sending them on a course of HGV driving, loading and securing, basic safety and maintenance. Once you had completed the course you had your HGV test, which, once passed, enabled Reyners to keep a steady flow of driving talent which could only have benefited both the company and the driver.

Geoffrey Reyner Ltd. was a founder member, along with other hauliers and interested parties, of the R.T.I.T.B (Road Transport Industry Training Board) whose purpose was to train people to safely drive and handle lorries with the goal of gaining an HGV licence. Reyners sent me to the RTITB school which used to be in Failsworth, Manchester. I undertook the course and passed my HGV test at the first attempt. At first I was given a flat back four wheeler ten tonner to drive.

My first run was a two drop journey to Norwich. I got there and had delivered the two drops by just after lunchtime. I rang the guy named Tommy M. at Reyners for my backload and I was sent to an old established hauliers named Ken Thomas in Guyhirn, in between Peterborough and Wisbech.

I was to collect nine tons of tinned peas which were for delivery to a cash and carry outlet in Stoke on Trent. I loaded, sheeted and roped it, and, not having a sleeper cab, booked some digs on the A50 somewhere near Markfield in Leicestershire, it's all a bit sketchy to me now.

Anyway, back to the story, I had tootled along the A47 and on through Peterborough heading towards Leicester where I picked up the A50. I had been driving along in the dark for some time when I spotted a blue flashing light behind me, it was a police car so I pulled over. I got out of the cab and met the police officer about half way along my vehicle. "where are you going ?" He asked. I explained that I was heading for my digs and he replied "do you know you haven't got a single light showing on the rear of your lorry ?" Obviously, I didn't know. I walked with him to the back of the lorry, and as he had told me, all my tail lights were out. I returned to the cab and tried my left and right flashers and they were working. "Well I can't let you goon your way without rear lights, where are you staying exactly ?" He enquired. I told him and he said he knew where the place was and that it wasn't too far up the road, so he offered to stay behind me as cover 'till I reached my digs.

I thanked him and we set off. After around ten minutes of driving he flashed me again to stop. He explained that the digs were only a hundred yards away up the road and asked me was I able to get my lorry off the road. I didn't know as I'd never stayed there before, so we both walked up to the place and saw that there was indeed room for me to reverse the lorry off the road onto a smallish car park at the side of the premises. He put on his blue flashing light in his car to stop any traffic that may have come along and I reversed onto the car park. He told me I was not to move from there the following day until I had my lights repaired, which I did have, by an auto electrician whom my company organised to come out to me. It meant I was to have a late start to my day, which was to be fair, a bit of a bonus for me. That was my first trip as a fully fledged HGV driver.

Another of my early trips in the ten tonner was to a Sainsburys regional distribution centre (RDC) in Basingstoke, Hampshire. I'd loaded ten tons of jams and marmalades from Robertsons Preserves in Droylsden in the late morning, and then left to run down to Basingstoke in order to deliver at a predefined time slot of 08.00 the following morning.

I'd never been to this RDC before but knew that it was in the town and not on the outskirts. When I got to Basingstoke in the evening I found a pub with some waste parking ground to the side of it which was shielded from the road by large advertising hoardings. I parked up there on what had become a really freezing cold night. I was going to "cab it" that night as I'd sorted out and old flat panel door on which I used to place a caravan berth mattress, which I'd lay across from the passenger door window, across the engine cowling and onto the drivers seat, it was all propped up and supported by blankets and cushions, then I'd tuck myself into a sleeping bag. I had an old curtain which I used to tuck behind the sun visors across the windscreen for a little bit of privacy. Primitive I know, but I didn't sleep in the lorry very much in those days.

As I said it was really….really cold that night, a freezing fog had descended on the town and I began to regret my decision to sleep in the cab, anyway after finding a chippy and eating them, I thought I'd go and have a few pints to help me sleep. I had more than a few and got back to my lorry at around 22.00. Even at that time everything was starting to freeze up. I sorted out my bed and bedding, hung my "curtain" and set out my clothes for the morning. I then got undressed and slid into my sleeping bag, and, with the aid of the alcohol I'd consumed, I soon fell asleep.

I didn't know how long I had slept, but I woke up absolutely freezing ! I found my little travel alarm clock and saw that it was only 02.20. I sat up and put on a clean tee shirt I had ready for the morning, that was cold too !. I tucked myself back into my bag and tried to get back to sleep, to no avail, it was just too cold. I sat up again and decided to put on my socks trousers and overall jacket. Whilst getting dressed I felt the urge to pee, this night was just getting worse. After dressing and putting on my boots and heavy waterproof coat I got out of my lorry and went behind the hoardings to do what was necessary. I then got back in my cab and started the engine, turning the "heater" on full blast.

Now for those that don't know, the heater in an H registered ERF with a Gardener 100 engine was next to useless ! You'd have to be driving at normal speeds for about a half an hour, before the heaters in those lorries would even offer up a slight bit of warmth ! I took off my boots and heavy coat and got back into my sleeping bag and once again curled up and tried to fall back asleep. The engine was running and, again for those that are not in the know, the tickover of the lorry was very erratic, so erratic that the cab used to visibly shake and vibrate, and outside, the blue smoke my vehicle exhaust was chucking out into the atmosphere would have given David Attenborough a heart attack.

As tired as I was, and being a light sleeper, I had no chance of kipping with all that going on, the noise, the vibration and no warmth whatsoever from the heater, so I got up again and turned off the engine. I got my heavy coat, took out the supporting blankets off my engine cowling and spread them over the top of me and once again got back into the bag. I lay there shivering until fatigue finally took over and I dropped off to sleep after who knows how long.

I woke up at around 06.00. The inside of my windscreen had ice on it, the outside of the screen was frozen solid, the freezing fog had dissipated overnight and the air was crisp and freezing cold. I decided that I would go to Sainsburys earlier in the hope I could unload before my booking time. I started my engine then I scraped off the ice inside my cab using a fuel card, I then climbed onto my front bumper and after an almighty effort, cleared a hole which was good enough for me to have reasonable vision to travel with. There was one other thing that I had to do which is not often seen nowadays, the air in my brake chambers had become frozen, I took a newspaper from my cab and lit a few rolled up tight sheets of it and set them alight, I then held them under my air tanks in an effort to thaw everything out which in turn meant the air could begin to circulate. I had to do this quite often in the early days, It would also be the method of thawing out diesel pipes in which the fuel could gel up in really cold weather. I checked my vehicle over and noted that the sheets and ropes covering and securing the load were all frozen solid too.

I then made my way to Sainsburys, the guy at the gate, who sits in a lorry height cabin, who lets you in, looked at me with awe as I pulled up outside his open window at around 06.50. "Bloody hell... where the hell have you come from ? are you booked in ?" I wearily told him my story and he must have taken pity on me because of the state I was in, he actually let me go in to a waiting area near the unloading bays but advised me that I may not get unloaded until my booking time of 08.00. I wasn't bothered, all I wanted was to get warm, have a hot drink and a wash.

It transpired that I didn't get unloaded earlier than my allotted time which I was grateful for, this meant I could then go inside the driver waiting area, where there were drink and snack machines and a toilet with hot running water in the sinks for me to use. Later though, I did struggle with the ropes securing the load, I had a really hard time undoing the dolly knots we used to tighten the ropes, they and the sheet covering the load were frozen solid, I had to climb on top of the load and pull the sheet up onto it to try to fold it up as it was impossible to drag it off as I normally would have done, it was so stiff that it may have dragged some the load with it.

The night I had just gone through was a nightmare. I swore to myself that it would have to be a last resort before I'd ever do anything like that again.

In north London there's an area that is known as "little Ireland", it's Kilburn. I was sent there with a load of small home DIY cement kits. They comprised of a medium paint tin sized tub of sand and with each tub came pre measured polythene bags of cement. I had nine tons of all this which covered the whole of the deck of my lorry.

I arrived at the drop, which was at a very well known Irish civil engineering company in Kilburn. This company had other sites in the UK and was probably the biggest well known firm of its kind. Anyway I arrived there just before lunch time to find

65

the gates to the very large site closed. At first I thought they may have been closed for lunch but there wasn't a soul in sight, which I deemed to be unusual at such a big site. I noticed that the gates to the site were not locked though, so I locked my lorry and tentatively pushed one of the gates open and walked in.

I had spotted a building around a hundred yards away and thought that there may be someone there so I headed for it. I had only reached half way there when a mans voice from behind me shouted in an Irish accent "Hey.. can I help you ?" I told him that I had a delivery for them to which he replied "not today you don't son, are you not aware it's Paddy's day ? There's nobody'll be working today" Only then did it hit me, it was the 17th of March, St. Patricks day.

He explained that he was the yard watchman and he'd been sat in a pub on the corner of the street where I'd turned into to access the yard, he'd seen me go up towards the yard, finished his pint and then followed me up to it. I asked him could I unload it myself, hoping he'd offer to help me. He took me to a clear spot in the yard and told me to put the stuff there, he then dragged an old tarpaulin over and asked me to cover it when I'd finished. He opened the gates fully and I drove my lorry to where he'd shown me he wanted the load putting. He asked for my paperwork and after a quick scan at it he said "right, I'll sign this now and when your done just pull the gate back to" then he was gone, probably back to the pub.

The load was all loose on the flat and had to be handled off so I started. It took me a good two hours to get it all off, I then rolled the tarpaulin over it all just in time to see the watchman coming back through the gate. He said "ahh I was just coming to give you a hand with all that". His timing was perfect and I just couldn't be angry with him, after all it's every Irishman's favourite day isn't it ?!!

Back in the days when some people worked on New Years Day if they didn't have enough holiday entitlement left, I was given a run to Bath and Bristol by one of the managers named Charles, who assured me, that considering it was New Years Day, all would be well and I would be able to unload all three of my deliveries. I was to go to Bath first and deliver two pallets of specialised paper. I then had two more deliveries of canned soft drinks to deliver to cash and carry outlets in Cardiff.

I had been out drinking on New Years Eve and I'd arrived home in the early hours of the new year after going to a friends party. I got up to go to work, and to say I was the worst for wear would be an understatement. I left Manchester at 07.00 and travelled down to Bath in a very sorry state.

The first delivery was at a high security complex which did some kind of work for the Royal Mint, concerning (I was informed) bank notes. I arrived there and entered what can only be described as prison like admissions. The place was surrounded by high barbed wire fencing with CCTV cameras every ten yards or so. I drove through the entrance gate which was then closed behind me. I pulled up to another locked gate in front of me, next to the security box cabin and opened my window to speak to the guard at the window. He asked me what I was there for, I told him that I had a delivery of paper and I was told it was expected there by my manager. He laughed at that, then told me that there were no staff in to unload me as it was New Years Day, he said I would have to come back the following day. I was really upset at this but, despite my pleas, I got no further with the security guard so I enquired if I could go in to turn around in order to get back out onto the road outside. He informed me I could but that I would have to surrender any cameras I may have had and also any cigarettes, matches or lighters.

I handed him my smoking gear and informed him that I didn't have a camera. He asked me to sit for a while whilst one of his companions came out to me as he would have escort me in my cab whilst I was on the premises. What a load of baloney ! I was only going in to turn around and leave. Anyway that's what I had to do, I left after collecting my smoking gear and dropping off my escort who had been with me for all of five minutes.

I drove to my next delivery which was a cash and carry wholesaler in Cardiff. I sensed something was wrong because when I arrived, there weren't any other vehicles whatsoever. I parked up and went to a closed roller shutter door, It was around lunch time and I thought that may have been the reason it was shut. I put my ear close to it and listened, I could hear a diesel fork lift engine running inside so I rang a bell by the side of the door. Nothing happened so after a few minutes I rang it again, a man came out of a smaller door nearby and asked me what I wanted. I replied that I had four pallets of soft drinks for him.

67

He replied that they were not accepting deliveries that day as most of the warehouse staff were off and the two men who were there were doing a stocktake, I would have to come back the next day. My headache was compounding by this time. Once again despite pleading with the man to unload me, I left the premises with as much on my lorry as I had gone there with.

I made my way to the next delivery where I found they were open and I was able to unload the other four pallets of soft drinks. The problem I had was that because I could not unload at the two previous drops, the four pallets for the final one were wedged in front of the the others, at the front end of my lorry. The guy who unloaded me was very understanding and managed to dig the pallets out that he required. I retrieved my signed delivery notes, sheeted and roped the remainder of the load and left to find some digs in which to stay for the night.

It was quite early in the afternoon but I did manage to book a bed in a B&B not far from the prison in Cardiff. I parked my lorry up on an empty car park and made my way to the digs. On the way I attempted to phone Charles to tell him that the day had been a waste of time and give him a piece of my mind, but there was no answer, which upset me even more as I realised that they too were off work.

I found my digs, had a wash and changed clothes, then went out to find something to eat. I ended up, after dining in a small cafe, going for a "livener" in a pub, and…yes… one led to another…and another and so on. All I was doing was topping up from the previous night and early morning. I don't know how I found my way back to the digs but I did. I awoke the following morning, attempted to eat as much cooked breakfast as my stomach would tolerate before leaving the digs on a cold and foggy morning, to find where I'd left my lorry. I couldn't for the life of me remember where, in my beer fuddled memory, I'd left it ! I did find it eventually and delivered the two other drops without hinderance. Happy New Year my arse !!

I mentioned earlier that Reyners had a contract with Harp Lager who had a brewery on the borders of the Greenheys, Moss Side and Hulme areas of Manchester. The brewery was taken over by Scottish & Newcastle Breweries who eventually merged with Courage Brewers. I once took two tanks of lager from there, weighing four tons each, on my ten tonner to the brewery at Newcastle Upon Tyne. I arrived there and emptied the tanks, all I had to do then was return to the brewery at Manchester with them.

I set off and stopped just on the outskirts of southern Gateshead to phone Reyners to enquire what my job would be the following day. After finding out, I was making my way back to the lorry when I saw two people, a lad who looked to be in his early twenties and a girl who looked around the same age, stood near the passenger door looking at the company name and where it was from. I asked them what was the matter and could I help them. The lad replied "are you actually going to Manchester ?" I replied in the affirmative that I was. The girl then said "wow... that's where we're going, could you give us a lift please ?" I had been weighing them both up as I was expecting such a request, they both looked clean and tidy and I'd presumed them to be student types so I agreed, after telling them that I didn't usually give lifts (due to the earlier incident I have mentioned in this book) but that on this occasion I'd take them down to Manchester with me. They were both very appreciative and we all got into the lorry. I placed one of my bed making cushions on the engine cowling which the lad sat on, the girl sat on the passenger seat, we then we set off south down the A1.

After about forty minutes the lad asked me if it was OK to have a smoke. At the time, I too smoked, but not very often in the cab. I replied that it would be alright for them to spark up as long as they opened the passenger window slightly to let some fresh air in. The lad leaned forward as the girl opened her ruck sack and brought out a tin, "ah..roll ups" I thought, I was busy concentrating on driving and not paying too much attention to what they were doing but as I drove along I got a whiff of something that definitely wasn't a tobacco smell. I looked across the cab in time to see the girl pass the lad a big spliff, he managed to take a draw on it as I said "Oi... what's this, I thought you meant a cigarette ?, I'm sorry folks but I'm not having any of that in here whilst I'm driving".

I have never smoked pot, weed or whatever else it may be called and I still to this day have no intention of having any. The lad looked a little put out and said as he passed it back to the girl "Come on mate, it's only a little pot" I replied that I didn't care and that they had to put it out right now. The girl then snappily chipped in "what's the matter with you ? It doesn't do you any harm" I replied that nothing was the matter with me and to put it out immediately. The lad was just about to add something as the girl took another drag on the spliff so I cut him short and said "right that's it ! I'm not arguing with you any more I have to concentrate on the road, I'm stopping here and you're both getting out" There was a lay by just up the road from us and I pulled in. I stopped the engine and ran round to the passenger door and yanked it open, they still had the spliff lit when I ordered them both to get out which they reluctantly did, muttering and cursing me under their breath but I didn't care, if they'd have put the thing out the first time I'd requested all would have been well, but they'd argued with me and I wasn't having any of it. I drove off and left them both there in the lay by. I don't know but I wouldn't mind betting that I'd have gotten high had I allowed them to carry on.

One of the last trips I did in a ten tonner before I was given an artic' was to Northern Ireland. I was informed that if I didn't wish to do the job I was free to refuse it. To me it seemed like something a bit different, so I agreed to do it.

I loaded seven tons of steel pipes from a company in Miles Platting in Manchester just before lunch time, I then set off to catch the ferry from Stranraer in Southern Scotland the following morning. I caught the ferry the next morning and sailed into Larne whereupon I set off for my first drop in the Glengormley area. My second and last drop was in Belfast itself. It was for a smallish engineering firm in the Falls Road area. Now at this time Northern Ireland was in the midst of what's now known as "the troubles". I found the firm, which was in a side street, and after handing in my paperwork I was asked to reverse my lorry into a little partly covered yard which I did. The cab protruded out of the gate into the street. I got out and removed my chains, then I began to nervously pass down the pipes one by one to the crew of lads that were putting them in place at the side of the yard.

To say I was nervous was an understatement, I had witnessed British soldiers walking back to back in twos, guns out, in a battle type stance and armoured vehicles roaming up and down the streets. There was also a gang of youths on the other side of the street facing the yard who had been eying me up as

I'd reversed in earlier. My lorry was painted with the livery of Reyners stating that it was from Manchester, so I was worried.

Then it happened…I heard a very loud bang, like an explosion, the yards corrugated tin roof shook. I was off ! I decked off the back of the lorry and began to run, to where I didn't know, I was like a headless chicken, one of the lads who were unloading me shouted something like "driver, what's up with you ? don't you be worrying about that. It happens now and then but it's OK here, get back on your lorry and we'll get you away before you know it" I calmed down a little and climbed back onto my lorry, we beavered away and as promised I was fairly quickly unloaded. I got my paperwork signed and one of the lads asked me did I want a cup of tea. I politely declined his offer because all I wanted to do was get in my truck and get out of Belfast as quickly as possible, although I didn't relay those thoughts to him.

I pulled out of the yard and drove through the streets littered with soldiers and the armoured personnel carriers that they used. To say I left quickly would be a lie as there were massive speed humps all over the place which would have thrown a person out of their seat if they were hit at speed, it was a really nerve wracking experience for me but I plodded on and left Belfast.

I drove straight to Larne and parked up to ring Reyners at a phone box. I told them I was unloaded and that I was getting the next available ferry back to Stranraer. The guy who dealt with back loads came onto the phone and said "don't come back yet, I may have a back load over there for you in the morning" I said that I didn't care if he had a load and that I would indeed be catching the next available ferry. He then passed the phone to the senior traffic manager Colin, he began to tell me that I was to wait and see if there was a load. I cut him short and told him what had happened earlier, I reiterated that I was going to catch the ferry no matter what the consequences. This statement seemed to do the trick and he said I could get the ferry back but he wasn't happy about it, he told me that once I reached Stranraer I was to go to Hills Doors, a company in Stockton Upon Tees near Middlesborough the next day and collect a load of fire doors for south Wales.

I came off the phone and went to book in at the ferry terminal. The story doesn't quite end there, whilst booking the ferry the operative informed me that I could go on the ferry that was leaving in the next half hour, he said that it was full with freight vehicles but I could go as a foot passenger on it. My vehicle would then come over on a later ferry unaccompanied, this would save me from hanging around the terminal until the later crossing, I could collect it at the dock in Stranraer later that evening.

This idea suited me as I had not planned where I was going to stay that night, so I would have a little time to find a B&B in Stranraer whilst I was waiting for it. I did just that, once off the ferry I found myself some digs for the night which were in a house near the docks. I had a walk round Stranraer whilst I waited for the ferry which my lorry was on. Later I found a spot near the docks and watched as the ferry approached and tied up, I then made my way to the gate where I explained what was happening to the guy there, I was then allowed to go into the vehicle unloading area to wait for my lorry coming off.

I waited for a long time before I approached one of the staff to ask what was going on, he took me to a supervisor who told me that as my vehicle was unaccompanied it had been loaded first, so would be coming off last.

This is what happened, it was driven down the ships ramp and then over to where I was waiting with the supervisor. I went to get into the cab and I noticed there were what looked like fish boxes on the rear end of the lorry. I climbed down and went over to the supervisor who was looking at me with a grin on his face. I asked him what the boxes were, he told me that they were indeed boxes of fish and that they'd been put on at the last minute by mistake in Larne and that they were going onto a freight train carriage which was in a siding at the side of the dock. I answered him by saying how could it have been last minute as my vehicle had been loaded onto the ferry first. He was goosed then, he didn't have an answer, he stuttered and said there would be a gang of men waiting in the train carriage as the fish were being taken away on it later that night. I replied that there better had be and drove my lorry over to the empty carriage.

There wasn't a soul in sight, I looked around and I could see that the dock crew were now reloading the ferry that my lorry had been on. I got close to the open doors of the carriage, climbed onto the back of my lorry and began throwing the boxes off, the first dozen or so landed on the carriage floor but as I threw more they landed on top of the others and began to fall sideways, spilling the ice covered fish out, I didn't care, I was fuming. I continued to chuck the boxes off, there must have been around fifty of them. I looked around as I was throwing the last few off and I spotted a guy coming over to me waving his arms about and shouting towards me. "stop, what the fuck are you doing ?, there'll be a crew here soon to unload them"

I informed him that he was too late and that they shouldn't have even been put on my lorry in the first place, I also told him to keep away from me as I was in no mood to be messed around. "There'll be hell to pay for this" he said. I replied that I couldn't give a flying fuck and with that I climbed into my lorry cab and drove off the dock. Nothing was ever said about what I'd done, I'd been conned good and proper. After that episode I advised Colin that I never wanted to go to Northern Ireland again, which I was in my right to do, and I never went again.

As a footnote to this story I would like to add that Reyners did many trips to Northern Ireland after my trip, I had been one of the forerunners. There were a certain number of drivers, four wheeler and artics' who were on the job regularly and went every week, backloading pet foods mainly. They all used to stay in Larne overnight as that was an insurance stipulation. I never heard of any driver being involved with anything that was occurring over there at the time, and that in the main, they enjoyed going over there.

It wasn't long after this that a unit became available for me and I was moved up onto the artics'. This too was a 'H' registered ERF, it had a 180 Gardener in it with a six speed David Brown gearbox. It was a hand me down but I didn't care. I took half a morning cleaning the inside of the cab as the previous driver had not looked after it to my standards.

On my way back from the first job I ever did in it, which was a load of Thermalite blocks delivered to a site in Deganwy North Wales, I reloaded at the Co-op margarine works in Irlam, Manchester.

At Irlam you had to reverse your lorry into an indoor loading bay which was built up on both sides to trailer height and which ran around the edges and rear of the trailer. There was a gap of around eighteen inches between the bays and my trailer on each side.

The load was to be manually stacked on the trailer by hand. Ironically the boxes of margarine were brought to the trailer loaded on pallets from which you had to take them off. It would be some time after before somebody finally had the idea of taking twenty empty pallets with you so that they could be exchanged for the full ones you were loading. It was even later on than this when GKN Chep brought in their system of providing companies with pallets (for a fee of course) which virtually alleviated the manual handling of goods off and onto pallets by drivers.

A pallet was brought to and lowered onto the side of my trailer, so I began to remove the boxes and stack them onto the floor of the trailer, the fork lift driver then went away to fetch another pallet and I was left alone until the fork lift driver returned with another one around five or so minutes later. This repeat performance continued and I had stacked around half the load (ten pallets). The fork lift had left me another one to unload and I was in the process of doing so when I stepped backwards and was swivelling around towards the pallet when one of the boards of the trailer flat cracked and gave way under me, it was one of Reyners older trailers and probably needed some boards replacing.

The upshot was that my right foot went through the hole, I completely lost balance and fell backwards towards the loading bay, twisting as I did so because I didn't want to hit my face on the steel protectors which adorned the edges of the bays. My foot was still stuck down the hole I'd made, and despite my efforts, I did hit the edge of the bay with the back of my head, the steel rail at the edge of my trailer then made contact on the right lower side of my back. I ended up hanging upside down in the narrow gap at the side of my trailer.

The bang to my head hurt me but the pain in my back was worse. My foot was still caught in the hole and I was lying on my back with my body angled downwards in between the bay and the trailer. I could not free my foot from the hole and, as there was nobody around, there was no point in me shouting for help, so I decided to try and pull myself up. I grabbed the rail with my left hand and, with great effort on my back, eased my way up to head and shoulder height with the bay and trailer, from where I could then free my right arm to grab the floor of the bay, and hauled myself clear. I then wriggled myself into a sat up position on the trailer and without any exaggeration, I was in agony. I looked down to see my shin which had been cut and bruised by the broken wooden edges of the board.

Somehow I managed to get to a sort of standing up position and wriggled my foot free from the hole. At this point the fork lift returned with another pallet just in time for him to see me gingerly lowering myself back down to a sitting position on the trailer. I'd rolled my trouser leg up and all you could see above the top of my boot was rivulets of blood from the scraping of my skin which covered a big bruise. He immediately came across to me and asked if I was OK. I informed him that I'd be alright in a few minutes and asked if there was a first aid kit around. He confirmed that there was and went away to get one. When he left I got up and limped to my cab, I had opened the passenger door and sat on the seat with my legs facing the bay.

He returned and between us we removed my boot and cleaned up the wounds on my shin. He had a bandage and some gauze in the box and we put that on my shin. He then said that he would go and report it to his supervisor. Surprising as it was, I told him not to bother, that I was feeling much better, and that I just wanted to finish off loading. It was in my head, despite the pain and discomfort that I was in, that this was my first trip out on my own with an artic' and I didn't want to rock the boat in any way. Silly I know, but that's what I was thinking.

The fork driver went to a tea machine and brought me one back. I gave it about ten minutes and then said I was ready to carry on. We covered the hole with some thick card and I continued to load. I did have a hard time sheeting the load afterwards, but managed it and returned to Droylsden, where the load was going on overnight trunk to its delivery in the south. My wounds soon healed, but years later that injury to my back would bring me quite serious problems.

My next lorry at Reyners was an Atkinson Borderer, reg. NJA 400M it had a Cummins 220 engine and a ten speed Fuller gearbox, you could catch pigeons with it ! Reyners bought it second hand off Barber Turnock transport in Stockport. I had the sleeping arrangements for "cabbing it" sorted out very quickly once I was given it to drive. I acquired a caravan single mattress attached to a board, and with some adjustments, I could fit it from the passenger door, over the engine cowling and onto the driver seat without the need for any propping up, it was quite comfy to sleep on.

I also had a set of proper curtains which were attached to a curtain wire which was fixed around all the windows. I got myself a one ringed gas primer stove, pots and pans and a little kettle for brewing up and to heat up water for when I had the need to wash in the vehicle.

My first trip was to East Kilbride near Glasgow with a load of chipboard which had come up from Kent on night trunk. I had no issues with that trip. Another load that came up from Kent was fruit for Liverpool market. Although hand balling was still prevalent, this load was on pallets, on a flat trailer which was sheeted and roped. It was loaded with plums, they were in open topped punnets which had four corners that protruded above box height so that other punnets could be stacked on top without crushing the plums below.

I arrived at Liverpool fruit market and went to the first of two deliveries I had there. I took off the ropes holding the load at the rear end of the trailer and asked the wholesaler could one of his forklifts raise me up to the side of the load on an empty pallet so I could roll back the sheet, this would avoid me climbing on top of the load and potentially crushing the produce. If I'd tried to drag the sheet off from ground level there was a very strong chance the sheet or one of its ties may have gotten tangled in the punnets and I might have pulled the load over and off with it. The wholesaler instructed one of his team to do as I'd requested and we managed to roll the sheet far enough forward to be able to lift off the eight pallets which belonged to him. After his portion of the load was all off, I reversed the operation to roll the sheet back over the load and secured it enough to travel the short distance to the next wholesaler who was at the other side of the market.

Upon arriving there, I again asked the proprietor if a fork lift could lift me up to do what I'd done earlier. He refused, he said that it was a health and safety risk and that his fork drivers were too busy. I explained the situation, but he wouldn't give in and told me I'd have to sort myself out. I went back to my vehicle and undid the rest of the ropes. I wrapped them up and then climbed up onto the rear of my cab to the front of the trailer where I could use the headboard of the trailer as a starting point. I clambered up the load slowly, it was around six feet high off the trailer deck, upon reaching the top of the load I very steadily raised myself up to a standing position on the front sheet. I managed to stand on the protruding corners of the punnets and rolled the sheets off to one side as the proprietor stood and watched me, I then slowly and very carefully lowered myself over the front of the punnets and down to the back of my cab.

Upon reaching the ground, I hadn't walked a few steps when the wholesaler came up to me carrying my paperwork and said "that produce is no use to me, you've walked all over it, I can't sell that to my customers you'll have to take it back, here's your notes" he thrust the notes into my hand and began to walk away.

I asked him what else was I supposed to do, he hadn't agreed to someone lifting me up to remove the sheets. He must have really had a mood on him that day because he then turned on me swearing and telling me that it was not his problem. I didn't argue back, I politely asked him could I use his phone to ring my boss and inform him what had occurred, he refused that as well and walked away. I went and asked another nearby wholesaler, after telling him what had happened, if I could make a transfer charge phone call to my boss from his office. He kindly let me do it after telling me what a prick the other guy was. I explained my predicament to my boss Keith, he asked me what number I was ringing from and told me to hang up and wait, not to approach the moody guy, and he'd try to sort things out.

I was there a good hour, I went and rolled up my sheets. The moody wholesaler came to me and told me to move my lorry. I told him it wasn't going anywhere till I'd heard from my boss, I then walked away from him and sat in my cab. As I said I'd been there a good hour when I was called to the office where I had rung Keith from. He told me that despite his efforts, the moody guy had refused to give in, and he gave me an address to re-deliver the produce to. It was at Safeways RDC in Warrington. With the help of the good hearted wholesalers forklift, I was able to lift my sheets back onto the load, open them out and safely get down. I thanked him for his help and he replied that we all needed to work together to make the job easier for everyone. I fastened the sheet down and re-roped it then left for Warrington. I had no problems there and everyone was helpful. I just wish that had been the case at my second delivery !

A similar story concerning a customers bad attitude happened to me whilst I was loading at their premises, which I will relate to you in the next story.

I was sent to a warehouse in the Strangeways area of Manchester, quite near the infamous prison which is still there. This particular company used to import clothing and handbags, then they'd repackage and sell them on to wholesalers and stores throughout the UK.

I arrived there at around 14.00, parked outside and then went into the office door where I met a lady who escorted me to a guy in an office in the warehouse, he was introduced to me with no name, but as the supervisor. I introduced myself and told him that I'd come to pick up a load for Sutton, an area in Surrey. He replied in a very brusque manner that he'd been expecting me before lunch and that the load was supposed to be in Sutton by 09.00 the following day. I apologised on behalf of myself and the company and explained that I'd only been told of the pick up at lunchtime. He huffed and puffed and said something like "well at least you're here now, there's a yard at the end of the building, reverse in there and we'll start loading you" he then walked off bawling at some lads in the warehouse to get the Sutton load ready as I was here to collect it. He was so rude to them and myself, no please or thank you, which I really do not appreciate.

I did as I was asked and reversed into the yard then prepared my trailer for loading. I waited for around 25 minutes and nobody came to me, so I went up some steps at the side of the loading bay and wandered into the warehouse. The staff didn't seem to be doing much and I was just about to ask someone what was happening when the supervisor came through a door shouting "right.. let's get some work done !" Everybody jumped up and started looking busy, he then turned to me and asked what was I doing in the warehouse, I replied that I'd come in to see why nobody had started loading me. Once again, in a very rude manner, he told me to go and wait outside with my vehicle and loading would begin when they were ready. He then went off barking orders at the warehouse staff.

I went back outside and at around 15.00 a pallet load of fairly large cardboard boxes was brought out to the loading bay on a hand pump truck. A lad came and got on a forklift truck, lifted the pallet off the bay, then brought it to my trailer, he then low-ered the pallet onto it, he then went back inside. I began taking the boxes off the pallet and stacked them at the front of the trailer.

This routine continued at a very slow rate. I stacked the box-es, which were very light and didn't feel full, two high, which brought them up to just below my height (I am 5' 10") I'd only covered a quarter of the trailer with the boxes when I asked the fork lift driver how many were to be loaded onto me in total, he replied that he would ask his supervisor the next time he went indoors.

Not long after that the supervisor came out onto the loading bay and shouted over to me " Oi' you'll have to stack them higher than that" I replied by asking how many boxes were there in total. He said "Don't you worry about that, it's a mixed load it'll all go on" I was really getting annoyed at his attitude, I told him that I would like to know how many so that I knew how high to go, and in what way to stack them, because at two high there wasn't a problem, I could just put them one on top of the other, any higher and I would have had to put a binding lay-er for stability. He replied, once again in a very brusque manner, that I'd need another layer but there were smaller boxes coming out later and I could put them on top. I decided not to push the matter any further and continued to load them in the same man-ner and whatever came later I would deal with as it occurred.

I'd loaded the full forty foot length of the trailer at two high when the light began to fade at 16.00, it was winter time, there were more boxes to be loaded. I asked the fork lift driver to lift me up onto the top of the load which he did, he then went back to the warehouse. I carefully stood on the boxes, trying to keep my weight where the four corners of four boxes met. The boxes, some of which were not full to the top, began to buckle and cave in a little under my weight so I kept away from the edge of them in case they did collapse inwards, possibly causing me to fall off.

A couple of pallets of same sized boxes came out and I stacked them on their sides three across which formed a binding layer. Then smaller boxes were brought, I managed to make a binding layer with them too. I was about third of the way along the trailer and it had virtually gone dark, I asked the fork driver if there were any lights in the yard, he replied that there were, but they didn't work. I asked him to lower me to the ground and I went inside and found the supervisor.

I explained that I didn't want to be on top of a load of unstable boxes in the dark unless he could provide me with some light. He replied in his rude manner that there was light coming through the door of the warehouse onto the loading bay. I had put up with his rudeness long enough and told him that I was not prepared to work at height on top of collapsing cardboard boxes in the dark, I asked him could I use a phone to make a call to my manager. He refused that and told me to get back onto my trailer and finish loading. I informed him in a firm but polite way that I didn't work for him and that he couldn't give me orders.

I left the warehouse to go outside and find a phone box, he was shouting at me that he would see to it that I was sacked for my behaviour. I ignored him and left. I found a working phone box (very unusual at that time in that area) and rang my traffic manager Keith. I explained the situation to him and he told me to return to my lorry, not to get back onto the load, and he would phone the customer to try and sort things out.

I went back and stood near my lorry. The fork lift driver came to me and said that the supervisor had asked him to get onto the load and finish the loading but he had refused on the same grounds as I had. A man eventually came out of the warehouse in a shirt and tie, he was looking around in the darkness at the broken lights and my lorry, he came to me and asked if I would mind coming back to his office and speak to Keith.

I followed him back through the warehouse, the supervisor was glaring at me as I passed near him, I then went into a small office where there was a phone off the hook, I was invited to pick it up and talk with my manager. Keith told me that I was to ask firstly, if I could spread my sheets over the load so as to keep it dry and protected, then drop my trailer in their yard and return in the morning when it was light to continue loading. He said that if this request was refused, I was to ask them to take the load off completely, by themselves, and I would then leave empty. I left the call open and put the first part of the request to the office man who was waiting nearby. He paused for a short while before replying that I could do as Keith had requested. I then told Keith that I had been given permission to do it, he agreed with me that the attitude of the supervisor was not acceptable and that I had done the right thing, I then hung up.

I asked the office man if I could have the assistance of the fork lift driver to lift up my sheets whilst I spread them and help me in any way I needed. He agreed to this and that's what I did. I left there in my unit after dropping the trailer, and returned the next morning as daylight began. I finished off loading, fastened the sheets down and roped the load. The rude supervisor never showed his face once. I collected my delivery notes from the office and rang Keith to inform him of my expected arrival time in Sutton.

I encountered swirling freezing fog in the Midlands and for the rest of the journey south, I arrived at the wholesalers in Sutton at around 14.50. I was expecting a hostile reception as I'd been told by the rude man that I should have been there at 09.00. It was quite the opposite, I was thanked for getting to them in such bad weather, no delivery time was mentioned, I was given a cup of tea before a crew of about six friendly lads helped me remove the sheets covering the boxes and unload the trailer. The owner then thanked me again and gave me a £10 tip. It's amazing how different two days can be, one where you're treated and spoken to like dirt, the next, where you're treated with kindness and respect.

There was a factory in Speke, an area in Liverpool, their company name was Goodlass Wall. They manufactured paint and Reyners used to carry loads of it to their satellite depot in Maryhill, Glasgow.

I went to load up for Maryhill there one afternoon. I was parked in the centre of the yard where the fork lift brought pallets of various sized paint pots from out of the warehouse and loaded them onto my trailer. The fork lift driver filled out the forty foot flat of the trailer with one layer of palletised paint pots, he then stacked another layer on the top of the first one and then another layer of pallets on top of that. As stated the pots were not all uniform in size and the load was undulating with sporadic slight differences in height. Once loaded, I climbed onto the trailer and then onto the top of the load in order to spread my sheets over it. I had done this many times and was always aware of how I moved on top of the paint pots in case I stumbled and fell off. This time I was unlucky.

I had rolled out my rear sheet (which was the practice, as the front sheet would then overlap the rear sheet once opened) and from the nearside area of the trailer I began to throw out the folded sheet over and down the sides of the load, as I did so I took a little side step, the pallet I stood on must have been on top of one that wasn't level, causing it to tip. The next thing I knew, I was falling off the load, from a height of around seven feet.

I put my hands out in front of me to try and break my fall and luckily I landed on the floor in a cat like position, hands first followed by my knees. I remember I had sharp pains in my wrists, which had taken the brunt of the fall, but I had no time to worry about that because I looked over my shoulder to see two pallets of paint had tipped outwards and the top one was just starting to topple off the one underneath it. I very quickly rolled over and away from the falling paint pots and luckily for me none hit me, they fell to the floor about three feet away from me. Several of the tin lids burst open spilling paint onto the floor, but again, luckily away from me, so I didn't get covered in paint. I had a few splashes on my boots but that was it.

I was still sat on the floor, examining my painful wrists when one of the warehouse staff ran up to me enquiring if I was OK and did I want an ambulance. I replied that I didn't need an ambulance but I was worried about my wrists. He helped me get up, then we slowly made our way over to the office in the warehouse where I sat down. I rolled up my overall trouser legs to have a look at my knees, which were also by now hurting me. They were both scraped and looked quite bruised, but compared to my wrists, there wasn't enough discomfort to worry me.

The man who had helped me must have been a first aider, he brought a medical aid box and cleaned up my knees. He examined my wrists and we both concluded that nothing was broken or fractured, they were badly sprained though, we put the details of the incident in the accident book. He then gave me some painkillers and brought me a cup of tea. I sat in the office for some time whilst the spillage was cleared up and the load was straightened out with replenished paint pots. It must have been around 16.30, when I was feeling a lot better and the pain in my wrists had eased up, so I went back to my lorry and finished sheeting and (rather painfully) roping the load down. I left

Speke at around 17.30 and ran my lorry out to a place in Skelmersdale where I parked up for the night.

I was quite sore in the wrist and knee departments the next morning when I left, and apart from encountering rain drops that froze solid as they landed on my windscreen whilst going over Shap Fell in Cumbria, I made it to Glasgow without any further mishaps !

In the centre of Manchester there is the Arndale Shopping Centre, a huge shopping mall with offices set above it. During 1996 it was the subject of a bombing attack. It was carried out by the Provisional Irish Republican Army on Saturday, 15th June. They detonated a 1,500 kilogram lorry bomb on Corporation Street in the centre of Manchester. It was, at the time, the largest bomb detonated in Great Britain since the Second World War.

When the centre was first being constructed I delivered twenty tons of thirty foot long steel pilings there. Pilings are driven into the ground during construction to shore up and stabilise earthworks so that concrete footings and the like can be put in place. I arrived at the site during the very early stages of construction, when all that was there was a massive deep hole in the ground. It was so deep that from street level the top half of a medium sized tower crane could be viewed. When I drove through the site access gates I had to traverse down a series of long gradual ramps which had been constructed to get traffic to the very bottom of the workings.

It was an extremely busy, huge site, with cranes lifting and swinging large cement mixers, steel girders, timber and all manner of construction equipment. There were dumper trucks, JCB's and all that sort of equipment, plus a lot of workmen. I was guided by one of the banksmen (people who safely watch moving vehicles on sites) to where I was to be offloaded. I was put in a position below one of the tower cranes, and after removing the chains which had been securing the load we began to unload the pilings which were lifted off two at a time by the tower crane. It must have been around forty five minutes before my trailer was emptied.

I had my notes signed by the foreman and it was then I thought "hang on, I've driven into a dead end here, there's nowhere to turn around, I'm going to have to reverse out"

I approached the foreman and began to explain that I didn't fancy reversing all the way out, up all those ramps to the gate. The foreman laughed and told me not to worry, he said that the tower crane was just doing a lift for another part of the site nearby, he asked me to unhitch my trailer, turn the unit around (there was enough room to do that) and then the tower crane would lift my trailer up into the air, spin it around in the opposite direction and then lower it down to the ground where I could hitch it back up to my unit. This is what happened and after around ten minutes I was ready to drive through, and up out of the site. On my rare return trips to Manchester nowadays I always look and remember back to the days when I was part of the construction process there.

In what is known as "the black country" in the West Midlands, there is an area called Smethwick, it lies to the west of Birmingham and just south East of West Bromwich. Reyners used to load at GKN steel reinforcements there. They made steel mesh sheets which are used to be set in concrete to strengthen it.

Constructed of bright steel in a criss-cross mesh fashion (think of a waffle) they were eight feet wide by sixteen feet in length and were stacked in piles ten high, they were rather loosely held together with metal wire ties which somewhat held them in position but they were extremely slippery. To load these sheets safely was an arduous process, you'd put on two lifts of ten and then secure them with "S" shaped hooks, tying them down with ropes to the trailer bed. You'd then put another two lifts on top of them and repeat the process and so on until you reached a height of about seven foot. That was your first stack, weighing around nine tons, you'd then load another stack behind it on the trailer in the same manner so you would have two stacks weighing in total around eighteen tons on the vehicle.

The securing process didn't end there, you then had to climb on top of the load and carefully move around as steel poles, eight foot long, were handed up to you, there would be eight of them and you had to lower one through each corner of the mesh stacks down through it to the trailer bed, a loading supervisor would then throw up to you a loop of rope which was tied and secured from every angle and direction of the pole as possible. This was then considered by the loading supervisor as adequate enough securing, it wasn't for me though, and I'll tell you why. I was there one day on my first visit when one of our drivers who was driving a ten ton rigid, loaded there before me. He had told the loading supervisor that he did not want to rope from each corner in every direction as he didn't think it was necessary, the supervisor had warned him that not to do so was dangerous practice and that he, the driver, would be responsible if anything unfortunate were to happen. He did not do anything more to secure the load and despite the supervisors pleas to take it very steady the driver left the works after weighing off the load.

The supervisor and I watched as he set off down the narrow street where there was a left hand bend before coming to the main road. The driver clipped the edge of the bends kerb with his nearside rear wheels and we both watched aghast as the load slid over to the offside to an angle of about forty five degrees. He ended up having to reverse back very slowly to the works and then wait until I had loaded before taking off the whole load in order to reload it. With this in mind I vowed to always load it in the fashion the supervisor requested with my own added precautions.

I'd firstly loosely fasten two chains over each already roped stack, once that was done I'd loosen the chains and then place 2"x 2" timbers along the top edge of the load to protect it and then re-tighten the chains (the timbers stopped the chains from digging into the mesh and putting it out of shape). I'd then go round and tighten any of the ropes that may have loosened slightly once the chains had been fastened. I never had any mishaps with mesh, you'd drive along and round a bend where you would see the load move ever so slightly, if you were unfortunate to have to brake hard it would move slightly forwards. It never moved enough to worry me though. I loaded there many times, always delivering the mesh safely. It had to be treated with respect, I didn't throw my vehicle around harshly and I always braked and accelerated gently. I did though have one unfortunate occasion whilst delivering a load of it to Liverpool docks, which was not of my making,

I'll explain. I had gone to the Isle of Man Steam Packet dock at Liverpool. The load was going over by boat to the island. After waiting for some time (as always on Liverpool docks at that time) a docker had instructed me to park in a certain position on the dock for unloading, he told me to remove my chains and ropes, take out the corner poles and wait to be unloaded. I asked the docker if I was to be unloaded where he had set me up telling him that once the chains and ropes were off it wouldn't be safe to move the vehicle. He replied in a very offhand manner that I was to do as asked and that he knew what he was doing. I removed the chains and ropes and took out the poles.

I stood by my vehicle and waited, A mobile crane came to my side and between us we removed the back stack of mesh, the crane then went off somewhere else so I waited for it's return. After a while another docker walked up to me and told me to move the vehicle around twenty yards across the dock to unload the rest. I told him that I'd been assured that I was to be unloaded where I was and that the load was very unstable in its unsecured state. As the other docker had done, he replied in an aggressive manner telling me that I had to move it or stay there all day. I didn't fancy re-roping and chaining the remainder of the load by myself and asked him whether he could give me a hand to secure it. He point blank refused. I, by now, was getting fed up with the unhelpful attitude of the dockers so I said that I would move as long as my paperwork was signed as the load being delivered in good order, and that I would not be held responsible for any damage whatsoever. He agreed to this and signed my paperwork as requested, muttering under his breath that I didn't know what I was talking about and how long he'd been unloading goods without any problems.

Once I had received my notes, I warned him that the load would be unstable and was he sure he wanted me to move. He replied "Just take it over there lad, for fucks sake, how many times do I have to say it ?". I got in my lorry, started the engine and set off very very slowly, and I do mean slowly, I was crawling along, the docker was walking in front of me waving where he wanted me to go, he signalled for me to veer off to the right and then straighten up. I didn't have the opportunity to straighten up though, because as I gently turned to the right the load started to slip and the front stack slid completely off the trailer landing on the dock ! All that was left on my trailer was the bottom stack of ten, half on half off it, with the ones that had been on top of them leaning up against the side of it and my trailer.

I got out to check if there was any damage to my vehicle which thankfully there wasn't. I looked across to the docker who was scratching his head and raised my arms in a "I told you so" gesture then got in my lorry and slowly moved away, allowing the remainder of the load which was still attached to my vehicle to fall off to the ground. I once again stopped and checked for any damage to my lorry as I thought the pointed edges of the mesh may have damaged my tyres or rear unit lights but apart from a few scratches on the rear mudguard there was nothing, so with that I got back in my lorry and drove away. When it's rusty, mesh doesn't slip around too badly, but it is very very slippery when new, treat it with respect. Some people just won't be told !.

During the Falklands war I, along with many other Reyner artic' drivers over the following three months or so, were sent to a pallet making works in Oldham. I was to collect a load of empty pallets for delivery to a Royal Navy supplies depot in Southampton. The pallet works was in a narrow, cobbled back street and we used to have to load one side of the trailer with thirteen stacks first, then carefully move across to the other side of the street to load the other side with a further thirteen stacks.

Average pallets are not very heavy, but the pallets we used to load there were. They were made of heavy hardwood, you could load twenty six stacks at twenty pallets high giving you a total of five hundred and twenty pallets on the trailer, the weight, we were told, was nineteen tons. I recall having to move very slowly to the other side of the street with nine and a half tons on one side of the trailer which was tilting at a precarious angle due to the unbalanced weight in order that I could finish loading the other side, it was quite unnerving.

Once loaded I had to fully sheet all the pallets which stood at around ten feet high off the trailer deck. During the loading process I'd put my sheets on top of a stack which would then be lifted onto the trailer so the sheets would then be on top of the load. I then had to climb onto the unit behind the cab then make my way up onto the headboard of the trailer and then mountain climb up the front stack of the pallets. The pallets had to be fully sheeted we were told as they had to be kept dry and free of any road dirt, my two main sheets were not wide enough to completely cover them so I first had to spread my fly sheet out then lower it over to cover one side, I'd tie off the fly sheet ties to the pallets on top then open out my main sheets ensuring they covered the top and the other side completely. You have to remember I was around fourteen feet off the ground so it was not a very safe way of doing things, but it was the only way at that time.

It never happened to me but one of our drivers was nearly blown off his load by a strong gust of wind, he threw himself flat onto the top of the load and clung on for dear life, one of his sheets however didn't beat the wind and was blown completely off the load and came down over the wall of an adjoining factory premises !

I myself have been on the top of these pallets when it was windy and it's quite a scary experience. Anyway I digress, so once my sheets were spread over the load I then had the task of getting back down to floor level to tie them off and rope the load. This was in itself an arduous job, I had to kneel down at the front end of the load, turn myself around so that I was facing the back end, try to get a firm hold on the sheet, digging my fingers through it to grab one of the batons on a pallet and then lower myself down, I'd try to find a foothold in between the gap at the top and bottom of a pallet and edge my way down like that until I got a foothold on the trailer headboard, from there I'd clamber down over my air and electric lines onto the vehicle duck board behind my cab then off there and onto the ground.

Luckily I always managed it without any injuries or mishaps. Once the load was roped I'd then go the same way to Southampton as I always did carrying those loads, avoiding low bridges.

The first time I arrived at Southampton I asked the guy who was unloading me, after he'd used a damp meter to check that the pallets were indeed dry, what were they for and where were they going, he told me that they were going out to the Falklands and would be carrying anything that would fit on them, foodstuff supplies etc. etc. I asked him what they would do with them when the conflict had finished and he told me they would be stacked into empty containers and then sunk at sea. He said there would be too much of a logistical problem to get them all back to the UK. I don't know if he was serious but he certainly seemed to be.

I can tell you that I took at least four loads there and I was one of many drivers from Reyners who did, we also delivered them to Plymouth so there's a fair few pallets made their way to the Falklands that never came back. Considering the quality of the pallets the cost must have been huge, it seemed an awful waste of money to me even though it was necessary.

There's a place in County Durham called Spennymoor, I'd unloaded a full load of jams and cake mixes there one Friday and I was then instructed to drive over to Hartlepool and load twenty tons of newsprint reels from the docks there, they were for the Daily Mail printers in Ancoats, Manchester for delivery on the following Saturday morning.

I arrived just after lunch time to find another one of our drivers waiting to load, and surprisingly we didn't have to wait long to go into one of the dock sheds to load. I went into one shed, Jack G, the other driver went into another shed, where, I didn't know.

The reels were quite big, they were about four feet in diameter and around seven feet in length, we used to lay them on their sides so that they could be rolled off the rear of the trailer at the printers. You would have the first one lifted on, tight up to the headboard of the trailer by a lift truck with a clamp to hold them. He would hold it whilst you wedged two small triangular shaped wooden chocks behind them to hold them in place. The trailer flat would be almost filled to its rear end like this, the last one being held with a back skid, which was a wooden triangular length of wood around seven feet long and it had rope attached to each end with which to securely tie off and wedge the reel.

The lift truck would then load some reels on top of the others in the valleys created by the lower reels. During loading, whilst up at the front end, you would lift your tarpaulin sheets up onto the top of the bottom row, once loaded you'd then spread your sheets to cover the load completely. On this occasion I got loaded and the lift driver asked me to pull out of the shed as there was another lorry waiting to load in there. I pulled out onto the quayside. I looked around to see if Jack was anywhere to be seen but couldn't see him.

I parked up and began to climb up onto the load in order to sheet it. There was quite a strong gusty wind blowing by this time. I put a sheet on my shoulder and carefully made my way to where the reels were stacked on top towards the rear, I lifted the sheet up onto them, then climbed on top of those reels. I opened the sheet out covering both sides and the rear of the back reels. I then proceeded to climb down to fasten it to the trailer. I was half way down when a gust of wind got underneath the open sheet and blew it right off the trailer onto the quayside. This had happened to me on many occasions so I just gritted my teeth got down from the trailer and folded the sheet again. I lifted it onto the back of the trailer, climbed up and then lifted it onto the back reel, climbed up that and lifted it onto the top rear reel. I then climbed up onto that and spread my sheet open again, the wind was still gusting now and then so I waited for a still period before once again climbing quickly down only for the sheet to blow almost fully off again. I was getting really peed off at this stage so I wrapped the sheet up and put it on the rear end of my trailer but then I got into my lorry and moved it close to a shed side wall hoping It would shield me from the wind.

Once again I went through the whole business of lifting it up in stages onto the load and clambering up to spread it open. I'd only got half the sheet open when a gust came and took the sheet half off the load, me nearly with it. I lay down on what bit of sheet was still on the load and waited for the wind to drop again. At this point I looked across to see Jack G sailing by in his lorry, he didn't have reels on, he had loaded wood pulp bales, and he must have been able to sheet up inside his shed, anyway, he saw me lay down on top of the load with my sheet blown half off, waved, and then carried on away from the dock. If only he could have heard what I called him for not giving me a hand, I was furious, it would have taken about five minutes for him to tie down the four corners of each sheet and then another five to tie the ends when I spread my fly sheet.

As it happened I did receive a hand from another driver who emerged from the shed I'd been in, he drove out fully sheeted, as he'd been the last one loading they let him stay inside out of the wind. He stopped and helped by securing the corner ties of the sheets. Once that was done I had no more problems and soon had the load sheeted and fastened down securely.

I did have a go at Jack the next time I met him, I told him in no uncertain terms what I thought of his behaviour that day. I would never see a driver struggle the way I had, I have helped strangers sheet up in high winds let alone workmates. He apologised in a half hearted fashion but things were never quite the same between myself and him after that.

During the long hot summer of 1976 Reyners were extremely busy, not only did they have their regular customers to haul for, they also had the Harp lager brewery (now owned by Scottish & Newcastle) in Manchester to service with trucks and trailers. During that year I, and many other drivers, were delivering almost always, lager to breweries all over the UK. As you can imagine, if you're not old enough to remember at that time, cold beer was in extremely high demand.

We delivered it mainly in twenty ton demountable tanks which carried the equivalent of 120 UK barrels, that equates to 4,320 UK gallons which in turn equals 34,560 pints, in one tank, a lot of lager !

One of the many breweries we delivered to was Scottish & Newcastle Breweries in Newcastle Upon Tyne, during that summer lorries delivered lager there from 03.00 in the morning, one tank every hour 'till 18.00, that's fifteen tanks daily for the five week days Monday to Friday. You'll agree thats a lot of lager delivered. This was only one of many breweries we serviced, here is a list of those I've been to that I can remember.

Scottish & Newcastle Brewery in Edinburgh
Scottish & Newcastle Brewery in Glasgow
Scottish & Newcastle Brewery in Newcastle
Federation Brewery in Gateshead
Jennings Brewery in Cockermouth
Thwaites Brewery in Blackburn
Mathew Brown Brewery in Blackburn
John Smiths Brewery in Tadcaster
Samuel Smiths Brewery in Tadcaster
Wards Brewery in Sheffield
Bottling Plant in Cleethorpes (can't recall name)
Guinness Exports in Liverpool
Isle of Man Steam Packet Company in Liverpool
Schweppes in Liverpool
Burtonwood Brewery in Burtonwood, Warrington
Guinness Brewery in Runcorn
Joseph Holt Brewery in Manchester
Courage Brewery in Newark upon Trent
Wolverhampton & Dudley Breweries in Wolverhampton
Holdens Bottling Plant in Sedgley
Canning Plant in Rugby (can't recall name)

Charles Wells Brewery in Bedford
Lockwoods Canning in Little Sutton, Lincolnshire
Morrells Brewery in Oxford
Greene King Brewery in Bury St. Edmunds
Greene King Brewery in Biggleswade
Buckleys Brewery in Llanelli
Courage Brewery in Avonmouth
Schweppes in Bristol
Courage Brewery in Reading
Courage Brewery at Tower Bridge London
Guinness Brewery in Park Royal London
Harp Lager Brewery in Alton Hampshire
Ushers Brewery in Salisbury

Quite a list I'm sure you'll agree, most of the bigger breweries like Edinburgh, Biggleswade, Avonmouth, Tower Bridge and J.Smiths Tadcaster all had multiple weekday deliveries (i.e: on the hour) I remember that Reyners had to hire lots of skeletal twenty foot trailers on which to load the tanks, in order to cope with the demand.

There were also five other companies with several contracted units and tanker trailers based at the Manchester brewery, working Monday to Friday every week as well. If I was given a Biggleswade, Bedford or an Avonmouth, which could be done legally there and back in a day, we used to get paid a bonus which equalled the cost of a night out allowance, it was because of the distances we covered, and it helped by getting the tanks back so they could be loaded for another run.

I had weeks where I did five days, Monday to Friday of going to Biggleswade or Avonmouth every day. It was a great money earner, with my wage and the five bonus payments. I can remember during those weeks it was so hot that I wore open toed sandals to work, there was no need to wear protective footwear as all the job entailed was driving.

I'd arrive at a brewery and put my tank at the unloading point and that's all I had to do, brewery operatives always did the unloading procedure, which involved pipes and air lines being connected to the rear of the tank. They would inform me when it was empty. I, in order to be sure, always checked that everything had been disconnected and made secure before I'd move away from the unloading point, I'd then set off back to

Manchester with the empty tank. It was good work for Reyners and it certainly suited me.

Reyners also worked for Brewliner, who did the transport operations for Wilsons brewery in Newton Heath, Manchester. We'd haul their beers in tanks and kegs to bottlers, canners and other breweries all over the UK, it was something a bit different from the Harp work and made a nice change.

There were times when drivers had to park up due to running out of time when they were not too far from home. As I lived in Manchester, and later on in Stockport, there were times when I'd park up at Keele or Knutsford services when heading back to the northwest. It was quite a popular practice to take your log book, or later on your tachograph card and thumb a lift off another lorry driver to somewhere near your home. It was known as doing a "dodgy". I knew which companies would more than likely be going my way and at that time it was a very rare occasion when someone didn't stop for you. I've parked at services and cafes on the M62, M61, A580 East Lancashire Road, A62 Stanedge Pass and the A628 Woodhead Pass.

This little story though involves one of my mates who was a lorry driver, he phoned me at home one night when I happened to be there, he asked me where I was going the following morning, this was common practice if you'd parked out of town and gotten a lift home, you'd ring around all your workmates looking for a lift back to where you'd parked up. I told him I was going down to London, he replied that it was perfect for him and he asked me could I take him back for his lorry which was parked at "the Jet" cafe on the outskirts of Rugby on the A5. I said "bloody hell lad ! that's a long way to thumb it home" he replied that he'd had a bad day and someone who he knew was there when he'd parked up who was going home so he'd cadged a lift off him, he said that as I was going back that way it was ideal. I arranged to meet him not far from my home the next morning and we set off early at around 04.45 on our way south.

In those days I used to often go to "the Jet" cafe for breakfast if I was heading that way, but on this trip I'd planned to go down to a cafe further south called "the Red Lion" near Northampton. We arrived at "the Jet" at around 07.30. As he was getting out of my lorry I asked him, "have you got everything mate ?" he turned towards me and showed me his folder

93

with his driver log book in it, patted his pockets and said "Yeah all good" then as he patted his pockets again a look of panic came across his face, "where's my bloody keys ?" he said in a very uncertain way, he began franticly looking for his lorry keys on the seat and around the floor of the cab, he then suddenly stopped and turned to me with a look of realisation on his now ashen face and said "I've left them on the sideboard at home, what the fuck am I gonna do ?" I said something like "well there's not a lot you can do mate, you're gonna have to ring and tell them you've lost them or something" The look on his face said it all, he looked broken. He said something like "I can't tell them I've done a dodgy from here they"ll fucking sack me" I said "well I can't help you with this one mate, just say you've lost them, I don't know what else to say". "Yeah you'd better get on your way Steve, thanks for the lift mate" he said, and with that I reluctantly drove away leaving him there with his big problem to sort out.

I spoke to him the next time I saw him and he told me that when he'd phoned his office to tell them he'd lost his keys, he was so nervous that the manager, had not believed him, he'd told him that he'd "better go home and get them" and that he wouldn't be paid for doing so.

It's around 100 miles from Levenshulme in Manchester to "the Jet" on the A5, I'd never consider doing a "dodgy" home from that distance, he did and committed the cardinal sin, he forgot his keys. Still, no harm done.

Before I got my HGV licence I was dating a girl named Pat. She was a nurse and lived a couple of miles from me in a suburb of Manchester called Fallowfield. We got engaged and two years afterwards we were married, it was 1977. We moved into our own little quasi semi house in Reddish, a suburb of Stockport, around a mile away from my family's home in Levenshulme.

I remember that I had a weeks holiday after our wedding which we spent making our house a home, we did have a sort of honeymoon though. There was a mate of mine called Mick who used to work at Reyners but had left to run his own lorry on mainly fridge continental work. Apparently he was coming through France on his way back to the UK with a load of frozen produce, something had blown into his open window and

94

lodged in his right eye. Despite eye baths and other attempts at shifting it he'd failed to do so. He decided he would come off route on the way to his destination at Edinburgh and go home to Oldham, where he was going to seek professional medical help with his problem.

He had phoned my friend John S and asked him could he take his load up to Edinburgh to unload it as it was on a time specific delivery. John S. had told him that he couldn't do it because of his own work commitments but that I was off after just getting married. He phoned me and asked could I do it, he said that I could take Pat and it would be a bit of a honeymoon trip for us both. At that time Pat had never been to Scotland and she said she'd love to do it, so with the promise of a sweetener for doing it we ended up at Oldham and got into Mick's DAF 3300 with its fridge trailer and set off for Edinburgh at around 17.00.

The load was due for delivery at 08.00 the following morning. Pat and I eventually drove through the dark streets of Edinburgh, looking skywards to the lit up castle on top of the castle rock at around 23.30 and parked up, backed onto the unloading bay with the fridge turned off, the doors, with their seals removed and opened slightly as per Mick's instructions. The delivery notes for the load were wrapped in a see through plastic bag, wedged between one of the trailer door handles. We then climbed into our bunk to settle down for the night at around midnight.

The next morning we were both up before the staff at the company started to unload us at around 08.25. We got unloaded, and after getting permission from the warehouse foreman to leave the rig where it was, we went for some breakfast.

We eventually set off from Edinburgh at 10.45 and headed for our pick up point near the town of Ayr to reload for France. We loaded twenty tons of hanging beef in the fridge and set off south to meet Mick at Knutsford services, he'd had his eye sorted out and was OK to drive so his partner drove him to the services there.

We arrived there at around 20.00. Mick thanked us for getting his load delivered on time and gave me some cash as a little bonus. I told him I wasn't interested in the money and that it was an opportunity for Pat and myself to have a little break on our honeymoon period whilst off work. He was insistent that I took it because he would have had to pay a penalty clause had the load arrived late, and after having a little chinwag he then set off south to Dover. His partner drove us home, we had a little supper and after watching the TV for a while went to bed, Pat was tired, it had been a long day for her but she and I both had enjoyed our "mini honeymoon cum rescue mission" to Scotland.

I returned to work at Reyners the following week and I recall that after being away from home, I was in my lorry going back to my house for the weekend when I found myself about two minutes away from my old family home in Levenshulme, I must have driven there on auto pilot ! I turned around and made my way back to Reddish where I now lived as a married man, with my own home ! I wonder how many people have done that ? Or is it just numpty headed me ?!!

1977 was also the year I was given a brand new unit by my employer Geoffrey Reyner Ltd. It was an ERF "B" series day cab with a 240 Gardener engine, its registration was VDB 10S. As with the Atkinson I soon had it kitted out for sleeping in and made it a comfy little home away from home for myself.

I remember in 1979 when our first baby, was born. My traffic manager Keith had been keeping me on local work anticipating her imminent birth. I was unloading at a warehouse in Mossley when he rang me to say that Pat had gone into labour, he told me to drop my trailer where I was and to get off home to be with her, this I did.

I arrived home to find Pat, (it was her Birthday) in the early stages of labour and soon after we were both in the maternity ward at Withington Hospital in South Manchester. Andrea, my first born daughter, was born some time later after Pat being in labour for twenty three hours.

I was picked up by my Dad from the hospital and when I got home I rang Keith and asked him what was going to happen with the lorry, he told me not to worry, I was to have a few days off and the lorry could stay at the place I parked it at near my house. He hinted "you may have some use of it" which of course meant, if needed I could use it as a sort of taxi. I was very grateful for this and thanked Keith for his kindness. I did use it too.

Chapter Three.

It's all change, then change again !.

It's funny how things can be changed by something else affecting you. This happened to me when Andrea became a toddler. I decided I didn't like being away from home whilst she was growing up so upon hearing that the lad who used to load the trailers at Harp Lager on a full time basis was suddenly leaving I decided to apply for the job.

I approached Keith, the articulated vehicle manager and told him I was very interested in doing the "shunt" job (shunting the trailers in and out of the loading bays at the Harp brewery) The job would mean me giving up my lorry and working five twelve hour days (06.00 until 18.00) Monday to Friday based at the brewery.

I was given the job and told to start the following day as the lad who was leaving would be getting paid that night which was a Thursday and they were letting him finish without completing his full week. He said that the Friday would be like a trial period and that if I didn't like it I could go back on the road. It was short notice but that suited me.

That night I went for a sort of leaving party, I ended up being with my brother in law Dave in our local working mens club. He had brought me home in his lorry which he left parked where I used to park mine, he was, shall we say, too inebriated to drive home so he stayed at my house. I too was three sheets to the wind so after having a little supper we took ourselves off to our respective beds and went to sleep.

The next thing I remember is Pat waking me up saying it was 05.30, I had to be at the brewery to start work at 06.00 so after rousing Dave, getting dressed and leaving the house without a brew or anything to eat we set off in Dave's lorry for the brewery at 05.45. Dave had deliveries at Liverpool and Birkenhead that day so it was on his route, little did I know what was going to happen to me. We arrived at the brewery at 05.58, the gateman, seeing it was a Reyners lorry let Dave drive in thinking he was there to do a brewery job.

Dave pulled up in the middle of the large yard and I got out. I ran over to the loading bays where the bay foreman, Jack D, was waiting for me. He said jokingly "Ahh you must be Steve, I was told to expect an ugly bugger" I laughed half heartedly and confirmed who I was.

Jack was straight into it "right Steve pull this tank out it's full, put tank forty one in, by the time you've done that this tank here will be full, drag that out find an empty tank and put in its place" and so on and so on and so on....... he went on like this for what seemed an eternity. I couldn't take it all in, what with my beer addled brain, no food or drink inside me, I didn't know whether I was coming or going !

I got on with what he had asked and when I eventually caught up with what he'd wanted, all the bays full and tanks being loaded he pulled me to one side and said "Steve, pray tell me, what's up with your mate ?" I looked around to where he was pointing and saw Dave's lorry, parked up where we first came in, Dave's feet and two lower legs were hanging out of the open cab window. I'd completely forgotten about him, Jack had had me running around in circles and I'd not even registered he was still there. I said something like "oh... he's tired, he hasn't had much sleep" Jack replied "well that's fair enough but can you go and ask him to move over to the side and park properly before all the big bosses start to come in, then you can go and get some breakfast in the canteen, you look a bit peaky" with that he smiled and walked off.

I went over to Dave's lorry and gently tapped one of his boots, "Dave.. move your lorry over there out of the way then we can go and get some brekkie" Dave pulled his legs back inside and sat up sharply, "OK" he said, he started his lorry and pulled away, he did a large U turn in the yard and drove off into the sunrise ! I went and had a breakfast in the subsidised canteen and then spent the rest of the morning recovering.

I spoke to Dave over the following weekend about how he'd just drove off and he told me that he'd gone straight to his first dock at Liverpool, after unloading there he went and had a full greasy breakfast at a dockside cafe, and then on his way through the Mersey tunnel he had thrown up out of his cab window all over the bonnet of a passing mini car !

I stayed shunting at the brewery for around eighteen months and had many enjoyable times there. I recall that on really busy days John S, who I've mentioned previously, would take over from me at 18.00 until everything that needed to be done was done.

The lads on the loading bay who loaded the tanks with lager were on split day shifts, 06.00 till 14.00 and 14.00 till 22.00 and there was one crew who were, shall we say, mischievous. This particular crew were always up for a laugh, you had to have your wits about you or you'd get soaked by a powerful hose operated by one of them. John S had been soaked on several evenings by this crew, that is until one evening he drove through the brewery gate in his unit, I saw he was dressed head to toe in a fully protective wet suit, it was from his feet to the top of his head, all you could see of John was his face.

The lads on the bay spotted him jumping down from his cab, laughing manic like as he started to walk to the loading bays in a robot fashion. I stood and watched as the bay lads turned on this powerful hose and train it towards the oncoming John. He just walked through it still laughing like a maniac until he reached the guy holding the hose, they were not allowed to leave the bay while tanks were filling so John wrestled the hose from him and absolutely drowned all three of them. It was so funny to see. There were pranks like that all the time when that particular crew were working, I enjoyed working there.

All things must pass as they say and after around a year I got a hankering to get back on the road. I relayed this to Keith and soon was back, albeit as a favour to him, he asked me to go to Tilbury in Essex and return with the lorry and load of a driver who had become very ill. I was back, doing distance driving again.

My time of shunting at Harp Lager came to an end once I'd done the "rescue job" of travelling down with another driver and bringing a sick drivers loaded lorry back to Droylsden. At first I was driving whatever was available, such as when drivers were on holiday etc. Then I was offered a new lorry, it had been offered to other drivers first who had all refused it, and the reason why ? It was drastically underpowered. It was an X registered ERF with a Gardener 200 bhp engine. I recall that when I was hauling maximum weight loads it would just die on hills, "it wouldn't pull your hat off" was what everyone used to say, but it was mine, it was new and I could kit it out the way I wanted, so I accepted the offer.

On my first trip out with it I went to Worcester with a load of paper reels. I arrived at the delivery point and after handing over my paperwork I was instructed to reverse inside the building through a roller shutter door. The street had low concrete boulders on the kerb edges, presumably to stop lorries going onto the pavements or to stop people parking up the kerbs. A bloke came out with me to watch the nearside of my unit and guide me as I reversed in, as it was quite a tight manoeuvre. This was before the advent of kerb mirrors which enable a driver to see what was happening below on the nearside of the vehicle.

I asked the guy to watch and warn me if I got too close to any of the boulders and began to slowly reverse in. I was going extremely slow and every couple of seconds I would stop and look towards the bloke who was gesturing with his hand for me to continue. When I got to the point where I thought I would be near the boulders I looked to him and gave him the thumbs up sign as if to ask "Are we OK ?" He nodded in the affirmative and waved me on, so I slowly continued. I stopped again a couple of seconds later and did the same thing to the watching man, again he waved for me to carry on so I set off. I hadn't moved six inches before I heard a cracking sound followed by a hiss of air so I stopped immediately, engaged the hand brake and got out.

The guy was stood there scratching his head as I looked to see that the very front corner of my unit had hit a boulder, the cab was made of fibreglass and it had caved in just in front of the passenger door bottom step. That was bad enough on its own but the hissing air I could hear was coming from a ruptured air line behind the shattered fibreglass which fed an air tank just below the front headlight. I said to the guy "I thought you indicated that I was clear ? why didn't you stop me ?" He replied almost crying "I thought you would miss it, honestly" Well I hadn't missed it, the ruptured air line soon drained all the air in the lorries braking system and resulted in the brakes being locked on, I couldn't move anywhere. I was completely blocking the street.

Pretty soon there was a crowd forming, car drivers were blasting their horns and it wasn't long before a guy in a shirt

100

and tie came out of the printers to see what all the commotion was about. I explained what had happened to him and I remember him giving the watching guy a withering look before disappearing back into the premises. To cut a long story short I was there for around an hour before a recovery vehicle and fitter arrived who bodged up the air pipe enough to get the air system working again, enabling me to reverse, this time under his watchful eyes, into the building to unload. I was exonerated from blame as I had been given a guide who hadn't done his job properly, obviously my bosses were not happy about a new lorry getting pranged on its first trip out though.

On one of my runs I was sent with an empty twenty foot container to load Carnation cream from a factory in Ashbourne, Derbyshire. My brother in law Dave was also sent to load another one at the same time as me. We both duly got loaded, from floor to ceiling, front of the container to the back doors, with boxes of Carnation. We both weighed off at the weighbridge and were both at our maximum weights, which at that time was thirty two tons.

The containers were for export and we were to take them to Seaforth container docks in Liverpool. We left together at around 14.00 after deciding that we would both take a "quicker" route, by cutting across and travelling to Stoke on Trent via the A52, which would take us across country through a place called Froghall. We had both never used this route before so it was all new to us, but it would save us having to go down to Uttoxeter and then across to Stoke. Dave took the lead with myself bringing up the rear and all went well until we reached a down hill stretch of road that dropped down to Froghall.

This is a hill which starts at the top at 323 mtrs. above sea level and is 4.3 km long. It has (although we had no idea at the time) an average gradient of 4.7 per cent. With around 100 mtrs. of it at 13.1 per cent which is very steep. When first entering the slope Dave and I slowed right down, put our vehicles in first gear, then we began to descend. Little did we know what was in store, the hill was not straight, it had curves and was engulfed on both sides by trees and shrubbery. There was a narrow kerb on either side of the road, I was around 10 mtrs. behind Dave, I was driving an ERF which had good braking systems, he was driving a Seddon Atkinson which didn't have as good a braking system as mine did. However we were in first gear which was holding us back somewhat until we rounded a bend onto a straight stretch of road, as I followed Dave I could see there was what looked like a sharp left hand bend ahead of us.

My lorry brakes were at this point starting to feel a bit 'spongelike' as they were starting to get really hot and fade. I made a decision to stop and conveyed this to Dave with a few flashes of my headlights. Dave had made the decision too and we both tried to stop. The weight of the vehicles was trying to push us down though so we both instinctively edged our near-side wheels along the kerb edge to help us slow down and stop, which we eventually did, with my lorry about four feet away from Dave's back end. To say I was relieved would be an understatement, I remember thinking "flaming hell Steve that was close !"

I got out of my cab and made my way downhill on foot to Dave, who was also getting out, he said something like "bloody hell, who's fucking idea was this ?!" We both walked around our lorries checking the wheel hubs which were all really really hot, you could have fried eggs on them. We made the decision to put ourselves on a break until the brakes had cooled off. We saw a guy walking up the hill towards us and we asked him if there was anywhere we could safely turn around, he replied that his gate which was some distance behind us was the nearest place we could reverse into but that we probably wouldn't be able to do it, he said that what we'd done happened regularly and that there was a guy in Froghall, at the bottom of the hill, who had a recovery truck which he used to get lorries up and down the hill. We both mulled over the idea and decided that would prove too expensive an option so we'd look for another way to get down.

We decided to walk down the hill to see what was around the bend in the distance. I recall the pressure on the back of my calves as we walked down there it was that steep. When we got to the bend we found it to be reasonably sharp with a fairly steep drop off on the uphill side of the road. Beyond that point the road went steeply down with a gentle curve at the bottom and from there it was a slight climb up to where the road then levelled out. We both walked back to our lorries very shakily, I got into Dave's to sit and wait for our brakes to cool down. After around forty five minutes I said "right, we can't sit here all

102

day, we're gonna have to make a move, we'll try and reverse to that guys gate" I got into my lorry and started it up, the brakes had cooled off by this time, I selected reverse and tentatively let out the clutch, the unit just shook, there was no way I could set off backwards, I left it in reverse and turned off my engine. Dave was stood in the road near my cab, I said "right Dave we'll have to go down then" he said something like "what ?! Around that bend ? We could end up going right over the fucker and over the edge !" I replied " well we can't sit here all night, if you go forward a few yards so that I can get out, I'll go first, give me about a minute then you come. I'll see you at the other side of the hill hopefully" Dave said "you're fucking nuts, take it easy Steve for Gods sake". He went back to his lorry and pulled forward a few yards and I thought to myself "this is it, I'm going".

I selected first gear again and very nervously set off past Dave's truck and down the hill. The lorry, with its weight, was trying to push me so I feathered the brakes and held it back as I approached the bend. I rounded it slowly, I'll be honest with you, I was absolutely shaking with fear. Once round the bend I let it go a little bit and changed up a few gears, I rounded the curve at the bottom and powered up the last slope to the top where I stopped. I listened for Dave's lorry and eventually I heard him rounding the sharp bend above me. He did the same thing as I'd done and he was soon coming up the slope behind me. I set off with Dave following and we both eventually pulled into Knutsford services where we parked for the night. We both had a laugh about it but underneath it all we knew that we'd had a lucky escape. I chose never to use that road when freighted ever again. The last time I was in the area, there was a much needed weight limit of seven and a half tons in operation on the road with that very dangerous hill.

I once had an overnight stop in Southampton, again I was with Dave, we had both unloaded our respective twenty foot containers at one of the container docks there and Dave had managed to reload another one which was for delivery at 11.00 the following morning in Llay which is near Wrexham in North Wales. I had arrived a little later in the day and had not managed to reload another container for myself due to time restrictions. I was told to be at the dock before shift change the next morning so that I could collect one and be in some sort of good time for its delivery up north.

Dave and I parked up at what then was a large city centre car park near to the docks which doubled as a lorry park during the night. It was a huge car park where there used to be a big modern swimming baths which are no longer there. You could use the baths for washing, or even get a bath in there. You could get a meal in a portakabin by the car park entrance and if you fancied a beer or two or a visit to a cinema the town centre was only a five minute walk away.

Dave and I had a wash and shave in the baths and then a meal before heading into town for a "walkabout", a loose term for drinkies, I think it was Dave's birthday or some sort of celebration so we had more drinks than we usually would have done. All thoughts of rising early for the pick up at the docks for me and an early start for Dave went out of the window, "I'll get up, I always do" I said to Dave, who had reminded me at some point in the evening. We both returned to our lorries quite late after having some late night supper from a chippy and went to sleep. I had a small travel alarm clock which I set for 04.30. The next thing I remember was hearing the roar of a lorry starting up next to me, I sat up startled and gazed at my alarm clock, it hadn't gone off because I hadn't set it correctly, I threw back my curtains to see Dave, who was parked next to me, getting himself ready to leave.

My clock told me it was 05.05 ! I'd overslept, something I very rarely did. I hurriedly folded back all my curtains without fastening them, threw my bedding paraphernalia aside then started my engine and drove away at about 05.10 in my unit and empty twenty foot skeletal trailer as quickly as I could. I was wearing only my underpants, no shirt, trousers, socks or boots.

It was a bright summers morning, I remember arriving at the dock gate and flying past the dock police box there with my empty trailer bouncing around and making a lot of noise, I didn't slow down until I reached the completely empty lorry booking in parking area at 05.20. I grabbed my pick up information notes and got out of my lorry, grabbing my tee shirt and trousers as I did and set off half running, half stumbling as I desperately pulled my tee shirt over my head and almost fell over trying to pull my trousers on as I made my way across towards the booking in office.

Heaven knows what the guys in the booking in office thought when they saw me, notes in my mouth pulling a shirt and pants on, no footwear whatsoever making my way over to them.

I entered the office, hair unbrushed, my tee shirt on inside out and bare feet panting "help us out here lads I've gotta get this box on before shift change" I thrust my collection details over the desk towards a smiling guy stood behind his counter, his mate in the corner was laughing out loud at the sight they'd just witnessed. The guy behind the counter said "nice try son but you're too late, they've already stopped the cranes and come down, it'll be after shift change now before you can get it" I was desolate, "Oh shit, my boss will go mad, can you at least stamp my notes with the time I arrived so I can tell him I was here early enough please ?!" He replied "aye we'll do that for you son but it'll be 07.00 before the next shift comes in and by the time you get your box I can't see it being before 08.00"

I told him that as long as my notes were showing I'd arrived early I didn't care. He processed my notes and told me to pull off the waiting area and park up at the barrier that let you onto the container loading area, to wait there and then I'd be first in when they started work. He also said something whilst laughing like "now get over there and get some sleep while you can because you look like you need it !"

I left the office and walked slowly back to my lorry, my feet felt every lump and stone in the ground surface and it was quite uncomfortable, something I hadn't noticed when I'd first arrived in such a panic. I also felt quite nauseous and had a headache.

It must have been around 05.30 when I got into my lorry and pulled it up to the barrier as I'd been instructed. I put my bed back in position, opened my window, closed my curtains and laid down in what I was wearing on top of my bed. I soon fell back into some much needed sleep. I don't know how long after it was but I was woken by a heavy banging on my cab door, I leaned up on one elbow and pulled my curtain back to see a bloke stood about four feet away looking up at me, he said loudly "I hope you haven't been here all night lad, you're not allowed to sleep on the dock" He was just about to say something else, but I was in no mood for little dictators and before he could say any more I shouted "FUCK OFF !!" Then closed my curtain and laid back down. He said "don't talk to me like that, I know the shop steward, I'll have you barred from the dock" I just shouted again through my curtains as I lay there "FUCK.....OFF !" I was thinking that if he persisted in bothering me I was going to get up and thump him, he obviously hadn't been in the waiting area office and checked, he'd pulled up to the barrier thinking he'd get first in the queue and then go and book in. He walked away and I didn't hear any more from him. The lads in the booking in office must have put him wise as to my situation and no more was said. I did eventually get my box and had no problems when I arrived late at the delivery point in Manchester.

As a footnote to this story I was later informed by Dave that he had left the lorry park soon after I'd gone and had only driven for about an hour before pulling up to have a "snooze" which lasted for about an hour, so he was late too, it made me feel a little better about it all.

Before the advent of proper sleeper cabs most drivers mainly stayed in transport digs, although some did sleep over the engine cowlings in their cabs then. If you asked lorry drivers where they had delivered to the most, apart from the ones who went to the same place on every trip, I reckon that most would say London and its surrounding areas. There is so much industry there covering all the ranges of business you could think of. I've had my fair share of London deliveries too. I, like many other drivers seemed to gravitate to the east and south of London to park up at nights.

Reyners had an office in Silvertown which is in the east end of London, (the story that I understand to be true is that it was called Silvertown because a giant Tate and Lyle sugar factory was based there) The guy who ran Reyners office there was named Jack Gillies, a real character who didn't suffer fools lightly, he said what he thought and could appear quite brusque but I knew him to be a caring man, great at his job, and as long as you did your best it was greatly appreciated by him. Not far from Jacks office there was a transport motel, "the Silvertown Motel", which was supposedly an upgraded transport digs. It had a cafe serving all kinds of meals, washrooms and was quite modern in design at the time. The lorries used to park on land belonging to the motel at the rear of the premises.

106

I remember parking there and it was always full. Lorries were jammed in, usually there was a yard marshal who asked what time you were leaving in the morning and, depending on how early you were going, he would try to park lorries in order, earliest at the front then departure times descending in order behind them. I recall the bed rooms had bunk beds in them. It was definitely three, maybe more, meaning at least six people in a room. There was a pub across the road called "the Rose of Denmark" where there would be a stripper performing on certain nights.

Another cafe not far from Silvertown was "the Four Oaks" on the A13 near Dagenham. That too was always busy. In south London I used to stay at a cafe in the New Cross area on the Old Kent Road called "Taylors". This too had multi bed rooms where you would sleep in your own bed with other drivers in theirs. The lorry drivers used to park up in the streets surrounding the cafe as there wasn't a designated lorry park there. I used to go to a pub near there called the "Montague Arms", like many London pubs did, they had strippers performing as well as comedians. I have been privileged to see comedian and actor Mike Reid in there and Jimmy Jones who both used to compere and tell jokes.

I remember one of Reyners drivers, a lad named Brian (the son of "Pop" I mentioned earlier) hauled a near naked stripper over his shoulder and ran out of the front door of the pub with her kicking and screaming, he brought her straight back though and nearly got himself barred.

The cafe owner at Taylors always made up plates of cheese, corned beef and ham sandwiches for the drivers returning from the pubs which they'd wash down with a cup of tea or coffee, they would just help themselves as Taylors trusted them to do the right thing and leave everything in good order.

Another stopover not far from there was a house that did transport digs in Stockwell, which I've mentioned earlier in another story, called "the Albion", there too, lorries parked in the surrounding streets, you'd be lucky if you were allowed to even drive up those streets in London nowadays, let alone park a lorry up overnight. I can also state that whilst my varied vehicles were parked in the areas mentioned, I never had my load or the lorry tampered with, something else that you would not find happening nowadays.

Sea Containers or "boxes" as we called them gave Reyners a lot of work. As explained earlier in this book, Reyners stored and repaired them but we also used to collect empty ones to load, and full ones which we emptied. We would take them for export to container ports all over the UK. Places such as Tilbury in Essex, Harwich in Essex, Ipswich in Suffolk, Seaforth in Liverpool, Containerbase at Urmston Manchester as well as at Garston Liverpool, and Salford docks. There were also container docks at Hull, Southampton and perhaps the biggest and busiest at Felixstowe in Suffolk. It was from there that I'd collected a box for a delivery in the north west of England one afternoon.

In those days you had to travel through Ipswich to get to Felixstowe as the new road and bridge over the River Orwell had not yet been constructed. On this occasion I had loaded my box in the late afternoon and decided that I would leave the port area and find somewhere quiet to park. I headed for Ipswich and upon reaching the outskirts of the town near Nacton had opted to pull off the road I was on and take a back road which ran somewhat parallel to it. This road was virtually deserted, I found a lay by that was sheltered by trees on both sides of the road and pulled in to park for the night.

It was a warm Autumn evening and I had been there for some time, having cooked myself something to eat and drink, boiled up a kettle of hot water to wash with and was sat in my passenger seat with my feet up, no radio or TV on just sat relaxing when out of the trees on my left, about twenty yards away from me walked a full grown deer. I sat perfectly still and watched as it slowly walked into the centre of what was the road and stopped. It was magnificent, stood proud with its head up, fully grown antlers atop of its head. I sat motionless, I didn't want to scare it off and hoped I wouldn't spook it. I didn't have a camera, but oh… how I wish I'd have had one then. It turned its head to look at me sat in the cab then slowly walked back from where it had come from and disappeared out of view. I can honestly say I've never been that close to such a beautiful animal in its natural state either before nor since.

There's nothing else much to talk about regarding this unit except for the fact that all the other drivers said I must have had "a heart like a lion" to take it on. Eventually I was offered another new unit, it was one of a pair of ERF's that came together. Dave, my brother in law was given B812 PBF and I got B813 PBF. By this time Reyners had started buying sleeper cabs and both our new ones were fitted with bunks. Along with having a bed to sleep on it had a radio. More importantly though it had a night heater which was fed off your diesel tank. I'll admit now that it was primitive compared to the night heaters nowadays, when used on cold nights it was very noisy, but it kept me warm. If it was on full power I could dry my hair with it !.

As I mentioned in the last paragraph, Dave had the twin to my unit, and on one trip, we were both sent to Southampton with twenty foot containers which we loaded before taking them down there. We'd both delivered our loaded boxes to one of the container berths and then had loaded an empty box each from a local hauliers yard. We were instructed to go and load them at a warehouse in Southampton, and once loaded, take them up to Salford docks for export.

We both arrived just before lunch time at this big warehouse in the Regents Park area of the city, it belonged to British American Tobacco who manufactured cigarettes etc there at the time. We sought out the warehouse supervisor who straight away informed us that everyone was just about to go for lunch, he invited us to go to the works canteen and then after lunch he'd sort us out.

The canteen was fantastic, good food at really low subsidised prices. We both had a good feed and went back to the warehouse area. We met the supervisor again and were surprised at what he said to us "we will be loading you both today lads but it's a very slow process which may go on into the evening shift, so if you'll back your trailers up to the loading bay over there and unhook them, we'll take it from there. If you both come back at around 08.00 in the morning everything should be ready for you, OK ?" I said that I'd have to check with my boss if it was OK and he told me that it was already sorted out with everyone concerned. We took his word for it and did as he'd instructed.

We left the factory at around 13.30 and made our way to the large car park near the swimming baths in the town centre, it served as a lorry park during the night time. When we got there the place was obviously full of cars but there was an area near the portakabin cafe there which had enough room for our two units to fit into. We parked beside each other before going to find a phone box to ring Keith our manager at Reyners to inform him what had happened.

He told us he knew all about it and that the job was paying enough money to cover us both doing nothing for the rest of the day "have a nice afternoon and stay out of trouble" he jokingly said. That was it, we had a free rein ! "What shall we do ? pub?" said Dave. I replied that if I started drinking that early I'd be slaughtered by dinner time that evening, Dave had hollow legs and could drink all day and night if he was in the mood for it.

It was a lovely sunny day so we both decided we'd get our wash things and go for a bath in the local swimming complex at the other side of the car park. We had a long hot bath each then returned to our units and got changed into clean clothes. "Time for a walkabout" Dave said, and so off we went, it was around 15.30 by then. We had a steady afternoon and, surprisingly, did behave ourselves. We had a meal out and must have got back to our lorries later that night. We both watched TV for a bit and then settled down to sleep.

We both left the lorry park which was now beginning to fill up with cars again at 07.30 and made our way back to the tobacco warehouse. When we arrived we could see the rear container doors were now closed so it looked as though the boxes were loaded and ready to go. They were indeed loaded, filled to the brim with cigarettes and sealed with thick padlocks on each container. The supervisor told us we could now hitch up to our trailers but not to move until he said it was time to. He was waiting for private security escorts to come who were going to shadow us all the way up to Salford docks.

He told us to go up to the canteen and have some breakfast whilst we waited. Once again we had a good feed there before returning to our lorries, the supervisor took us to his office and gave each of us our respective paperwork for the loads, he told us that we must follow a certain route up to Salford and gave us detailed instructions of which way to go. I presume it was for security purposes as the route he specified was not one I would normally take. Without going into details it involved travelling across country through Wiltshire and up to join the M5 in the midlands, where we were to stop and have a stipulated break at a service station before setting off up the M5 and onto the M6 towards Manchester and then on to Salford. He told us that we should both stay as close as possible together and that we would be shadowed by security guards in plain unmarked cars for the whole of the journey. The reason for going onto the specified services on the M5 was so the security guards could swap over personnel, he told us that we would not know how many or where they were but that they would be keeping a close eye on all the proceedings. He said that they would shadow us both until the boxes had been lifted off us at Salford and put straight onto a waiting ship.

That's how it panned out, I never noticed anyone shadowing us and overall the job took a day and a half to complete, we were travelling on a Friday and by the time we'd both been unloaded at Salford the day was almost over. We had been on a one off trip hauling cigarettes from Southampton to Salford, having been such expensive and high value loads to have warranted that much security.

Whilst talking of high value loads here's a little story that may interest you. I have told you previously about sea containers or boxes, as we call them, which were what it says on the tin, boxes with doors at one end, but there were variations. One being completely open sided with no roof, the front and back ends could fold down to make them flat, they came with heavy duty plastic tarpaulins to cover whatever you may have needed to cover.

There are also open topped containers, these had a front, back with doors and sides but no roof, they had a heavy duty tarpaulin which is rolled out over the top of removable bars which were put in place across the width of the box. The tarpaulin, which has eyelets all around the edges of it, was then fastened down by placing the eyelets over lugs that are welded onto the box about a foot down from the top of it and along a swinging retention bar above the rear doors You then feed two thick security cables, one on each side, through the eyelets from front to back and then down through lugs fitted onto the doors to the container door handles. These cables have slots at the end which you then pass a security seal through. This means if the seal has been tampered with or changed that the doors had been opened.

I collected an empty one of these containers from a yard in Trafford Park and was sent to load in the countryside near a place called Tuxford in Nottinghamshire. This unassuming works made mining equipment and I was to load what people call a "mole" which was the front end of a machine that is sent underground and breaks up and chews stone and earth to form tunnels. The head of the mole was made of very hard wearing expensive materials to cope with the tearing of rock and the like. I reversed into a works shed where the mole had been assembled. With the help of the lads there we rolled back the top tarpaulin and opened the doors before swinging the top retention bar over and out of the way. A team of lads then got inside the empty box and began to assemble and fix a hardwood cradle and supporting front and side timbers to the box.

This, as you may imagine, took some time and I noticed there was one particular guy who was instructing and overseeing the whole of the procedure.

Once the cradle had been fixed in place, a crane then lifted the mole off the floor and slowly brought it to the rear of the box, with the guy I mentioned guiding the crane driver as he carefully manoeuvred it into the box. The mole was attached to machinery which made it spin, the width of the round mole head being around seven feet in diameter, the machinery behind it was a little narrower than the head, the whole length of the outfit was around sixteen feet and it weighed nineteen and a half tons.

Once it was where the guy supervising was happy with, it was lowered onto the cradle. The cranes holding chains were undone and removed before the team of wood workers got back into the box and began to add the finishing securing timbers around the mole and its engine.

I had been watching all this and was amazed by their professionalism, I mentioned this to the guy who had been supervising it all. I asked him where it was going and he told me it was Australia, he said that around three containers containing all the moles paraphernalia had already been loaded and sent. This was the last one with the head of the tunnelling machine. He told me he was going to fly down to Australia in around a weeks time to assemble the whole thing on the site where the tunnelling was to be done. I said "Australia, bloody hell you get around don't you" He laughed and replied that he'd been all over the world doing the same thing, he mentioned Canada, China, Russia and the USA. I said he must like travel and he said it was just part of the job. I asked him how long it would take to assemble the whole thing and he said that putting it all together and testing it would take around six weeks, he then added, in a very serious manner "and I hope there's no problems because I've booked a two weeks holiday in Scarborough with my family" which I found highly amusing. A world globetrotter going to Scarborough. Don't get me wrong, there's nothing wrong with the place, but I'd have put fiver on a guy like that going to somewhere, shall we say, a little more exotic !

We closed the whole thing up and fed the security cable through all the lugs before sealing it at the back doors. I then took the container to Felixstowe for the beginning of its long journey down under.

Felixstowe, as I've mentioned earlier, is about the biggest and busiest container port in Great Britain, it deals with 48% of Britain's container traffic. In 2017, it was ranked as 43rd busiest container port in the world and 8th in Europe, handling the importing and exporting of 3.85 million twenty-foot equivalent units. It goes without saying that I've been there many many times. On one visit there I'd had my box offloaded onto the dock for export, I was then sent to another berth to collect a forty foot box which was to be delivered to the US Airforce Base at Alconbury in Cambridgeshire at 13.00 hrs. It's a huge base which although belonging to the RAF, was, and still is as far as I know, wholly occupied by American Airforce personnel and was around an hour and a half drive from Felixstowe.

I arrived at the base around lunchtime and was greeted by a rather scruffy looking guard at the security gate. I recall thinking that "our boys wouldn't be allowed to be on duty in that state". He checked me over and then the inside of my cab, ensuring that I didn't have any cameras or recording equipment. He and a fellow guard then checked out my lorry exterior, mirrors on sticks to check the underneath, climbing a set of steel ladders on wheels and looking at the top of my unit and container and then ensuring the security seal and padlock on the rear doors had not been tampered with. Once that was done he directed me, with the aid of a site map, to a stores warehouse in the heart of the base, telling me that I must not go off route whatsoever.

I found my way to the stores department to find they were just going on lunch break, I was informed that I too could use the "mess" and they told me where to go. So off I went.

When I arrived at the "mess room" I joined the rear end of a fairly long queue, upon eventually reaching the front end of the queue I could see the menu board on the wall behind the food serving staff. I was quite surprised to see that all the prices were in US dollars and Cents. I didn't know what Pastrami was and there were other meal combinations and names I didn't have a clue about too. I opted to have a hamburger and fries to save myself any embarrassment and confusion about my lack of US gastronomical knowledge. Of course, I did not have any US currency on me either, so upon reaching the cashiers till I enquired about the price in Sterling. What followed was like when a stranger walks into a saloon in an old cowboy movie, everyone within earshot went quiet and looked at me like I was from another planet. I quickly explained my situation, how I was a delivery driver and had been sent there by the stores department, once I did that everything was OK and I was allowed to pay for my food so I sat down and, rather embarrassed, ate my meal.

I returned to the stores afterwards and passed my delivery notes, which were in a sealed envelope, to the supervisor in the office there who opened and checked them. I was then instructed to accompany the supervisor to the rear of my vehicle whilst the seals were removed. I asked the supervisor at this point what was in the container, he informed me if was full, front to back, with boxes of denim jeans, jackets and shirts. I was quite astounded by that, but upon reflection there were a lot of personnel on that base who stayed in Britain for long periods of time so I suppose off duty clothing was needed.

I used to park up for the night sometimes at Huntingdon which is the nearest biggish town to the base, you could see lots of Americans and their vehicles around the place. I'd sometimes go and watch a film at the cinema there and most of the audience would be Americans too.

The products were unloaded without incident and I returned the empty container to a haulage yard back at Felixstowe. I have delivered many boxes to US and UK bases, one twenty foot container I delivered to RAF Mildenhall, a base not far from RAF Lakenheath, which is also wholly operated by USAF personnel was full of Coca Cola cans and bottles. I also took a trailer full of new two wheeled trailer water or fuel bowsers to what was the US base at Burtonwood near Warrington, which, at that time, was just used to store military equipment for the Americans, that too had a "mess room" which had its menu in US currency. I still stand by what I said earlier though, I'm certain that British service personnel always dress much more smartly whilst on duty, I found the US forces to be rather slovenly dressed, not all of them mind you, but enough for me to have noticed and to be able to recall it.

I did another job from Felixstowe, which involved me collecting a forty foot container and taking it the short distance to a house, on a new estate in nearby Ipswich. The box was full of household furniture, clothing and equipment and had come from a home belonging to an English couple, one of whom had been in the army based in Germany.

I arrived at the estate just after lunchtime, and after carefully slaloming through bendy avenues and between parked cars (which always amuses me, why don't people use their driveways ?) I came to the last house of a cul de sac with a turning circle at the end. I nosed my vehicle right up to the fence which was beyond the turning circle so that the back doors of the box were near the short driveway to the house I was delivering to. The lady of the house came out as I pulled up outside, as did half the people on the avenue ! She checked the security seal, and after seeing it hadn't been tampered with, I opened the two rear doors to see all household regalia from the back doors up to the front. It had not been loaded professionally and a lot of space had been wasted, things had fallen over too, due to not being packed correctly. I climbed up and into the box but did not start to pass anything down as I wished the lady to see what condition her possessions were in.

I rummaged around and found a pair of stepladders, I lowered them onto the floor at the back of the box so she could climb a few steps to see for herself. I told her that I could not be held responsible if anything had broken in transit, I asked her who had loaded it and she told me it was her husband and a few of his friends. She told me not to worry and asked could I start to pass stuff down. Now I'm not a lazy person, but I thought "hang on, who's going to carry all this stuff into the house ?" I was in the box, about to bring everything to the back doors and help lower it down to…who? the lady of the house ? I asked her if there was anyone else to help carry the furniture and possessions indoors. She said that there wasn't, she thought I'd have someone with me to help. I explained that I was just the driver who delivers containers to be unloaded and that I was not even insured to get inside a container to load or unload it. I said that I was willing to help on jobs like this one but I could get into trouble for being inside a box.

This insurance stipulation came into effect when containerisation first started to become popular, it stated that only the employees of the company or person who was taking delivery or exporting the goods were to handle them. The UK dockers unions enforced this and if you were found to have broken this "ruling" you could be barred from carrying and loading or unloading containers. I took many containers carrying all sorts of cargos and apart from opening and closing the doors had nothing to do with the handling of goods in them.

So what were we to do on this particular trip ? The lady told me that her brother lived quiet near and that she would phone him and ask for help, she also said she would ring other friends and acquaintances. This resulted in me just passing down light things for her to take inside, we did this for around forty five minutes after which time a car pulled up nearby and two guys got out of it. It was her brother and a mate of his. Five or so minutes later another car pulled up and another guy and his girlfriend got out who were there to help. With three lads and the two ladies carrying the stuff in, the job speeded up somewhat and after stopping for a brew for ten minutes or so we had the whole box empty at around 16.45.

I was knackered, I'd been inside the container on my own, hauling everything to the back doors, it was a hot day and I was sweating profusely, my hair plastered to my head with sweat. I climbed down from the box and, after checking that it was completely empty, the brother told me I could close it up. I was about to go to my cab when he shouted to me "don't go yet driver, my sister wants to see you before you leave" I waited at my cab door thinking "oh… I may be getting a little thank you tip here boy" a minute or so later she came round the back of the trailer and walked up to me, she said "I just want to say thank you for your help, would you like a cold drink or something before you go ?" I thanked her for the offer but I still had to go and get the empty box off my trailer at Felixstowe and it was getting quite late, so I would leave the drink. I returned to Felixstowe having had to reverse my lorry out of the cul de sac past even more parked cars, why do people not use their driveways !!

There was a lad at Reyners called Dave who, after tramping around the country for many years, had ended up being the day shunt driver. He unloaded the articulated trunk vehicle that came through the night from Kent. If he had enough time he'd also load it for its return down south the same evening. Dave was a lovely man, he was over six feet tall and heavily built but he was a gentle giant with a happy go lucky attitude most of the time. The job meant that he didn't go away from home, always pottering around locally which suited him as he'd had a son who was, at the time of this story, a toddler.

I was making my way down to Felixstowe one day with a forty foot container which I'd loaded at some place or other. At the time I used to go through Bedford and across to St. Neots on my journey to the port, I had stopped in between the two towns in the early afternoon to find out what Reyners had planned for me regarding a return load. I was in a phone box and said jokingly to Howard, one of the transport clerks "what load of crap have you got me to come back with then ?" I began to chortle waiting for some smart remark to come back to me, but there was a moments silence. You know the feeling you get when you know somethings wrong but you don't have a clue, well I got that feeling then. I said "what's up Howard, what's wrong ?" He replied "you haven't heard.... have you ?" There were no mobile phones then so I didn't have a clue. I said "heard what ? what's happened" He said "Dave S....... died today, we think his lorry had a front wheel blow out on the M63, he went off the road through a fence and down an embankment, the lorry rolled and his cab was crushed, he died at the scene"

I remember feeling numb and dizzy, I'd only spoken to Dave recently and now he was gone. Howard said "are you OK Steve, I'm sorry to give you such bad news over the phone, are you alright to continue on, you can park up if you like, nothing

117

much seems to matter now" I took a few moments to gather myself and replied shakily that I would continue. Howard reiterated that I could stop there or wherever I wanted if I needed to, he said most of the drivers who'd he'd been in touch with had called it a day. I decided that I would try to get to Felixstowe and then park up. Looking back, I should have stayed where I was, my mind wasn't fully on the job, all I could think of was Dave and how he was no longer with us.

It was a very sad day at his funeral, all of the Reyner drivers and staff were off, most were present. There was a wake held at "The Bush" which had been Dave's local, he'd only lived around the corner from it. I recall being in there when his wife and little boy came into the pub, she'd only come in to say thanks to everyone who'd turned up, I looked at his boys little lost face and I couldn't contain myself, I left the pub and went outside where I burst into tears. Another lad who'd seen me hurriedly leaving came out and asked was I OK. I said through tears "that poor little lad of Dave's, he looks so lost, it just broke me" He told me he was upset too and I had nothing to be ashamed about, he then coaxed me to clean myself up and come back inside whenever I was ready.

There have been other workmates that have passed away during my lifetime but Dave's was in such tragic circumstances. At the time I thought that it could have been anyone of us drivers, nobody knows what's around the corner. It was an accident, nobody's fault, which resulted in a child losing his Dad, and a wife, her husband. We at Reyners lost a lovely gentleman and workmate. RIP Dave.

My brother Peter was once a second man for me on a wide and long load I did to Loughborough in Leicestershire.We used Reyners extending trailer which could be opened up from forty feet to sixty feet long. The load was made up of two overhead crane beams which were sixty five feet in length and twelve feet in width at one end each. The wide part of the beam was where the crane could be operated from, there were two beams laid side by side with the wider parts being both laid to the front and rear of the trailer.

We loaded the beams before setting off without a police escort, we had our route, which at the time the police gave you, so we set off towards Oldham where we could pick up the A627(M) after which it was virtually all motorway driving to Loughborough via the M62 and the M1. We made it to the delivery point without incident, unloaded then closed the trailer up to its running length of forty foot and set off back towards home. Perhaps it was the Friday traffic, I don't know, but I reckoned in my head that it would be quite a push to make it back to the depot in the busy traffic. It also began to snow, lightly at first, but it was snowing.

I asked Pete if he'd mind staying out overnight, I explained that it would have been late getting back and that I had two bunks in my cab, one of which I used for storing gear on but which he could use to sleep on. As explained earlier, I had a night heater in my cab and a spare sleeping bag so we would both have been warm, we could park up somewhere and have a few pints then run back to Droylsden the following morning. Pete was up for this so we made our way up the M1.

We'd decided that as it had started snowing we didn't fancy cutting across country over the Pennines in case the roads over them got blocked with snow. I pulled into Chesterfield, famous for its leaning twisted church spire at around 18.00. I found a spare piece of land and parked up.

I had all the gear for cooking us some food, which I did. We finished that, then I boiled up a few kettles of water for us both to have a wash. It was by this time snowing quite heavily. We both watched a little TV in the cab and I began to get a little worried that I may have made an error, what if it continued snowing all night and I couldn't get out of Chesterfield the next morning ? Pete said "no point worrying about it Steve let's go and have a few beers, whatever happens... happens" We got changed and went for a walk around the town, slipping and sliding in the snow. It was some time later that we went into a pub and had our first pint. We walked around after that, going into another two pubs, we then found ourselves back near to where the lorry was parked, there was a pub around two hundred yards from it so we decided we'd go and have our fourth and final pint in there then call it a night.

The pub was very busy, filled with locals, it was one of those bars where when a stranger walks in everything would go quiet and everyone would look at you. It was quite unnerving, anyway we ordered our beers and stood by the bar to drink them as

119

there were no spare seats. Pete and I had changed from our overalls, we were similar sizes although Pete is a bit taller than me. I used to carry sets of clothes to change into when I was away, I had a couple of shirts and a pair of black trousers. Pete had brought an overnight bag with him containing a change of clothes and some washing gear as he'd thought he may not get back home the same day. It came to last orders at the pub and we decided to have one more pint. The bar staff served us our beer but were eying us up suspiciously. Pete and I noticed this but we knew we hadn't done and were not about to do anything untoward so we slowly drank our beer.

I needed the toilet so went to find it, as I opened the door, two men who were in there were talking and I thought I heard one say "those two at the bar". They abruptly stopped talking when I came in and no more was said. I went back to our Pete and told him. I said "somethings going on here and it involves us two, I think we'd better drink up and piss off" We looked around the room as we finished off our pints and noticed that most people had finished or almost finished their beer but nobody was leaving, we were being surreptitiously observed by several of the punters in there. It was then it dawned on me, I said to Pete "this lot think we're coppers and they're all waiting for after time, we've both got blue shirts on and dark clothing, they think we're scuffers". Pete and I both laughed at the realisation, it was the only explanation that made any sense, we both finished our pints and made our way towards the door, on the way I turned towards the bar and said loudly "right you can all have a drink now, we're not coppers, thank you", and then we were out of the door.

We both laughed as we walked back to the lorry. It had stopped snowing by this time, we went and got ourselves some supper from a chippy near my lorry then got back into it. We had ourselves a brew before turning in for the night. Me and our kid….coppers !!? I still laugh about it.

It was one morning in the Summer of 1981 that I went to the Harp Lager brewery in Moss Side, Manchester to collect a tank which had been loaded for John Smith's Brewery in Tadcaster, Yorkshire. It was a 03.00 delivery slot which was a regular run in those days. Those of you who are old enough to remember may recognise the month and year in question, it was when the Moss Side riots took place.

Almost opposite the gates of the brewery on Denmark Road stood the Moss Side police station. As I arrived in the area in my unit at around 12.30, close to the brewery I saw lots of people on the surrounding streets, there had been a lot of tension in the area previously but I was not aware of what was about to take place. When I reached around a hundred yards from the gate a fairly small crowd of people were outside the police station, angrily shouting and waving in its direction. The security men on the gate at Harp lifted the entrance barrier just as I got to it so I drove inside and went round to where I could collect my delivery notes which had the trailer and tank identification numbers I was to take, on them. The security officers had closed the barrier behind me straight away.

I collected my paperwork and went to find the trailer with the tank on that I was to deliver. After I had hooked up to the trailer and done all the checks necessary I got back in my vehicle and drove over towards the gates in order to exit the premises about twenty minutes later. As I approached the security I noticed that the officers in there had completely closed the outer high wrought iron gates. I stopped and parked up around a hundred yards from the gates. I left my lorry and walked over towards the gatehouse where the security officers were intently watching what was going on outside the gates, the crowd had swelled a lot since I had been inside collecting my tank. It now half filled the road outside and there were a lot of angry shouting, people throwing things in the direction of the police station and generally being unruly.

I went into the gatehouse and asked the security what was going on, it was then that I learned that people were besieging the police station. I told them that I needed to leave pretty soon in order to be on time at Tadcaster. They advised me to sit and wait to see how things would pan out. Now I had finished around midday the day before in order to be able to start early for the delivery, I had gone to bed at 17.30 and risen at 23.00. I told them that I had no intention of waiting, the way it was going outside, I could see it was only going to get worse. I asked them to go out and open the gates as I approached them, whereupon, I would exit the brewery and take my chances getting through. They eventually but reluctantly gave in to my request,

121

I returned to my lorry, started it up, engaged gear and set off. Two security officers, one positioned at each gate, opened them as I approached, I'd put my hazards and main beam headlights on and I was pressing hard on the lorries horn, which was very loud. I held my breath and thought to myself "this is it Steve, don't stop for anything" As I passed out of the gates the security men closed them straight after me and I was on my own.

The crowd outside had heard my horn and seen me approaching, I can assure you, I wasn't crawling along ! the crowd began moving towards the police station, making enough room on the road for me to pass through, I was scared beyond belief, hoping that everyone would get out of the way, the crowd had now turned really ugly and I had no intention whatsoever of stopping. Luckily for me I did get by them all without incident and I left the area as quickly as possible.

I recall that I didn't take the tank back to Harp after I'd unloaded at Tadcaster, I took it to Reyners yard in Droylsden as the rioting had got much worse after I'd left the brewery. I believe that every window in the police station had been broken and twelve police vehicles had been set alight. Shops and businesses in the area had been looted as well. I also heard that a police officer had been shot in one of his legs by a crossbow bolt. Lots of roads in the area had to be closed after the riots, gas main pipes had been damaged by blazing cars and barricades that had been set up by the rioters which had to be repaired. The rioting had begun on the 8th July and ended on the 11th, although its memory lived on for some time after for many people, I will never forget the night it affected me directly.

I was in a works canteen in Hollinwood near Oldham one lunch time, I had got my meal and was seated at a long table at which around ten people could be seated. A guy came and sat down opposite me, he had the overalls on showing he was a worker at this particular works. He put a plate down with a meal containing meat, veg and gravy. He also had a bowl with a sweet and custard. He went and got a jug of water and a glass and returned to the table. In one motion he picked up his sweet and custard and tipped it on top of his dinner containing the meat, veg and gravy. He then took a spoon and began working the two meals into a mash like substance before devouring it all at a speed that was hard to fathom ! I sat gobsmacked watching him whilst trying not to stare. He'd stop occasionally and take a drink of water in between shovelling the mess down his throat. He ate the lot in a very short time, took a last drink of water then got up and walked out of the canteen. I said to another guy at the table "what was all that about ?!" He replied that this particular guy did this every day and that he went straight to the bookies once his "meal" was finished. It's strange but true, there are some weird people out there.

One day my brother in law Dave was approached by a lad we both knew who I'll name as John H. He had set up his own small company providing his units to haul other peoples trailers.. He asked Dave if he fancied coming to work for him as he'd ordered a new unit which when it arrived would be given to Dave to drive. The wage was quite a bit higher than he was on at Reyner's and there was also an added work related bonus on offer so after some thought and a chat with my sister Anne, he decided to accept his offer and began working for him. He drove a Volvo F12, the unit that John used to drive. John had moved to an administrative role whilst waiting for the new F12 to be delivered, he also had another unit, a Volvo F10 that another lad drove for him. They both hauled trailers for RH Stevens who were based in Macclesfield.

One weekend Dave came to my house and said that John had told him that the lad who drove the F10 was leaving him, probably because he had been promised the new unit and the other lad hadn't. He'd asked him to ask me if I also fancied changing jobs and go to work for him. I had a good think and talked it over with my wife Pat. The lure of more money for doing the same thing as I was, was too much, and despite being at Reyners, all told, for seventeen years, I decided to go and meet John, which resulted in me leaving and joining his firm. Dave and I were back working together.

Chapter Four.

Snow, toxic gasses, it's all part of the job.

Life whilst working for John H, I thought would be much the same as I'd been doing. I was totally wrong, it brought about some big changes. John preferred that we left the lorries at RH Stevens' yard in Macclesfield when we got back there for weekends, so I eventually bought a car, it was a second hand Ford Granada Ghia 2.0 litre.

We were paid weekly, so either Dave or I would drive the other up to where John drank at a pub in Glossop on a Sunday lunchtime to collect our wage slip, the driver not drinking (much). We'd use the time there to have a chat about how the week had gone. At first I didn't mind this but it could be a bit of a bind if Pat or myself fancied doing something else. Dave, who had bought my old house in Reddish, (we had moved to another bigger house, also in Reddish) would sometimes go on his own and collect the packets or I'd do the same for him whilst he had a break from going.

The job itself was pretty much the same but I worked quite a bit harder than I had at Reyners. I didn't mind as I'm not frightened of hard work and the financial bonus for more productivity on my part was quite well rewarded. We were virtually under RH Stevens traffic office rule. We hauled their trailers doing mostly their work, which was plentiful and varied. John had told us that we weren't to argue about anything we were asked to do, if we had any gripes then we could talk it over with him at the Sunday get together in the pub. He did say however that if either of us sensed that a job may be asking too much of us or seemed not worthwhile doing financially then we could voice our concerns to the traffic manager without going "over the top".

Although the pay whilst working for John H was better, I had managed to get home the odd night at Reyners, I was away all week whilst working for John H. Sometimes I may have ended up in the yard at Macclesfield mid week, finished at say 19.00 so I'd stay in my lorry for the night at Macc' as I invariably had an early start the following morning. It was too far for me to travel home and could take me up to, or even over an hour and a quarter travelling, then around forty five minutes to get back in the very early hours of the morning, it just wasn't worth it.

I was paid in accordance with night out rate from Monday to Thursday and if I was away on the Friday expenses for that would be added too. I'd usually have a shower at the yard and then go to a local chippy if I didn't fancy cooking my own dinner. There was a pub quite local to the yard in Macc', I think it was called "the Dolphin", I'd often go there with yard and traffic office staff, or other drivers, and have a few beers and play some pool before retiring to bed in my lorry which had a lovely comfy bed in it but no cab heater.

As stated earlier, the work at RH Stevens was plentiful and varied, there wasn't any brewery work as there had been at Reyners but one contract that RH did have was carrying a very dangerous chemical called Bromine. It is a chemical element with the symbol Br and atomic number 35. It is a volatile red-brown liquid at room temperature that evaporates readily to form a similarly coloured vapour. Its properties are intermediate between those of chlorine and iodine and if inhaled or digested can cause breathing difficulties as well as skin and organ burning in humans. RH Stevens used to collect it from Felixstowe in sea container tanks and smaller one ton tanks for delivery to ICI (Imperial Chemical Industries) plants across the UK.

My brother in law Dave was once involved in a potential spillage of it whilst delivering a tank of it to ICI at Grangemouth. Without going into detail, Dave had been asked to move his vehicle at some point by the staff who were in charge of the unloading process, there was a pipe that fractured and some of it escaped. The plant was put into its protective safety measures and all production was halted.

After a full and thorough investigation, Dave, and RH Stevens, were fully cleared of any blame.

I did not work many Sundays whilst I was a driver, those were days I wanted to spend with my family and were precious to me. At most firms I've worked at there were always the lads that actually WANTED to work them, and if I was asked to work one I'd always refer the fact that there were men who wanted to work them, and usually I would get out of doing so

125

by that method. I did however work one whilst subcontracting at RH Stevens. I was to take a load of fertilizer to a mushroom growing company in the countryside not far from Hailsham in Sussex. It had to be there for an 08.00 delivery slot on the Monday morning. As I left RH's yard just after lunch time on this particular Sunday, it began to snow, and did so on and off for most of the journey south.

I arrived at the delivery point at around 19.00 in the dark. The night security guard let me into the yard where I was to be unloaded the following morning, he parked me up at the place where the unloading would take place. By this time the snow was falling quite heavily and had settled on the ground. The security man told me there was a country inn around ten minutes walk up the lane outside, so after having a wash and change, I walked the short distance to it and had a few pints and a packet of crisps. When I left the inn it was really snowing heavily, it had settled on everything, I got back to my lorry and made myself ready for bed, had a cup of coffee whilst watching a little TV, then retired for the night.

When I woke up the next morning at 07.30 I drew back the vehicles cab curtains to see nothing but white, the windscreen and both side door windows were completely covered in snow. I got dressed put on my coat and boots, then opened the cab door to get out, I knew as I pushed it open that something was different, a wall of snow fell from the door and its window down to the ground, well I say the ground, it was about five inches deep in snow, what made it worse was that it was still snowing. I'd not seen snow like that since the bad winter of 1963. The load I had on the trailer was covered with tarpaulin sheets and they had a layer of snow on top of them of around five inches too.

I found a guy who seemed to be in charge of what could only be described as chaos. He told me that I was positioned correctly for unloading but that I may have a long wait before they could start as half the staff had phoned in saying they were either stuck in snow or were not even attempting to leave home. I wasn't too concerned about this and asked if there was anywhere I could have a hot wash and a brew. He pointed me to what I'd asked for and said that he'd let me know when to remove my sheets for unloading.

It must have been around 10.00 when he asked me to take off my sheets. The place was still in a chaotic state although the snow had relented a bit and was not falling as heavily. Staff were out with brushes and shovels trying to clear some sort of pathways and areas around the place I unfastened and removed the ropes and proceeded to wrap them, I had on a pair of cloth gloves and before I was half way through wrapping them my gloves and the hands inside them were thoroughly soaking wet and freezing cold. I unfastened the sheets and went to ask could a fork truck pick me up so I could get on top of them as I'd have no chance of pulling them off with the weight of the snow lying on them, my plan was to wrap the sheets up on the top of the load. After around fifteen minutes one came out of the works and slipped and slid its way over to me. The driver positioned himself next to the load, whereupon I stood on one of its forks, he then slowly raised me up to a height where I could step onto the top of the snow covered sheets.

A brush was thrown up to me and I began to shove the snow on the front sheet off and down on one side of the load. It was still snowing and at the time it felt like I was totally wasting my time.

It was really hard work trying to push five maybe six inches of snow off a tarpaulin, it didn't want to move, I slipped and fell over a couple of times during my efforts to remove it, I was sweating although it was bitterly cold. I did eventually remove the snow from the sheets after quite some time, I then pulled them up onto the load to wrap them.

The unloading process took a long time, a pallet would be lifted off, taken into the works and I wouldn't see the fork truck again for ages, presumably because there was only one fork lift working who had to cover jobs that another ones should have been doing but there were no staff to operate them. The trailer eventually became completely empty at around 13.00. I phoned RH's traffic office to find out where I was supposed to be back loading from, they told me that I was to make my way to Sheerness in Kent and put on a load of newsprint reels for Manchester. They said I was to cover my trailer flat bed as it would have to be dry in order to load the newsprint. I obviously had let them know earlier what the situation was and I could only laugh when he asked me to do it. I informed them that it was still snowing but I would try my best to clear my trailer of as much of it as possible.

127

I went and asked someone for the loan of a brush, upon receiving one I clambered up onto the rear of the trailer and began to sweep the snow off its bed. I was fighting a losing battle, the snow began to fall a little heavier so as I swept it was landing behind me and settling where I'd been ! I changed tack then, I went to the front and swept an area big enough for me to partly roll out my fly sheet, covering the area I'd swept. I did this all the way along the trailer bed for the full forty five feet of it, so the fly sheet covered it all. I then fastened the sheet over the headboard and along both edges of the trailer and to the rear of it, so I had it all securely covered. Once I was travelling the flat would then dry out enough for me to load at the docks in Sheerness. After changing my wet trousers and tee shirt for dry ones, I had something to eat before setting off for Kent at around 14.15.

The roads, those that were open that is, were treacherous. The snow was still falling, quite heavily, I crawled along ensuring I kept the lorry moving, slow and steady. I recall at some points the snow ploughs had cleared the road but it was like going through a canyon of snow. Sat high up in my cab I could barely see over the top of the ploughed snow. It must have been around 16.00 when the traffic office rang me on the cab phone to tell me that the area of Sittingbourne in Kent was completely snowed in. At that time you had to pass on the outskirts of Sittingbourne to reach Sheerness so I was advised to make my way towards the Dartford Tunnel and park up around there, they would see if they could find me a load from somewhere else. I plodded on through the snow, heading north towards the Dartford Tunnel before getting another call from the traffic office, they told me I was to go to an oil distributor based at Purfleet in Essex the following morning to collect a load of oil drums for delivery to the Birmingham area.

I ended up parking up for the night on a snow covered road in West Thurrock which is now the home of the Lakeside Shopping Centre in Essex, which at the time was still under planning. Nowadays you'd be lucky if you could find a place to stop for a minute without being clamped but in those days there were areas where you were left alone to park for the night as long as you were gone before premises opened in the morning.

That night there was packed snow everywhere and it was snowing on and off through the night. I phoned my boss John H and told him of my situation and he told me I could leave my engine running all night with the heater on if I felt it was necessary as I didn't have a fitted cab night heater, and by doing that it would have kept the diesel flowing as well, diesel could gel up in very low temperatures before different pipes were used to prevent this phenomenon happening.

I did do just that, it was bitterly cold. I had two door keys for the lorry, one for the drivers door, which also was used to start it, and one for the passenger door, meaning I could leave the engine running and secure the vehicle, once the curtains were closed nobody would know if someone was in the lorry. So after having a wash and something to eat in the cab I got changed and then went for a very slippery walk to a local pub that drivers frequented whilst in the area. I had a few pints before returning and bedding down for a very uncomfortable night in my ticking over lorry, but I was warm enough at first to fall asleep without too much trouble.

When I awoke in a very cold cab the next morning at 05.00 it didn't take me long to work out that my lorry heater had packed up, it was now blowing cold air instead of hot. I got myself dressed then made a brew before setting off to find the company I was to load at in Purfleet which, under normal circumstances, would have taken me around twenty five minutes, instead took nearly an hour.

It had snowed during the night on top of packed snow and the roads, especially the side roads were treacherous. I arrived at the company at around 06.30 to find the gates closed. I could see into the premises yard and it was completely covered in snow. My heart sank, I couldn't see a soul, the place looked as if it was shut. I sat outside for a while waiting to see if anybody would turn up, after all it was only 06.35.

At around 07.00 a car pulled up at the gate and a guy got out to open it, I climbed down from my lorry and made my way over to him. I told him I was there to collect a load for Birmingham. He told me that he wasn't sure how long I would have to wait before I could start loading as he, at that time, was the only one there. He asked me to sit tight and he would come and let me know what was happening when he himself knew better. To cut a long story short I was sat outside for over six hours. More staff had turned up but presumably not enough for normal operations to take place. The guy I had spoken to came to me and told me that as it had by now stopped snowing, they were going to try and clear the yard and access to the loading bays after lunch. He apologised for the wait I'd had, telling me that there had been production jobs and yard clearance that needed doing before I could begin to load. I had been in contact with the traffic office at Macclesfield telling them of the situation, they had told me to stick with it as there wasn't an alternative to back load with at that time.

After lunch they began to clear the yard, a fork lift truck with a sort of home made contraption for pushing the snow to one side was used and people followed with shovels, brushes and bags of grit behind it. I also got myself a brush and mucked in with them, more to get myself warm, as I'd been sat around in the cold for some time. Enough snow was cleared for me to be able to turn into the yard and, with some difficulty, reverse onto a loading bay. I undid the ties holding the fly sheet and rolled it forward to the headboard at the front of the trailer, I lifted it up and balanced it on top of the headboard where I held it until the first two rows of forty five gallon drums were wheeled on with two wheeled trolleys, I could then roll it back onto the drums ready to roll out once I was fully loaded. Sixty drums were eventually loaded onto the trailer.

After using the fly sheet to cover them, I roped them down securely and at around 16.00 set off from Essex and its snowy situation to head for the three deliveries I had in and around Birmingham. I had informed John H that my heater was not working and he told me that he'd book me in at a Volvo dealership at Newcastle under Lyme near Stoke on Trent, he'd asked could I put up with no heater until then, I couldn't see what else I could do so I accepted that, it would be repaired once my load was off even though my feet in particular were absolutely freezing, I swear I had ice on the inside of my boots it was that cold !!.

That night I parked up at the Watling Street Cafe on the A5 just off the M1 at Flamstead in Hertfordshire. On the Wednesday morning as I travelled northbound the snow fizzled out, up past Luton and on towards Northampton was clear of it, however as I passed Coventry I noticed that there was snow lying on the ground there.

I arrived at my first delivery in the Coleshill area of Birmingham at around 08.00. I took off twenty drums there without many problems, the delivery point had been covered with a layer of snow but it had been cleared enough for me to get in and get the drums off.

I then made my way across to the Tyseley area of Birmingham arriving there at around 10.00. As in Purfleet, the yard outside the premises was covered in snow, and as before, I was asked to wait until they had time to clear the yard before unloading could take place. I sat outside and waited for around an hour, I only had ten drums for them so I thought to myself "sack this for a game of soldiers, I'll get them off myself !" I walked into the warehouse there and asked the foreman if he had anything soft I could drop the drums onto, he asked me "like What ?" I replied "tyres, cushions, sacking, anything soft to break the fall of a drum, I'll roll them onto it, then onto the floor and roll them in" He told me that there was an old van tyre in the stores area and said I could use that, he also told me that I would be held responsible if there was any damage or leakage from the drums. I agreed to this and went to get the tyre.

Once I'd taken the tyre to my trailer, I undid my ropes and rolled the fly sheet forward to get access to the drums that were required. I dropped my two main sheets down on the floor and placed the tyre on top of them at the rear of the trailer. I then got onto the trailer and mauled one of the forty five gallon drums over and let it fall on its side onto the trailer floor, I then rolled it to the rear of the trailer and off that onto the tyre. The tyre and the sheets did their job and cushioned the fallof the drum which bounced gently on them.

I climbed down and proceeded to roll the drum along the floor and into the gate then on down the yard to the warehouse door. I don't know if you have ever rolled a forty five gallon drum on its side through snow but I'll tell you, it was bloody hard work ! As it rolled it gathered snow, as a snowball would do. I had to keep stopping and clearing the snow off it before I set off rolling it again. I did this with all ten of the drums without causing any damage to speak of, one or two had dints in their side where they had landed slightly off kilter but it was minimal and I got a clean signature for them on my delivery notes.

I re-sheeted and roped the remainder of the load and then set off for my third and last delivery cold and soaked through. It was timed for 14.00 at a big car plant in Castle Vale in Birmingham, I think at one time it was a Rover car plant, it is still there now and something to do with the assembly of Jaguars takes place there.

I had thirty drums for them, it was all well organised there, the snow had made no impact on the running of the factory so I was unloaded without incident. By the time I was unloaded it was around 15.30. I phoned RH's traffic office and told them I was empty and that I was going to get my heater repaired. They were a little apprehensive about this as they said there may have been another load for me to collect from somewhere in the Midlands but it hadn't been confirmed at the time. I was aware of what John had told me regarding arguing with RH's traffic clerks but I had had enough of being cold, I explained my situation to them calmly and asked them to speak to him to confirm that he'd booked me in at the Volvo dealers in the Stoke area and reaffirmed my decision to go to the garage for the much needed repair.

They reluctantly agreed to this, so that evening I arrived at the repair garage at 16.45. After booking my vehicle in at reception I enquired if the company had a shower I could use. They told me it was in the gents toilet area which was next to the customers waiting room and that I was welcome to use it. I was still wet from mauling the drums around at Tyseley so I collected some clean dry underwear and socks plus my washing and shaving gear and went to the shower room. I removed my wet clothes and had a long hot shower which was heaven sent.

Afterwards I dressed in the dry underwear, I washed my socks and underpants then carried them and my damp trousers and overall jacket into the customer waiting room where there were hot radiators dotted all around. I hung all my washed undies and clothes on the radiators and sat down in only my underwear and tee shirt whilst they dried ! I also turned my boots upside down and laid them across the top of a radiator to dry. I don't know what the staff in reception thought of me as I sat there like an underwear dummy in a mens shop but I didn't care, I was warm and clean and soon enough my lorry would be fixed so I was happy.

It eventually got repaired at 19.00 so I stayed in my lorry in their compound that night. It had taken me from Sunday lunchtime to Thursday morning to do one trip, one trip I will never forget.

132

There is another trip that was equally as bad as the last story I've just related to you, only this time for different reasons. I had set off from High Wycombe in Buckinghamshire where I'd parked up with a loaded trailer one October day in 1987. I was hauling a trailer on which there were five deliveries. The first drop was boxed cellophane rolls which went to a company in Newhaven in Sussex. The second delivery was in Hove near Brighton and then I drove across to Portsmouth where I made another delivery of boxed goods.

Whilst driving across to Pompey, as it's known, I passed some woodland near to Arundel castle in Sussex, what's unusual about that ? I hear you say, well it had at one time been woodland but as I passed there, every tree had been blown over, all falling in the same direction as one another, away from the coastline. Do you remember the great storm of that year ? Well for those that don't, a weatherman named Michael Fish forewarned of an impending storm which he at the time allegedly said was a false prediction (although to be fair to him he always maintained he had been misquoted) Well that storm in which Michael said "don't worry there isn't" after being informed there was, blew down around fifteen million trees ! With gusts reported to have reached between one hundred to one hundred and thirty miles an hour, whole swathes of forestry were flattened. Have you ever watched Thunderbirds on TV. ?, well, when Thunderbird two makes its way to the launch pad and all the trees fold flat so it can pass over them, well that's how it looked.

Sadly eighteen people were killed due to it, homes and businesses were without power due to trees blowing over onto electricity and phone lines, roads and railways were blocked by falling trees, ships were blown over and a ferry was blown ashore near Folkestone in Kent, the damage is said to have cost almost six billion pounds in todays money (two billion then). If the storm had hit during the day time rather than when it did, at night, many more people would probably have died, as it was, most people were in bed asleep. Evidence of the storm was all along the South coast but thankfully it didn't affect any of my delivery points so I finally drew up at my second to last one in Yeovil, Somerset at around 16.30. I delivered plastic extrusions

133

there and decided I had done enough for the day, by the time I'd unloaded it was around 17.00.

I asked permission to park outside the premises I'd unloaded at and began setting my stall out for the night. I rang RH's traffic office and told them where I was up to. They were not happy, "what time did you start ?" I was asked, I replied that I had started at 06.00 I was then told that the last drop, which was on an industrial site at Plymouth, and which was only a couple of pallets of metalware was expected that day. I replied that they'd be shut by the time I got there as it was around two hours drive from where I was. They retorted by saying "I can assure you Steve they're waiting for this gear, there'll be someone there to unload you, you'll have to go, if you leave now you'll be there in an hour and a half" I knew they were talking rubbish about the running time but if someone was waiting for this stuff urgently then I had to go. I wasn't very happy but I packed my stuff away and set off for Plymouth at around 17.15.

I arrived at the company to.......yes you've guessed it.......find it was closed. It was 19.10 and there wasn't a soul in sight. I phoned RH straight away, there was a lad on duty to deal with any emergencies and all I got was "well there's nothing I can do about it, you'll just have to wait 'till tomorrow", all the day staff had gone home, including the one who had told me to go there that night.

I was fuming, I was on an industrial estate miles from anywhere, I looked around and saw a light in a building a few hundred yards away and made my way to it. It was a bus garage and a couple of lads were in there servicing buses. I asked one of them if they knew what time the company I was delivering to closed and he said it was usually around 18.30 before everybody usually left. I was desolate, I asked him would he mind if I had a wash and brush up in their washroom to which he said yes. I got my gear and by the time I had finished it was around 19.40. I asked him where the nearest pub was, as all I wanted to do was have a few beers and try to calm down a little. He said there was one around a mile away, so after deliberating whether it was worth while going there or not I set off walking at around 20.00.

I found the pub and had a few beers but one thing I did was totally out of character. I'd packed in smoking quite some time before this episode but I bought a packet of cig's from a machine in the pub and began smoking them, that's how rattled I was with the whole episode. The next morning I got on the phone, and forgetting John H's words not to argue with the staff at RH's I gave the lad, who'd told me I must go, a right rollocking, I told him of how it had all been for nothing. I also told him that I'd done quite enough the previous day and that his pushing me to do more was unnecessary. Of course he took the ear bashing, probably holding the phone away from his ear whilst he did something else. He sort of half apologised when I'd finished and said that he'd been assured that they wanted the gear and that someone would be there to unload me. With my anger now suppressed after my rant it was back to work as normal, only now I had started smoking again. Another trip I won't forget in a hurry.

Does the year 1988 ring any bells to you ? That was the year when a few days before Christmas a Pam Am Jumbo jet, which had taken off from Heathrow Airport on its way to the U.S. was blown up in mid air by a terrorist bomb, wreckage was spread over hundreds of miles but most of the planes body fell and crashed onto the town of Lockerbie in Southern Scotland. It resulted in the deaths of two hundred and seventy people, there were two hundred and fifty nine on the plane and eleven in Lockerbie.

I was going up to Scotland not long after New Year which of course fell into 1989. I was travelling on the old A74 which was the main route into Scotland from the M6, it was a dual carriageway which passed next to the town of Lockerbie, before we got there I found the southbound traffic had all been diverted onto the northbound side making it just one lane in either direction. The reason why became crystal clear when I passed the scene where the planes wings, virtually full of fuel, and some of the undercarriage had come down and crashed onto some houses right next to the road, exploding with a huge fireball. It had created a huge gash in the earth, completely destroying the houses and sadly some of the residents inside them. The crater was around twenty five feet deep and around one hundred and fifty five feet long, the wreckage had impacted slightly on the southbound side carriageway and that was the reason it was closed at that point.

Apparently it was later disclosed that the bomb should have detonated somewhere over the Atlantic Ocean but as the plane had been delayed at Heathrow it happened instead over Lockerbie. It's a very sad memory, and one I will never forget.

My wife and I visited the garden of remembrance at the Lockerbie Air Disaster Memorial fairly recently, it's at Dryfesdale cemetery which lies around a mile west of Lockerbie on the A709 Lochmaben road. It was quite an emotional experience, thinking of all those innocent people who were all probably looking forward to Christmas, which of course they never saw. I believe the scars will remain with the victims families and the townsfolk of Lockerbie who are old enough to remember it.

In the beginning I was paid a bonus for the work I did, unfortunately the bonus's over a long period of time began to reduce, I was working as hard but I was being paid less than I had been for doing the same work. It was because the rates of the jobs that were given to me, which was all a quite a bit above my control. That, along with my now underlying aspirations of running my own lorry someday brought me to the decision to leave my brother in law and John H behind and try something else which would help me to achieve my ambition. I put in and then worked my notice with John and left the company. A new and somewhat different chapter of my life was on the horizon, a chapter that would bring me a new found freedom but would end in a lot of stress and heartache.

Chapter Five.

Business, carpets and a move to North Wales….it happened.

I went to the local job centre and found a vacancy for a delivery driver, the job entailed driving a seven and a half ton van delivering carpets, vinyls and flooring accessories around the North West and North Wales. This was exactly what I was looking for because there were no nights away from home, that meant it would have afforded me the time to get the wheels in motion for running my own transport business whilst still earning a wage, albeit a much reduced amount to what I was used to. I applied for the job and after an interview I was given the position and would start work the following Monday. There was a twist in the tale however, which I will come to shortly.

I would now be working for and be paid by a guy from Bolton who had won a contract to supply drivers and vehicles to Hadfield's Carpet Wholesalers in Stockport. They distributed to shops and carpet fitters all around the North West and North Wales. I arrived back home after the interview and told my wife Pat that I'd got the job. We were both happy that I'd quickly found another position and that it would entail me being home every night, and with no weekend work at all, I would have so much time with the family that I'd never properly had before.

I had an uncle in Liverpool called Sammy, who used to deliver carpets in North Wales, Cheshire and Wirral and I decided to give him a call on the telephone over the weekend to see if he could give me a few tips and advice on how to go about the job. Sammy asked me who I was working for, I told him it was a guy from Bolton who was contracting for Hadfields in Stockport. There was a minutes silence before he asked what areas I would be covering, I told him it was North West England and North Wales, another pause followed before Sammy spoke again, and this is the twist in the tale, in a very slow and quiet tone he said "you've got my job Steve, that was my area"

I was a little confused and asked him what he meant. He told me that he'd worked for Hadfields from a warehouse in Bootle, Liverpool but they had made him and the staff at Bootle redundant and closed the operation down there, the work had then been subbed out to another company who would employ their own drivers and vehicles to do the job working from Stockport. I was gobsmacked.... the realisation of what he'd just told me really shook me. I told him that I had no idea about what had happened and apologised to him for taking his job. He said "don't be silly lad, if anything I'm glad that you got the job, it sort of keeps it in the family, if you need any help at any time give me a shout and I'll do my best to help you out" I sort of stutteringly apologised again and thanked him for what he'd said, then, realising that he didn't want to talk any more about it I said my goodbyes and hung up the phone. Pat had been listening and saw my ashen face, I explained it all to her, she too was shocked but she soothed me by saying what Sammy had said, that it was still sort of in the family.

I was still apprehensive about the whole thing when I reported for work at 07.00 on the next Monday morning. I didn't mention it to the staff at Stockport who would have known of Sammy's fate as the whole operation had been overhauled in a "streamlining" of the business. I was asked to assist in the loading of my vehicle so I would know where the delivery goods were on the van. I then received my delivery paperwork which had been put in delivery drop order and before I knew it I was out on my own, "thrown in at the deep end" so to speak. I soon learned the route and delivery options, which varied from day to day, and before the end of the week, I had it all sorted out to suit me and the shopkeepers. I would always recall my Uncle Sammy's words though, they haunted me for some time after whenever I was in the Merseyside and Wirral areas.

At the end of my time with John H I'd been doing lots of research on what I would need to be able to run my own lorry, I knew I would need an operators licence to run a heavy goods vehicle and a CPC (certificate of professional competence) would be required to apply for the licence. I enrolled myself on an evening CPC Goods National course at Stockport Technical College which I passed after completing it. I then enrolled myself on a small business management course, also at the same college which I completed with a pass certificate.

Meanwhile I was working during the day, I'd start at 07.00 and once I'd sorted myself out job wise, I would finish, usually around 14.30 to 15.00. This was alien to me, I could collect the kids from school and for once in my working life I only saw one five-o-clock in a day !! After saying that, there was the occasional early start, I would go fully loaded to Somerton in Somerset, then come back empty. I'd get down there at around 09.00 and be back home by my usual finishing time. I also collected new carpets from manufacturers premises, I'd go to Kidderminster in Worcestershire or sometimes locally to Leigh near Manchester. These runs, though rare, were a welcome change from the usual repetitive deliveries I made.

I was at one of these routine deliveries in Bromborough, Wirral one day. The shop was the last one in a street which became a pedestrian zone after 09.00. The shop was at the end of the street which ran off the main Birkenhead to Chester road so I'd pull up just past the road and then reverse around the corner until my vehicle was off the main road where I'd stop and park up, the back end doors would then be almost at the entrance to the shop. The shop in question used to buy full rolls of carpet, twenty five metres in length and weighing in at various weights depending on the type of carpet, but they were bloody heavy !. On this particular day I had a few really heavy rolls to carry in. There was no way I could lift one on my own so the two lads from the shop me. We worked it out of the back of the van and onto our shoulders, then, like pallbearers do, we'd shuffle our way slowly to the door entrance, once there we had to, as one, bend at the waist with our legs straight and then roll the carpet onto our backs so that we could carry the roll in through the narrow doorway as that was the only way it would go in.

Once inside we simply tipped it off our backs either onto the floor or onto a stand which allowed the carpet to roll freely so lengths could then be cut off it. After we'd taken the last one in I was offered a brew which I politely refused because I was parked at the very end of a pedestrian zone, I walked to my vehicle to find a traffic warden writing a ticket out for me. I explained that I had just delivered carpets to the shop behind us. He was unrepentant and said "there's a free car park up the street and around the corner which you can access without coming down here, you should have parked there" He then proceeded to hand the ticket to me and started to walk away, I tried to explain that the carpets were heavy but he just waved me away and walked off. The shop owner had seen this and re-offered me the cup of tea. "you've got your ticket so you may as well have a brew Steve" he said.

I did have the tea and whilst it cooled he advised me to contest the ticket, as the warden had done the same thing to other delivery drivers. I did contest the parking fine, I explained that if I was delivering cartons of Mars bars or similar, then I would have used the free car park, but I was delivering really heavy rolls of carpet which needed three men to carry them, not boxes of chocolate !.

The ticket and the fine were rescinded on that occasion, although I was warned that I would need to find another way to deliver them in the future, such as delivering at an earlier or later time, as I could face being booked again. I explained this to my boss back at the warehouse and within a few days a two wheeled trolley on which a carpet roll could be balanced enabling you to wheel the roll into premises with ease was delivered to all the drivers including myself, to do the difficult task with, it was an absolute godsend !.

My time working out of Hadfields was a short one, one Friday just before finishing for the day I was asked if I'd mind doing a holiday relief for one of Hadfields sister companies, Walsh's carpets and flooring supplies, who were based in a warehouse at Longsight, an area of Manchester, it was not too far for me to travel to so I agreed that I'd go and cover for a driver who was supposedly having a fortnights holiday, I was then supposed to return to Stockport and continue as before.

The following Monday morning I reported for work at 08.00 at Walsh's. I was told that I would cover several areas in a week, Mondays was Manchester, Stockport, Ashton under Lyne and surrounding areas. Tuesdays run would cover Warrington, Deeside, Flint, Abergele, Colwyn Bay and occasionally a wholesaler on Anglesey. I would then deliver to shops in Wirral, Liverpool, Southport, Wigan and St. Helens.

Wednesdays I would cover the Cheshire areas of Frodsham, Northwich, Winsford, Middlewich, Sandbach, Crewe and Chester. Thursday was the Warrington, North Wales and Merseyside areas again and finally on Fridays I would cover the Manchester, Stockport, Ashton under Lyne and surrounding areas again.

By the end of two weeks I was well into the swing of it all, I was asked by the manager at Walsh's would I mind staying on the job for a bit longer as the lad who had supposedly been on holiday had put in a weeks notice because he was moving to a new carpet wholesaler which was just setting up. They had decided to let him have his weeks notice without having to work it for them. I was only too pleased to agree to stay there, as Walsh's let the drivers take their van home which saved me having to cycle the mile and a half or so to work and then back home. To cut a long story short I ended up being asked to stay permanently as the bosses at Walsh's thought I was doing a very capable job.

I didn't know it at the time but the previous driver and two former managers at Walsh's were the ones who had split away from them and formed a rival company not too far away from them. I wasn't concerned, my new position suited me just fine thank you.

I could tell you stories about being attacked by dogs many times whilst delivering carpets, and by geese...... yes geese, one house where a carpet fitter lived in North Wales had a goose as a sort of guard dog ! I would pull up in the van at the rear of his house, he would rarely be there but he had told me to put the carpet in his conservatory where I'd find an envelope with either cash or a cheque (it was a payment on delivery operation) He would promise me that his Alsatian dog and the goose would be locked away elsewhere, however there were several occasions when either the dog, or worse, the goose for whatever reason, were not locked away and I'd end up running faster than Linford Christie out along the back garden path to escape either of them, slamming the back gate shut as they were on my heels !

I was very happy with my situation, being a seven and a half ton van driver on local deliveries was a piece of cake to me and everything seemed to be moving in the right direction.

It was during my time at Walsh's that I experienced one of the worst times of my life. In 1989 on Saturday the 15th April, I and my next door neighbour Seamus, along with some other lads went to watch the FA Cup semi final between Liverpool and Nottingham Forest at Hillsborough Stadium in Sheffield.

We entered the Leppings lane end of the ground along with all the other Liverpool fans and I found myself being herded towards one of the tunnels that fed the infamous terrace where so many people died. It was the strong right hand and arm of Seamus who grabbed my arm and pulled me over saying "we're over this way Steve to the left", within a couple of minutes we were sat in the stand to the left of the stand watching the carnage to our right.

I won't go into the rights and wrongs of the day, all I will say is that if the kick off time had been delayed by thirty minutes in order to allow everyone in comfortably then it may not have resulted in so many deaths. There are obviously other factors involved but that is my opinion. The other lads, Seamus and I were very fortunate on that unforgettable day.

Most the staff at Walsh's were very sympathetic to me on my return to work on the Monday morning except for one, an Everton fan who stuck newspaper photos of the dying people on the walls of the toilet there. He did apologise later though and admitted it was in bad taste.

One day the warehouse foreman who used to supervise the lads cutting the carpet lengths and the loading sequence for my van decided to leave, I saw an opportunity and decided that I would apply for his job, it would mean coming off the road but it was a slightly higher wage and the foreman had the use of a company car. I got the job without any problems, The lad who was leaving was working his fortnights notice, Walsh's interviewed applicants for the up coming driver vacancy and I ended up showing the guy who was selected to replace me the ropes of the job. Everything fell into place, although there were some bad feelings towards me from the other two warehouse lads, one of whom thought that he should have got the foreman's job. It hadn't been my decision, it had been the bosses at Walsh's who decided which person should be given the job. The atmosphere at work was very bad for a while before one lad left and the other was dismissed for a work related offence. New staff were employed and things soon got better and back to normality.

Whilst happily working for Walsh's and studying at college three nights a week the wheels of big business were in motion. Hadfield's and Walsh's were swallowed up by a larger flooring distributer. A decision was made to streamline the businesses and it was decided that Walsh's would move to a much bigger warehouse and office premises, merging with Hadfield's who had by that time, already moved into the new premises in Greg Street, Reddish. This suited me fine, it was even nearer to my

142

home, I could walk it in around five minutes, which was a good job because the streamlining meant that the car I'd been using was taken from me. I remained the supervisor in our section of the warehouse as Walsh's and Hadfield's were still being run independently although owned by the bigger group. A new senior foreman was brought in from another branch owned by the group and, slowly at first, things began to change, and not for the better for me. There was a lot of consternation and some members of the old management were not happy. Fall outs occurred between Walsh's staff, it became a kind of "them and us" culture.

I had by this time completed and passed my CPC and small business studies courses and thoughts of having my own lorry were coming to the forefront of my mind again, that is until' something I was completely not expecting, happened. One of the managers at Walsh's, Gordon, asked me to go for a pint with him after work in a pub near my house, he said he had a proposal for me. We met later after work and over a beer he told me he was not happy with the way things were going at Walsh's and that he had been sounding out carpet manufacturers and flooring supplies companies, he had decided to start his own firm, doing what we were already doing, he knew I had a CPC so I could run a goods vehicle, which such a firm would need. After explaining it to me he said that we could start the firm as co-owners, partners if you like. We would own fifty per cent of the firm each. I told him that I didn't have money enough to set up a company like that, it would require premises, a van, a forklift truck, shelving and all the paraphernalia required to be a successful business. Once again he informed me that he'd sounded out suppliers who were willing to help us get started, he had been in carpet wholesaling all his life, he knew a lot of people in the game, we would start out as a small business and see how it went.

I said that I would have to consider it and talk it through with my wife Pat and we left it at that. I did talk it over with her, over several nights and after a lot of soul searching she and I decided that I should go for it. It was an opportunity I'd never before considered but I was confident in my ability and work ethic to see it through. I relayed this to Gordon and we, in any spare time we had, surreptitiously began to put the wheels in motion. Gordon would deal with the suppliers and I began to sort out pricing on a seven and a half ton van, a forklift and shelving for the warehouse. We also found a warehouse with a small office in Denton that was for rent, and after viewing it decided it would be ideal for us. Whilst attending the small business course I had been tutored by a guy who was a multi business man, he introduced me to an accountant named Bernard.

Gordon and I arranged a meeting with Bernard and told him of our plans. After listening to us both he said that he thought the idea had legs, we were both accomplished at different aspects of the flooring and distribution industry and he could see no reason why it would not work. He would be our accountant, so together we all drew up a business plan which Bernard took to a few bank managers. One of these managers called us all back to meet him and after seeing and hearing the plans from us both he informed us that the bank was willing to back us and help us in any way they could. We had thought of the firms name, it would be G & S Carpet Wholesalers (I know, not very imaginative !).

It was strange at the time, all thoughts of lorry driving had gone from my mind, I was about to be a partner in a carpet and flooring wholesale business. Between us we set up deals securing the premises, the van and a service contract with a local garage, and a fork lift. We then bought second hand shelving and erected it on our own, this would hold the rolls of carpet. We set up a deal with a printing company for the stationary we would need then and then finally came the stock and carpet sample books from various manufacturers both here in the UK and Belgium. We were set up, we organised a grand opening bash, inviting as many carpet shop owners and fitters as we could, Gordons contacts were plentiful, so they, along with Bernard, and our respective close families attended what proved to be a very fruitful exercise. G & S Carpets were up and running.

During this period I didn't do much long distance driving at all, though I did go out delivering now and again and talking to customers whilst I did. I ran the van operations, routing, loading and maintenance, whilst Gordon looked after the running of the warehouse and the stock. We took turns at representing the firm by going out to shops and selling whatever we could face to face and all seemed to be going well. We had employed a lad in the warehouse and a van driver too. Things however did not remain that way, we were a small operation in a cut throat line of business. The bigger companies, as they do, could undercut us, they had more stock and resources and so after a while our sales began to dip, and without going into other factors that affected the business we both realised that we could not maintain it, we came to the conclusion, after consulting Bernard (who advised us not to) to wind up the firm.

I know that I had put all I could into making the business a success, but, as I have stated, there were other factors that were beyond my control and after around two years of trading, after paying the VAT and our suppliers what we owed, we closed.

As partners we still owed the bank money though and it wasn't long before they went for repayment, unfortunately it was me they went for first. I was summoned to court and pleaded my case, I was in the process of selling my house to repay the bank so I didn't get any court judgements passed to me, the judge overruled the banks efforts to take my home as we were showing good faith in our repayment efforts. Without going round the houses it resulted in the sale of my house to pay the bank a large amount of the proceeds, this all took a good length of time though so we were not homeless. It did however cause Pat and myself a lot of heartache and stress, it was a terrible time for us both.

By this time Gordon and I had been approached by another wholesaler in the area, he said he was looking for someone to run a franchise he wanted to set up in North Wales, he asked if one of us was interested. Gordon had no intention of doing it as he had not at that time been approached by the bank and had another job in the offing, but I, with the prospect of soon being homeless thought "What have I got to lose ?" so I went and met the owner and he spelled it all out for me.

The deal would involve me going with a van full of his stock and selling it to the shops and trade in the North Wales area for a trial period, he would provided the van. I was to do this for a while, and if I was successful the plan was to find some premises there and move to the area to run the franchise as our business under his company name. Once again Pat and I discussed it, we thought "what have we got to lose ?" Also the prospect of moving the family away to the North Wales coast was very appealing to us both so I agreed to take the offer.

145

I was successful in selling carpet from the van, I was also sounding out old and new contacts in North Wales at the same time, letting them know that our franchise would soon be operating in the area if they needed any flooring supplies. The "mother" warehouse in the Manchester area always held plenty of stock and would deliver it to our premises for us to distribute to them. we were to pay for the stock weekly and we would operate a pay on delivery system for us, it all seemed a great idea.

We found a small warehouse in Colwyn Bay, the franchise owner came across and gave his approval, he kindly provided us with the van I'd been using in the trial period which we would pay off weekly until it was ours, he did the same regarding an old but reliable gas fork lift and some carpet shelving. We cadged a lot of showroom type carpet displays and set them up in the spacious office we had there.

We set up a bank loan for the initial stock of rolls and supplies wewould be taking, after opening up our hearts to a bank manager and telling him exactly what our story was, he listened and said he believed that we deserved another chance and wished us every success, so, after another opening day presentation, we were back in the wholesale carpet business, albeit in a franchise situation.

Whilst all this was going on we had found a house we could rent for a year in Rhos on Sea, we found respective schools for our two girls and Pat would travel back to Manchester every Friday night to do a twelve hour shift as an SRN at Withington hospital, we were both working extremely hard.

At first I was going out and delivering any orders we had, Pat was in the office taking phone and trade walk-ins. This wasn't sustainable, I was out and carpet lengths may have needed cutting off rolls which meant that I had to do it when I returned from delivering, we needed someone else to help. One of my good customers named Elwyn told me there was a young lad who was a carpet fitter, he was sensible and hard working and he wanted to have a sales type job in the industry. His name was Nigel, he came to see us, we explained what we would like him to do and asked would he be interested. He was, and we liked what we heard from him so we employed him there and then.

Nigel was a great attribute to our little set up, he had a licence so he could go out on deliveries when necessary, He soon

146

learnt how to drive and handle the fork lift safely but more importantly, he knew carpets inside out, he was very knowledgable about the fitting side of the job too. He was also very I.T. savvy, he set up a stock keeping system on an old computer for us, he also set a programme for printing off our customer invoices for us, all in all he was the ideal employee.

We became more than employers to Nigel though, we'd socialise with each other and we'd always give him leeway if he needed time to do something that wasn't anything to do with the job, he became our friend and a vital part of the team. It wasn't long before the word got round that there was a wholesaler in Colwyn Bay. People would walk in off the street looking for cheaper than the shops carpet, obviously it was not in our interest to upset the trades people so we would only serve them if they came in with a carpet fitter or a carpet shopkeeper, they would then pay the tradesman rather than us and everybody seemed happy with that.

Our delivery area was the whole of North Wales, as far east as the border with England at Deeside, as far west as the Llyn Peninsular at Abersoch and all of Anglesey. We delivered down to the south as far as the Shropshire border at Oswestry. Business was good, on the whole most customers paid on delivery. We took on another lad named Paul who did the van deliveries for us, all seemed to be going well.

When our year long house lease finished in Rhos on Sea we got another years lease on a house in Colwyn Heights, we continued to flourish business wise. We had a few good outlets where, after trading with us for some time, they asked us could they pay weekly, we agreed to it reluctantly and in the main they were very reliable. One customer however ordered two rolls of Axminster 80/20 carpet from us, it was to be fitted in a social club on the Welsh coast. He said he couldn't afford to pay the somewhat considerable cost of the carpet and fittings up front and asked could he pay us a deposit with the balance to be paid when he'd finished the job, it was a very big order for us so after discussing it between each other we decided to let him do what he'd proposed. We took a hefty deposit but it still left a balance of almost £2.300.00.

I suppose you can guess what happened next..... after the job had finished we didn't get paid. I had to pay my supplier in

147

Manchester, that was a given, agreed to by both parties, so I did pay him.

I managed to contact the fitter who had done the job on the phone and he said that he himself hadn't been paid. After a week or so of excuses I'd had enough, I asked him where exactly had he laid the carpet. I didn't tell him of my intentions and after telling me he'd do his best to go and get the money I hung up, loaded a few tools in the van and set off to find this club.

I walked in just as it opened in the afternoon, there on the floor was the Axminster we'd provided. I spoke to the guy behind the bar, "are you in charge here sir ?" he looked at me warily and said that he was the steward, it was the committee who ran the place. I told him I'd come to pull up the carpet as it was mine and it hadn't been paid for, I told him I was going to do it there and then so he'd better get onto somebody quickly and sort out a payment to the carpet fitter who'd done the job, I said I'd give him half an hour before I took all the carpet up and away. I was fuming, the guy could see I meant business and asked me to calm down whilst he spoke to someone about it. I went and sat down, I was determined I wasn't going to leave unless I had either the payment sorted or the carpet back, even in its cut to fit state. Within ten minutes a guy came through the door and showed me a receipt he had for the payment to the fitter. I was desolate, I apologised for the way I'd come in all bull like and explained that the fitter had told me a pack of lies. The committee guy was very understanding and apologised to me for the carpet fitters behaviour.

I went back to the van and decided I'd go to the fitters shop in a local coastal town. When I arrived there I found it empty and closed, I made a few enquiries and learnt that he'd only rented it on a short term lease and nobody had seen him for a while. That dealing cost us our business, I would never make that money back and run the day to day cash on delivery system. I tried to explain it to my supplier who was sorry to hear about our problem but he had a business to run as well, he did offer some help which we were very grateful of, but it wasn't enough to get us out of the mess we were in. His words were "Steve, he's actually taken money out of your pocket, you'll have to find one way or another to get it back" He was right but what could I do ? The fitter had disappeared and we were left high and dry.

148

There was only one way out of the mess we were in, we decided that we'd have to cut our cloth accordingly and ditch the warehouse and fork lift. We put it to the owner of the franchise in Manchester who agreed to keep supplying us with cuts of carpet rather than rolls on a daily basis. By this time we'd paid for the racking and the fork lift so we sold them all to a guy who had a good business and needed bigger premises. We found a small workshop in Colwyn Bay that had once been a dairy, it wasn't ideal but it was a lot cheaper to rent than we had been paying for the warehouse and it meant that we could keep trading.

Paul had left already when we decided to move to smaller premises, Nigel realised that we couldn't really afford to keep him on and he too reluctantly left us soon after. Another old trade friend of ours, Roy, helped us out whenever he could, we couldn't pay him a full time wage but he was good enough to take whatever we could afford to pay him, he understood our position and we'll always be grateful to him for his guidance and kindness.

We should have seen it coming really, another non payment from a chancer in Shotton finally saw us off. It wasn't a huge amount but it was enough for us to always be playing catch up with payments. I also had unproven reports from the guy I'd sold the racking to that a rep' from another franchise had been in our territory undercutting me. As I said there was no proof of this and at the time I never found any evidence of wrongdoing but the word had got round that we were floundering and I suppose people will take an advantage if they can. So after two and a half years of hard work, it was all for nothing. We came out of it better than we had done with G & S though, we sorted settlements with the bank and the franchisor who I'll always be grateful to. We had managed to get a mortgage and were buying a nice semi near the promenade in Rhos on Sea. Pat was still going to Manchester on Friday evenings to do her night shift at the hospital. It was time for me to find another job, but I wasn't quite ready to go back on the road just yet, I'd try one more thing first.

Chapter Six.

It ends badly, dig out my boots, I'm away again.

I had heard that a local company, Hotpoint, who were a massive employer in North Wales and were based at Bodelwydden near Abergele were looking for temporary staff for a line they were opening up there. I applied and was given a job with a year long temporary status, not on the assembly line, but driving the little electric stand on fork lifts that were used to fetch the various parts of the machines to the line for assembling. It was a great job, I went with the intention that if I kept my nose clean they'd see I was reliable and may then take me on permanently.

For the hours I worked, from 07.00 to 15.00 five days a week I was paid extremely well, if I did any overtime I was really coining it in. It had a subsidised canteen and whenever there was a factory holiday shutdown they paid you double your basic wage. I didn't want it to end, I loved it, but, it did. The whole line I'd been working on were all given their last but one payslip with a letter thanking us for our temporary work, we were all going to be out of work in one week.

There ended the "off the road" period for me. It was time to find a job doing what I had done for most of my working life up to then. Get my boots back on and find a job back on the lorries, I had to start earning and that was something I knew I could do without any risk of me losing my house, although it would mean me losing my much accustomed to home life.

I finished at Hotpoint on a Friday afternoon and decided to look for a class one driving job the following week. My close old mate Dangle, whom I'd known from childhood, Express Dairies and Reyners, had been in touch with me to inform me that his Dad had passed away, the funeral was to be in Manchester during the week I was going to look for work, so I told him that I'd be there.

I got in touch with a company who were based in Cheshire, in between Stockport and Macclesfield, I won't mention any names because this venture didn't end well for me. I arranged for the interview to take place on the afternoon of my mates

Dads funeral which was taking place mid morning on that day. After the funeral I attended the interview and was given a position. I'd explained that I lived in North Wales to which they assured me that would not be a problem as they had a lot of work over that way. They told me they'd ring me the following Saturday and let me know what vehicle I would be driving and which trailer to pick up and deliver. I got the call as promised and was to collect my unit, an ERF EC Olympic, and a loaded trailer from the depot which had been preloaded for…Hotpoint in Bodelwyddan. Yes the company I had just left just over a week before ! The guys who I knew on the unloading bay at Hotpoint had to take a second look at me when I turned up there at 07.00 on the Monday morning, they must have thought I had a double !

My time with this particular company was short lived though. The work was plentiful and varied and they always did get me a load back home at the weekends as they had promised. On one occasion, and this is where things get awry, I was in one of many warehouses they used, this one was in Warrington.

I had rung them at around 18.00 to find out what I was doing next, they told me to drop the empty trailer there when I'd unloaded and make my way to a distribution warehouse near Runcorn to collect a loaded trailer which was for a timed delivery in Norwich at 08.00 the following morning. I was nowhere near being unloaded at the time, there were a lot of lorries in front of me and I reckoned it would be at least two hours before I was empty. I relayed this to them and said that I would do my very best to be there as soon as possible. I was told quite bluntly that it HAD to be there at 08.00. I once again explained that I could not possibly do it with the time constraints involved. The guy I was speaking with reiterated that it had to be there at 08.00. to which I said "well it won't be, I haven't got the time to do it, but as I said, I promise I'll do my very best to get it there as early as I can" The guy went off the phone and he must have thought he had the mouthpiece on it covered, but I heard him say something derogatory about me and how I'd not agreed to get the load there for 08.00. Whoever he was talking to said to him, "tell him to finish unloading, drop the trailer and ring the office in the morning", he also said that they'd find somebody who would get it there on time.

After that episode things weren't the same for me. I'm not saying they were deliberately awkward with me but I didn't get, shall we say, "a fair crack of the whip". When I'd had enough I decided that it was time to find pastures new, so I put in my notice and started to think about my next move.

I finished at Cheshire on a Friday lunchtime and made my way back home to North Wales. The following morning the first thing I did was to get in my car and head west. I drove to Anglesey and made my way to Gwynedd Shipping's depot and head office in Holyhead.

I walked in and enquired if they needed any class one drivers. They replied that they were fully staffed at that time, they asked me my age, where I lived and what had I done before. I informed them that I had done virtually everything, roping, sheeting, containers, abnormal loads in fact everything but petrol and livestock. They took my details and told me they would hold them on record, they asked me had I tried a firm called H.F. Owen in Bethel near Caernarfon. I knew of this company and I had every intention of going there later that morning should there be no openings for me at Gwynedd Shipping. I relayed this to them and they said I should speak to Harry, the owner. I thanked them and made my way back over the Menai Bridge to the mainland and within thirty five minutes I was at HF Owens yard at Bethel.

Harry was in the office and after talking to him for a while he said that it seemed that I had enough experience so he offered me a job. I started for him the following week. HF had somewhat different work than what I'd been used to, there was a lot of general haulage, he also hauled Gwynedd Shipping trailers, he also had a contract with a toilet and kitchen roll manufacturer. His main work though was to collect bricks from a works in Caernarfon and transport them to building sites and DIY wholesalers all over the UK. Up to that particular time I'd never operated a trailer mounted hiab crane which was sometimes necessary whilst hauling bricks. Nowadays you have to have a "ticket", a sort of licence to use them but at that time it wasn't a thing that was necessary.

I had a very quick induction on how to operate one on my first day, with Harry showing me the ropes. "This lever moves you backwards and forwards on the trailer (the hiab was on

152

rollers and traversed the length of the trailer) This lever lifts the arm up and down, this lever swings the arm left or right, this lever extends the arm further out and back, This lever closes the clamp onto the bricks and this lever with the red tape on it opens the clamp, DON'T touch it whilst the bricks are in the air !" This was more or less what he told me and I didn't forget it...... except once !

I was on a site where houses were being built near Newton Aycliffe in the north east. I arrived late in the afternoon at around 17.00. Most of the site workers had finished at 16.30 but there was a site foreman still working in the office there. He told me that the fork lift driver had gone home but as I had a hiab grab I would be able to unload myself, he took me with my lorry to where he wanted the bricks putting, he checked how many stacks I had for him, which was a full load weighing twenty four tons, he signed my delivery notes and left me to it.

Normally it would take an experienced hiab operator around half an hour to unload a trailer but I was still fairly inexperienced using one, it wasn't my first time, but I'd not done many. I removed the netting which we used to put over the bricks in case any worked loose out of the packs and fell off. I then started the hiab and began to carefully take off the packs from the rear of the load.

The weather was not great and to my dismay I heard the distant rumble of thunder, "Oh damn it" I thought and continued to to get on with lifting off the bricks in a slightly quicker manner. It wasn't long before I could see lightning flashes getting nearer, by this time I had about two thirds of the load off, stacked on the floor beside the trailer. It began to rain heavily as the storm was almost upon me, I lifted a pack and was swinging it over the side of the trailer when a lightning bolt shot across the front of me, I was standing on a metal plate and all I could think about was "what if any fucking lightning strikes this hiab ?"

I was panicking now and whilst intending to extend the arm out I pressed the wrong lever..... the one with the red tape..... the grabs opened up and the pack of bricks dropped out about four feet from the ground. I don't know if you know how many bricks are in a standard pack but it's a lot, around four hundred. This pack hit the floor and broke the bands holding it all together and spilt all over the area they landed in. It took me a good three quarters of an hour to find a pallet and re- stack all those

153

bricks, well, those that hadn't been broken by the fall. I did some of it in the thunderstorm which lasted around ten minutes before it passed over me, I was soaked to the skin when I'd done and I still had to take off the rest of the load, I never made that mistake again !

Whilst working for HF Owen I worked a couple of Sundays. On one particular Sunday I was given a job which involved collecting my unit from the yard at Bethel, driving to Holyhead port on Anglesey where I was to collect a trailer which had come over from Ireland on one of the ferries the previous night. HF had already started to do this kind of work, unloading and reloading trailers which had come over from Ireland on a regular basis.

The trailer I was collecting was to be taken to Dover port where it would travel over unaccompanied to be delivered somewhere in Europe. I was then to collect a trailer from Dover which I would have to either deliver somewhere in the UK or take up to Holyhead to go once again unaccompanied over to Ireland for delivery.

I went to bed early on the Saturday night as I wasn't feeling too well and awoke in the morning feeling really ill. I got up and went to work, it was too late to ring in sick as HF wouldn't have been able to cover the job at such short notice. I collected the trailer at Holyhead and set off for Dover at around 08.30.

I wish I could give you a little detail on the trip but all I remember is getting progressively worse by the minute. I cannot recall the trip, it was like, I'm here..... now I'm there, and not remembering anything, I was so ill. I do however remember leaning with both elbows on the steering wheel as I wasn't able to sit up straight in my normal driving position. I can only tell you what time I arrived at Dover was by looking at my tachograph for that day a few days after I'd got there, it was 17.35. I had stopped quite a few times, what I did or didn't do, I can't recall, but I arrived there safely, which when I look back at it, was a blessing in itself.

I do remember though that I'd dropped the trailer on the dock side compound and the trailer I was supposed to collect was coming in that night on an overnight ferry so I had to park up somewhere until the following morning and collect it then. I don't know whether it applies now or not but you were not al-

154

lowed to park in the compound on the dock, but I did. I must have found an empty space near the dock office and parked there, pulled my curtains closed, took off my boots and got into bed and fell asleep.

I awoke the following morning at 05.15, still feeling ill but nowhere near as bad as I was on the Sunday. I changed my clothes and went to the washroom in the dock office to use the toilet and had a wash. I then went to the drivers window in the office to ask about my trailer. I got a right royal bollocking off the guy in the office for parking on the dock, the shunters who load and unload the ferries on the dock had tried to wake me several times, to no avail, and had eventually given up. I explained how ill I'd been, and although he wasn't happy about me doing it, I think he got the picture and eased up on me. He gave me the paperwork for the trailer I was to collect and after asking me if I was OK to work I thanked him and assured him that I was, even though I was really nowhere near fit enough. This is where the second part of this story begins.

The trailer I'd picked up had two deliveries on it. One was for a shoe making company in Northamptonshire and the second was for a distribution centre at Bedworth near Nuneaton in Warwickshire. I had no issues delivering to both places and once the trailer was empty at around 13.00 I rang HF to find out whether I was to reload it or take it empty to Holyhead. I was told to ring back in around an hour, so I had something to eat, which was the first proper food I'd had since the Sunday morning. I still wasn't feeling great and felt really drained. When I rang back I was asked to go to a toilet and sink manufacturers in Stoke on Trent and load there for Ireland. I was then to take and leave the trailer at P & O Shipping dock in Fleetwood, Lancashire, for a night ferry crossing.

I set off and arrived at Stoke at around 15.30 in a heavy blustery wind and pouring rain. I was hauling what is known as a "tilt" trailer, which had a plastic tarpaulin covering the top, both sides two thirds of the way down them, for the length of the trailer, and the back which also came to around two thirds of the way down. On its roof the tarpaulin rested on removable metal bars that hooked into the sides about three feet apart along the length of the trailer and provided stability to it, whilst also giving the tarpaulin something to rest on. The tarpaulin was held in place by eyelets, which ran down front posts (one either side)

155

then along the two sides, up two posts (one either side) and then down and across across the back. The eyelets then fitted over lugs that were fitted onto the posts and opening drop down flaps, these flaps could be opened by lowering them down on hinges fitted onto the trailer. Once closed, you ran a security cable through the lugs from front to back along the length of the trailer and around to the centre of the back of it, from there it could be sealed with a security tag.

As stated earlier I'd had no issues unloading the trailer as both deliveries had been taken off through the rear opening flap, after undoing the cable and lifting the tarpaulin onto the roof at both delivery points. To load at Stoke I had to completely open one side of the "tilt". I pulled the security cable through from back to front on one side and with the help of a fork truck driver I folded the tarpaulin up and onto the roof so one side was completely open. I was parked in the centre of a yard at the factory and it was hammering down with rain. I watched as the fork truck loaded the goods which were in sturdy wooden crates, onto the trailer floor. He filled around two thirds of the length of the trailer deck in quite a short time and then informed me that he had finished.

I secured the load at the back end to stop any rearward movement, raised the side flaps and then asked the fork lift to raise me up so I could pull the tarpaulin back off the roof into position for fastening. It did come down but not all the way down in its centre, because with all the rain a large pool of water had gathered where one of the metal supporting bars was missing (that sort of thing was commonplace) I climbed back onto the trailer and tried to push the tarpaulin sheet up from inside to drain off the rainwater (as a shopkeeper would do with a sun/rain canopy) but I couldn't do it as it was really heavy, I was still unwell and felt as weak as a kitten.

I tried for some time to force the eyelets over the lugs, trapping my fingers in the process, the wind and rain were ceaseless and at around 17.45 I was asked by a member of staff at the factory if I could move my lorry off the premises as they wished to lock up and go home. I reluctantly agreed and after getting my delivery documents for the load I pulled my vehicle out into the nearby road where I once again tried, in vain, to secure the tarpaulin. As fast as I pushed the rainwater off the top, by the time I'd got back, outside the pool of rain had reformed on top. I was

156

crying in frustration, I was soaked to the skin, my hair couldn't have been any wetter if I'd dived in a swimming pool and my fingers were also bruised and aching.

I had a sudden brain wave "I'll set off in a straight line and brake hard that should shift it" I thought. I tried that, it shifted some water, but as before the rain pool reformed. I then thought that if I found a steep hill and drove up it, stopped, then reversed, the water should move off and not reform. Luckily for me there's plenty of steep hills in Stoke. After stowing away the security cable I set off, I found one and did exactly what I'd thought of.

This did work after a few attempts, on the last try I reversed down the hill quite quickly and slammed on the brakes, I could see the water cascading off the rear of the trailer so I put on the hand brake and jumped out of the cab and placed the now movable eyelets over the lugs. I then put the cable through them which in itself was another arduous task in the wind but I eventually managed it and set off for Fleetwood. I ended up doing fifteen hours that day, a day I never ever wanted a repeat of.

I recall once being en route to Basingstoke after a delivery in Swindon, the route involved me travelling via Newbury in Berkshire and then taking a left onto the A339 towards Basingstoke. This road, just outside Newbury, went past the Greenham Common air base. This is where around ninety six cruise missiles were kept by the U.S. air force.

Those that are old enough to remember will know of the women's peace camp there, it was started by "the women for life on earth" protest group, women from both the UK and the rest of the world were encamped outside the gates to the base. They would try to blockade the mobile nuclear weapons as they left the base on huge purpose built trucks to go and do practice exercises in the large area of woodland near to it. They would track them and disrupt their training regimes too.

On that particular occasion I did not see any missiles, but whist traversing that road in later times I have had to stop when military vehicles blocked the road, I then witnessed the missiles come out of thick woodland, cross the road ahead of me and disappear into more forestry on the other side of the road. I would then be allowed to carry on once they had gone. The protesters were there from 1981 until the missiles and the base personnel returned to the US during 1991/92. I often drove past there and recalled those brave women who suffered ridicule, attacks on them and hardship for the sake of their peaceful cause.

During my time on the road I've seen many accidents, I mean bad accidents where vehicles have been written off and people have been seriously injured, or even worse, when they've died. I was working for HF when one of them occurred. I was approaching the Conwy tunnel one early morning in the Westbound carriageway and as I was around a hundred yards from the entrance I saw a car, leaving the Eastbound bore of the tunnel, "what's unusual about that ?" I hear you say, well this car was on its roof. It had completely flipped over after apparently hitting both sides of the tunnel walls and it came sliding out, spinning around on its roof. That driver was miraculously relatively unhurt, the car however was a write off.

On another occasion when I worked for Reyners I was on what is now the A14 heading Eastbound for Felixstowe. Somewhere near Bury St. Edmonds, early on a beautiful sunny morning I was passed by a parcel van, a seven and a half tonner, he was flying along. I thought nothing of it and within quarter of a mile or so I saw him about five hundred yards in the distance start to go under a road bridge, in an instant I spotted him veering across the carriageway in what looked to be right underneath the bridge, he ploughed across onto the opposite carriageway and smashed into the bridge stanchion there.

I'd already began braking when I saw him swerve, I put on my hazard warning lights and positioned myself in the centre of the road before coming to a stop gradually. After checking that nobody was trying to pass my lorry I got out and ran to where the van had hit the stanchion. As I ran up I could see what had happened, the driver of the parcel van had seen a bright yellow crew carrying van parked in the slow lane of the carriageway right under the bridge. He'd swerved to miss it but had caught the back offside corner of it, this had caused him to veer off sharply to his right and career across the carriageways.

I ran straight to him, his cab window was open and he was sat in his seat upright with a ghostly white face. I asked him if he was alright, he said he was but that his legs were trapped

158

under his steering wheel and dashboard, which had been pushed back by the collision with the stanchion.

By this time I could see people coming out of the crew van, about four of them, all looking dazed and one or two with blood on them. A man, who announced himself as a doctor who had been travelling Westbound ran to us, he asked was the van driver conscious to which I replied that he was but he was trapped, I pointed to the guys coming from the van and asked him to go and check them out.

Somebody somewhere had found a phone, as there were no cell phones then, and help was on its way. I stayed with the van driver, I asked him what had happened, he said that he was attempting to swat a wasp as he approached the bridge, he'd seen the crew van stopped at the very last second, the low bright sun in his eyes and the van being under the bridge in its shadow had messed up his clear vision. He'd tried to swerve around it but had hit the corner of it. Another driver and myself managed to pull his door open between us and we saw that he was indeed well and truly trapped.

The doctor who had first come to us came back and took me aside, he told me that the driver of the crew van had had a shattered windscreen and had stopped to knock the glass in. He'd been at the front of the van with a rubber hammer knocking out the glass when the parcel van hit the rear of his, causing his own van to run into and over him with the force of the collision. He didn't think the driver would survive his injuries. Two of the crew inside the van at the back had been thrown forwards by the impact and had received cuts and bruises, but they like the other two were all conscious and relatively unhurt. The police and an ambulance soon arrived, and after giving the police a statement when the carriageway had been cleared, I was allowed to carry on, quite shaken up, with my journey.

Much later in my career I was held up on the M6 near Middlewich at junction eighteen for five hours after a heavy mobile crane had crashed into a lorry which had been coming off a slip road and then careered into the opposite carriageway before turning over onto an oncoming car killing the driver. An oncoming lorry driver who smashed into the overturned crane and car also died as did the crane driver, a fourth person involved also died. That was an extremely horrific scene to pass even five hours after it had happened.

I have witnessed a Land Rover having a front wheel blowout, causing the front end to drop which resulted in the heavy vehicle being thrown upwards, somersaulting through the air before crashing to the ground.

I've seen cars leaning up almost vertical on lamp posts. I've witnessed caravans snaking wildly before jack knifing and flipping over, dragging the towing cars with them before being smashed to pieces. I have passed where lorries have smashed into the rear of other vehicles causing immense damage and fatalities. There was a crew of Reyners employees once, collecting the broken bottle tops of taxable spirit drinks that had been in an overturned Reyners vehicle carrying a container which had also dragged the vehicles unit over causing the driver quite serious injuries in the process.

I was once driving over the viaduct on the M63 near Trafford Park, when a car in the middle lane, driven by a disabled man, had a blow out causing him to veer into the crash bars on the side of my trailer. There was minimal damage to my vehicle but his was in a bit of a mess, thankfully nobody was hurt whatsoever in a relatively minor accident, although it did cause mayhem on the motorway on that busy Friday evening.

Of course, all accidents are horrible, I have seen many, luckily for me I never had a serious one.

Chapter Seven.

Days to nights, nights to days, job to job.

My time with HF Owen was relatively short. I left after a fairly minor disagreement and a health issue, but it will never cloud the good times I had there, I worked hard and covered many miles. I'll always be grateful to Harry for giving me the job but it was time to find something new.

The next decade or so was quite turbulent, not in my home life, that was, and still is very good, it was work wise. I have always been in work, the odd day or maybe a week or two between jobs away from it, but I've always found employment, some good, some bad. What follows is a brief run through of my working life after HF Owen with the some stories thrown in.

My first job after leaving HF Owen was for T.D.G. (Transport Development Group) who ran the contract for the transport operations out of Kimberley Clark Tissues at their huge works in Flint. At first I started doing long distance deliveries on days. I would leave with a loaded trailer on a Monday morning and deliver toilet rolls, kitchen rolls or sometimes wet wipes, which were just out on the market at that time, to regional and national distribution centres, cash and carry outlets and sometimes shops all over the UK. I would then invariably reload waste paper bales from dealers which we returned to Flint. The waste was then recycled and used in the making of more products.

I recall that as tissue was very light, the trailer heights at TDG were virtually at their maximum so that more product could be squeezed onto them. We had fifteen foot six inches, fifteen foot nine inches and some at sixteen foot one inch which is five inches short of the maximum you can have whilst running on UK motorways (the minimum bridge height being sixteen foot six inches)

Quite often I would get multi delivery loads to London, which I dreaded. I'm wasn't concerned about the congestion and warren like streets and roads there, it was the bridges I was worried about, mainly railway bridges. I had to plan my delivery route in exact detail. There are so many low bridges, especially in south London, it was a nightmare. I didn't use a sat-nav at that time. I purchased a lorry drivers UK road atlas. It was expensive but worth every penny. It showed all the bridge heights, one way streets and weight limits for lorries. I would receive my delivery notes at Flint and spend as much time as necessary to plan a route which avoided the low bridges. Believe me, some of the diversions I've had to make to avoid bridges were huge. I never hit one or got stuck, and that was down to me planning my route very carefully.

It was whilst I was working for TDG that the UK foot and mouth epidemic started. Those that are old enough to remember may recall that over six million cows and sheep were destroyed during this torrid time. I can remember that I'd delivered a load in Aberdeen and had reloaded some farm machinery from a village around thirty miles west of there.

Once loaded, I travelled down to a lay by which was on the old original A74 which ran parallel to the dual carriageway just south of Lockerbie in the county of Dumfries and Galloway. This area, I found out later, was the second worst affected region in the UK, with over one hundred and seventy seven outbreaks, the worse region being Cumbria, which had eight hundred and ninety three. It was a warm Spring evening when I had almost run out of duty hours, I pulled into the lay by and began to set myself up for the night. I took out my gas cooker which had two rings and a grill, filled a kettle with water from a five gallon container I had, lit a gas ring to boil the water up so I could have a wash and a brew.

I'd opened both windows and it wasn't long before this foul odour permeated the air around me. I couldn't see anything around me in my line of vision so I got out of my cab and walked to the rear of my vehicle. It was then that I saw the black smoke pall of a fire in a farm which lay directly behind my lorry in the near distance. The smell was putrid, I've been in the countryside and had many differing whiffs and odours but this was something different, then it hit me, it was the smell of burning flesh, cows flesh. That is how millions of animals were destroyed during the epidemic.

I had to close the windows that evening, the burning went on until I finally climbed into my bunk for some sleep and as far as I know it continued on through the night. It had started in February 2001 and was officially declared over in January 2002. Over that year I saw many palls of black smoke all around the

162

country, a grim reminder of how a disease can cause such extreme measures to be used to eradicate it.

Whilst delivering to NDC's, RDC's and cash and carry outlets I also delivered to shops. Shops of varying sizes, a larger store may have taken four pallets of kitchen and/or toilet roll whilst the small shops would usually take one or two pallets. One small shop I once delivered to in south east London, which I only had one pallet for, proved to be a real pain to deliver to.

As stated earlier I always planned my route out as best as I could to avoid problems, but this particular shop turned out to be so demanding it stumped me. I got to the area and after driving around in circles for a while I stopped on the main road at the outward exit from the one way street it was on. I could not get to it with an artic' the size of mine. It was in a two lane one way street in pure suburbia. The narrow streets from which to access it were all one way too and had parked cars nose to tail down both sides of them meaning that if I'd have gone down them I would have found it impossible to turn to access the street at the inward end of the one I needed to get into.

I parked up with my hazard lights on just as a traffic warden came out of the street in question, I ran across to him and told to him of my dilemma. I told him that I'd tried every way I could to get to this shop and had found it impossible, I also informed him that I only had one pallet of goods for delivery there. He agreed with me, telling me that there was no way I would be able to drive to the shop with a lorry the size of mine. He said that he'd seen lorries delivering there that were much smaller than mine.

He then astounded me by telling me to pull forward from where I was parked, he was going to stop any traffic movement and I was to reverse into the street and make my way up the street against the flow of traffic until I reached the shop, which to compound the problem was facing a zebra crossing. I reversed the wrong way down the street with a traffic warden holding cars and vans up whilst I did it. I stopped on the zebra crossing at a point in between two railings on either side of the crossing blocking its use. The warden then told me I had ten minutes to get the goods off and wandered away. Needless to say I did unload the pallet in ten minutes, leaving most of the packs of toilet rolls on the pavement outside the shop for the owner to take in himself, which he had agreed to.

There was another delivery in Bow, east London that I went to, again this was in a road that I could not access from one end as the streets to access it were much too narrow for a big lorry. It wasn't one way but it meant that I first had to approach a raised roundabout the wrong way facing the oncoming traffic to line myself up with the road I needed to be in, I then had to reverse around four hundred yards down this busy road to get to the delivery point. It had to be done that way in order to be able to just drive away in the direction of where I'd come from. TDG did send lots of goods there and all the other drivers used to do what I had done.

Eventually, after a lot of complaints from drivers, TDG acquired a short twenty five foot trailer with self steering rear axles which could get around the tight corners of the streets around the delivery point and that was then used for deliveries to there and any other situations that may have arisen where it was needed.

Life was good at TDG, the pay was above average and you were not "chased" around by greedy or inexperienced traffic managers and I was quite happy until one fateful day.

I was given a delivery in Nottingham, it was a full load and I left Flint in time to arrive there for the booking time of 08.00. I arrived as the staff at Nottingham were winding up the big roller shutter door of the warehouse. I was asked for my delivery documents and to then open the side curtains on the trailer, they would then begin to unload me.

I was opening the first curtain, the nearest one to the warehouse, I unclipped all the buckles holding it and had began to drag the curtain towards the front of the trailer (as they would start to take the goods off from the back) sometimes a curtain would stick, they were on runners along the top near the roof and sometimes the runners would catch up and ride on each other, usually you'd take them back a foot or so and try again but this one was really stubborn. I wrapped one of the buckle harnesses around my hand and gave an almighty tug, but in doing so I stumbled as I was falling backwards, my hand was wrapped in the buckle harness and I ended up spinning round as I fell. It was at this point I felt an excruciating pain in my back, on the right lower side, this was in the same spot as the injury I'd had at the margarine works many years before. I will not exaggerate, the pain was unbearable, I was hanging at first but I managed to work my hand free and fell to the floor crying out in pain. One of the warehouse staff saw what had happened and was soon at my side. He told me not to move whilst he went and brought another staff member out, they both got me off the floor and virtually carried me into the warehouse office. I was in agony as they slowly sat me down on a chair.

I've never ever felt pain like it. The warehouse supervisor asked me did I want an ambulance to which I politely refused, I thought it was just a temporary injury and would soon get better. One of the guys made me a cup of tea and gave me some pain killers. One lad finished off unloading the trailer and closed it up when he'd finished whilst the other stayed with me. I was wrong about it being a minor injury, the pain, although not quite as bad had barely diminished. I rang the traffic office at Flint and told them of my situation.

They offered to send out a car along with another driver who would then bring the lorry back and I would go back with the car driver. I refused this, I knew how long it took to get to where I was, they would have to find a car and a driver and I thought it would all take too long. I said that if somebody could help me into my lorry I would then drive straight back to Flint whereupon I would see how I was feeling. The office reluctantly agreed to my wish and told me to be very careful, there was no rush to get back and to ring them on the cab phone if things changed.

My decision was the wrong one, I felt every bump in the road, I had really sharp pains in my back and had to stop many times to recover slightly before setting off again. I got to the yard at Flint around three and a half hours later and the shunter there helped me out of the lorry, I put my arm over his shoulders and he half carried me to the traffic office.

The manager there could see I was in pain and after asking did I wish to be driven, which I refused, told me to go home and let them know the following day what my situation was. I left my lorry, with all my night out gear in it, clothes, cooker, sleeping bags, pillow and blankets, the whole nine yards. I never saw my gear again for just short of a year.

165

I sought medical advice that evening and without going into details, the upshot was that I'd torn a muscle in my lower back. I still maintain that the injury I'd sustained as a young man many years before had somehow damaged that muscle and I was now paying for it.

The company were very good to me, I was on full basic pay for six months which reduced to fifty per cent afterwards. I had to go for physio several times a week when the initial sharp pains wore off and the tear began to heal. I also tried acupuncture which didn't do any good whatsoever. Eventually though I became fit enough for work and was signed off by the medical staff who had been looking after me, it had been all but a year I was off work. TDG took me back after I'd asked could I go on night duties, this would involve me mainly taking loaded trailers out to drivers who were parked up within striking distance of the depot.

I would run to say Carlisle, pick up a trailer that a day driver had dropped, and leave him the loaded one to deliver in Scotland. I would then return to Flint. This suited me as it didn't involve any mauling, it was mainly driving and I continued to do that until I aggravated the back injury again one night unloading empty pallets, putting me back off work. I eventually left the company some time later when I was offered redundancy.

As a foot note to this story, I later took the advice of a union solicitor and tried to make a claim in court for the damage caused to me and the loss of earnings I'd sustained by the injury. The claim hinged on there not being the right equipment to free a jammed curtain, the case was found to be not proven and was dismissed, much to my surprise. Upon reflection the company had been good to me throughout my time there and during my injury period so I was not at all too disappointed and left the courthouse with no hard feelings.

I searched the local job centre and newspapers for driving jobs and saw that a local dairy wanted an HGV class two driver to do deliveries around North Wales to shops and outlets. I applied for and got the job, I went out with one guy for a week to learn the ropes and then I was given his job to do whilst he took a well deserved holiday break. I hated it, it wasn't for me, too

166

much heavy work involved, dragging milk crates around in a freezing fridge van, I stuck it for two weeks and left.

My next job was working through an agency who sent me to Hays Distribution, who were running the contract to deliver beers, lagers and spirits for Scottish Courage brewers out of a depot and warehouse in Trafford Park, Manchester. This was possibly the best job I ever had. The manager for Hays at Trafford Park was an old workmate of mine from Reyner's called Keith Tayler. He offered me a job there on a full time permanent basis.

I did some day deliveries for them at first but I eventually went onto permanent nights. I loved it, the money was the best I'd ever earned and the work conditions were superb. The down side was that I lived in North Wales but I overcame this by asking my brother in law Peter, who at the time was a bachelor, if I could sleep in his spare bed during the day at his house in Reddish. It was ideal, we were like ships in the night, barely seeing each other, so it worked. I would stay at his place Tuesday to Friday and go home to Wales after my shift on Saturday mornings.

As with all good things, they come to an end, and so did this arrangement. Peter began seeing a girl (Pat, who is now my sister in law) and things got serious, I realised that I could possibly be in the way when they were making plans for their future so I reluctantly put in my notice at Hays and left. I will always be grateful to Peter for giving me the opportunity to stay at his house and thank him for his kindness.

My next job after leaving Hays was for a North Wales company based in Ruthin, the company name was L.E. Jones and although being specialist UK and European livestock hauliers they also ran a general haulage operation. I was taken on there as a "tramper", a driver who leaves on a Monday and roams around the UK delivering a load somewhere and hopefully not driving too far away to pick up another one for delivery wherever it needed to be, you'd then return to base with a backload at the end of the week.

The job was OK except for the a few little niggles, one was that when I started they did not provide me with any uniform or protective gloves. I was taken on because I could rope and sheet and I did a lot of it, gloves were a necessary thing in that line of work and I had to provide my own. The work was varied and I

167

didn't know from one job to the next what I'd be doing. The second niggle was that after I'd been there a while I discovered that they had different pay scales. This meant that I was being paid less for doing the same work as some other guy who was on a higher pay scale. I questioned this and was told that the higher earning lads had worked there a lot longer than me and they were rewarded for that in their pay. I couldn't accept this, they could have been paid a loyalty bonus or something along those lines but to give them a higher rate of pay for doing the same work rankled me so I put in my notice and left. The manager there said he was sorry to see me go and that I would always be welcome to return if I so wished to do. In that respect we parted on good terms but I just couldn't work for less than another driver doing the same as me.

I found my next job at the local job centre, it was a company named Londis, who are a general grocery supplier. They were opening a satellite depot near Holywell and were looking for a crew of drivers to work out of it. I went for an interview and after having a driving assessment I was offered a job driving a wagon and drag, which for those who don't know, is a rigid vehicle (in this case it had three axles) which towed a two axled trailer behind it.

I went, along with eight other guys, down to Londis's head office in Andover, Hampshire for a week long induction course. The company put us up in a hotel near the complex and that's where we learnt what was expected of us.

Unlike the previous job I came home fully kitted out with all you would need for work, uniform, boots and gloves. We were all given fuel bunkering cards and allotted a loaded lorry each to drive back to Holywell with and that was where we parked them up, in a corner of another transport company's yard that we were to use as a base. The job was great, at that time. Myself and two other guys would come in at 18.00 and take our lorries, which were part loaded with empty grocery cages, down to Hopwood Park service station on the M42 in the midlands. There we would meet another three drivers who had come up from Andover, we'd swap vehicles and return with the loaded ones they'd brought up, they were filled with groceries for the day drivers to deliver to Londis outlets all around North Wales the next day. We'd get back to Holywell then swap the boxes off the trailers onto empty rigids which made it six lorries to go out and deliver each day.

The process was reversed in the evenings ready for us to come in and go down to the midlands again that night. On one particular night I and another driver called John, who lived near me and would eventually become my daughter Joanne's father in law, had done our runs and were back at Holywell, the third driver was running a little late behind us as he'd had to wait for an extra ten minutes or so for his lorry at Hopwood Park. He didn't turn up when we expected him to and it came as a surprise when I received a phone call telling me that he'd turned the drag trailer over onto its side around fifteen minutes from Holywell on the A55 near Mold. John and I finished what we had to do and we then made our way to the A55 to see if Colin, the driver, was OK and if we could help in any way.

When we got there it was carnage. The westbound carriageway was completely blocked with Colins trailer which was slewed across both lanes on its side. We found Colin who was alright but a little shaken. He told us that he'd been following a car which suddenly braked without signalling to turn off at a rarely used road which led to an industrial estate, he'd braked and swerved to avoid the car and the momentum turned the trailer over causing it to break away from the rigid unit. He was very lucky that the whole thing didn't turn over.

Meanwhile at Andover they were already picking a new replacement load which would be brought up the whole distance to Holywell by one of their staff down there.

The A55 is a major arterial road and the main route for Irish traffic heading to the port of Holyhead, many lorries who couldn't take the diversions created must have missed ferries following the accident and the replacement lorry coming from Andover would have meant late deliveries to the shops waiting for their groceries, but, thank God, Colin was OK. Goods can be replaced, people can't.

The job we were doing, going to the midlands was only a temporary one. Eventually a purpose built warehouse and depot was completed at South Elmsall near Pontefract. There was a new transport manager in charge there and without going into detail the job changed dramatically. Whilst running to the midlands and back I used to do around nine hours a night, finishing around 03.00. This was good for the day men, some of them

169

started at 04.00, so to have the vehicles back, fuelled up and ready to go was ideal for them. Under the new manager I was expected to do much more than I had been doing. It was quite complicated, but I had to do what amounted to one and a half trips to South Elmsall, I had to deliver a Scottish based drivers load.

I used to meet him at Birch services after I'd been and swapped my boxes and he would rest in my lorry, whilst I had to go back to South Elmsall with his load and swap boxes before going back to Birch to retrieve my own vehicle and then return to Holywell. That meant me getting back to Holywell later than I had been, where I'd find aggravated drivers waiting for their loads to deliver. I wasn't being paid any extra for working longer and that bugged me. I didn't say anything but began looking for another job and within a day myself and John, the other night trunker, who also felt the same way as myself, found our next employer, put in our notice with Londis and duly left.

John and I both got jobs with City Transport who had a depot in a cardboard manufacturing company in Winsford, Cheshire. I was given a Scania unit and was to be a "tramper". I was back at being away from home all week. Once again the work was plentiful and varied although at the time City were one of the main distributers of Coca Cola products from bottling and canning factories based in the UK. I'd usually leave on a Monday loaded with cardboard and would invariably end up hauling loads of Coca Cola to RDC's and cash and carry outlets all around the UK for the rest of the week. I wasn't with them too long, they were a company who grew very quickly, too quickly some might say, and they eventually folded. John and myself left not long before they went under.

My next employer was City Link who were a parcel delivery company. They were looking for a night trunk driver to travel from the small warehouse they had in Gaerwen on Anglesey. The job involved me starting at 18.00. I would part load my trailer with overnight parcels which were in big "wheelie" cages. I would then travel to another City Link warehouse which was much bigger than Gaerwen, it was near Ellesmere Port in Cheshire, where my trailer and two other lorries would be filled out with cages. I would then take the whole thing to the

170

main hub which was a huge complex in Willenhall in the West Midlands.

There, I, and around one hundred other lorries which had travelled there from many towns and most cities in the UK, the furthest being Glasgow in the North (which was double manned and had two drivers), Plymouth in the South West and Kent in the South East, would all back into loading bays and the parcels from my load and all the others would then be sorted out and be put onto a lorry which was going where the parcels needed to be the next day. We all in essence swapped our loads around, each vehicle returning to its base loaded with parcels for that area.

I was supposed to leave the hub at 02.00 as it took around three and a half hours to return to Gaerwen. By the time I got back and unloaded the cages I would finish at around 06.00 so on average it was a twelve hour night. Once again, I was happily going to work, it was well paid and steady.

At one point during my employment I was given a newer lorry to use, I swapped over units one night at the hub and drove the newer one back to Gaerwen, whilst doing so I noticed a not so pleasant smell in the cab, it wasn't too bad but noticeable. I arrived there, unloaded, and then took the whole empty rig back to a yard in a farm near where I lived at Colwyn Bay, where it was left parked until I started work again in the evening. I returned to it that winters evening and once the heaters had warmed the cab up, the smell in the cab had really ramped up I thought at first that the driver who had the unit before me had left some food or something in the cab and decided I would take a look around the cab upon arrival at Gaerwen.

I didn't make it to Gaerwen, on the journey I noticed a couple of flies buzzing around the cab, then some more, the smell got worse and then many more flies. I did not have any windows open as it was cold outside and I wondered to myself where they had come from. Many flies turned into a whole lot of them so I pulled up at a lay-by on the A55 and opened both cab windows. I got out and went around to the passenger side and opened the door wide too. The smell was now really bad and I discovered that it was emanating from the heater outlet near the open passenger door. I climbed into the cab, wafting away flies and grabbed an extra large tin of dash polish that I had, I climbed back down and directed the nozzle into the heater outlet giving it a good long blast. It's hard to describe

171

what happened next, almost immediately a cloud of flies flew out of the outlet, I sprayed them as they came out as best as I could then gave the outlet another big blast of polish spray,. More and more came out, I've never seen so many flies in my life in one place. I emptied the can, spraying all over the cab, those that could still fly left via the doors, others dropped and died in the cab.

I had another unused tin of polish which I almost completely used up before there were no flies buzzing around in the cab. I phoned Gaerwen and told them what had happened and explained that I was going to be very late getting there as I would have to clean my cab out completely of all the dead flies and make sure there were no others anywhere else in the cab. I took me over an hour to do that, I used a full packet of wipes and finished the polish before I was happy that I'd cleared and cleaned it enough to travel. I don't know what the bosses at the hub must have thought when they heard why I was so late, all I do know is that I demanded my old lorry back, which they agreed to do.

Later on during my time there I found out that many drivers, those who travelled from areas nearer the hub were not doing as many hours as myself but got paid just as much as me. I spoke to one who only did six hours maximum a night and got the same pay as me. I composed a letter to the HR department explaining my grievance, laying out facts, such as, that I did a much longer shift than a driver from Coventry or Leicester, I asked could they review my pay.

The next time I went down to the hub after they'd received my letter, I was asked to go to the managers office. He told me that he'd read my letter and that he thought I had made a good point but as we were all salaried drivers they could not offer me any more money, he apologised and said I'd have to take it or leave it. I decided after sleeping on it that I would leave it and put in my notice. I was on the move again.

Whilst serving my notice I saw an advert in the local paper which was for the opportunity to become a driving test examiner with the DVSA at their training academy in Cardington, which is an area of Bedford.

I applied for this and after undergoing a driving assessment with one of their senior examiners in Wrexham, I was enrolled

172

to begin a month long course at the academy which, after training lead to a theory test, which was followed by an advanced driving test which lasted around ninety minutes. During this test I was trained to take in all forms of traffic conditions where I was expected to show, through absolute concentration, a highly consistent standard of observation and planning which would result in the ability to safely control the aspects of speed and vehicle stability whilst showing a courteous and positive attitude. I passed the theory and driving test modules but failed on the third module.

This was where I was taken out in the role of an examiner, taking a driver for their car test. The "car driver" was a senior examiner and was fully competent in handling the car in the way a new driver may have but was fully trained in ensuring that the "test" was undertaken in a safe way by myself, him or her self, and equally as important, the general public, both on and off the road where the test took place.

As stated, I failed this module, and as it was a pass or fail contract I was dismissed the next day. I was advised by my trainer to re- apply and go through the whole process again but I had lost heart, I had been on the course for a month, travelling back to Wales at the weekends and I really didn't feel I wanted to do it all again and that was the end of it.

I came out of it as a far better driver. I, like everybody who passes their test, thought I was a good driver, the training I undertook whilst there showed me that I wasn't as good as I (and probably 95% of drivers) think they are. An advanced driving training course, if taken by everyone, I think, would result in a lot less vehicle related accidents on our roads. Here ends the lecture.

My next job was with a pharmaceutical company that was based in Walton le Dale near Preston, Lancashire. At the time the company was called Unichem. They were advertising for four drivers to fill jobs that had been created by streamlining the way it had been run previously and also by an expansion of the business area. I wrote off for an interview which resulted in me getting a position with them. I had to go up to the head office at Preston, along with three other lads who had also got jobs with them. We had a days induction and were then each given a van to return home with. The job involved delivering pharmaceutical drugs, controlled drugs and the like to chemist shops and doctors surgeries around North Wales.

We were joining an out-based operation which already had three drivers working for them. We all received the products from a lorry which drove down from Preston each morning to a designated place which we would all meet at. It would have all the mornings orders for the shops in trays of differing sizes, which were then sorted onto each vehicle for us to take to the shops on our delivery round. After I'd gotten used to my delivery round I would always have delivered to my shops and be home by lunch time. After lunch I would then go back to where we all met where a smaller van would come from Preston with not as many orders, I would then set off on my round delivering to the shops again. I'd then go home when I'd finished.

This procedure happened five days a week but we also had to do a morning round every Saturday, finishing at lunch time. The job was OK, it was well paid and I was home every night.

As before, all good things come to an end, the company changed its name, new managers were employed who wanted to put their "stamp" on the way things were run. It became nigh on impossible to get holiday dates that I wanted as staff couldn't be found to cover me, and working five and a half days a week was getting me down.

Whilst life was moving on, things had happened in my family which would indirectly affect me. My Mum had separated from my Dad and the upshot was that she had moved to live around the corner from me in Rhos on Sea. This prompted my sister Anne, who was married to Dave, my brother in law who I'd worked with at Reyners and John H in the past, had also, after a problem in Manchester, moved with their sons to Rhos on Sea, they lived around the same distance from my Mum as me but in the opposite direction.

It was all getting a bit too much for me at Unichem which had by now rebranded as Alliance Healthcare. When my brother in law Dave told me that the company he was now working for was looking for another driver, he asked was I interested to which I of course replied "Yes !!" After a few hiccups I was finally given a position with the company which was called Harsco. I was on the move again, back to long distance driving.

The company Dave worked for was named Harsco, they were contracted to carry steel coils from the giant Shotton Steelworks in Deeside, North Wales.

I got the job with them and after an induction I was given a unit to call my own. I set it up for being away from home, filling it with the gear I'd need to live a somewhat "easier life" and began work. The job was tramping, I would collect a trailer loaded with coils and go to say... Cardiff, I'd unload there and then go to the huge steelworks at Llanwern near Newport, where Harsco had an office, or Port Talbot, an even bigger works in South Wales. From either of these, I'd load and then take steel coils or plate to anywhere in the UK, backloading usually for either the North West or South West and Wales, but really it could have been anywhere.

The job there didn't last long though, to everyones surprise Harsco walked away from the contract and all the drivers and staff were to be made redundant.

Another company, Gwynedd Shipping were given the contract, they took on most of the old Harsco staff to work for them, but not me, I hadn't been with Harsco long enough, and so I was expendable. Dave was absolutely disconsolate about it all, he had been moved over to Gwynedd and I, who he had kind of brought there, hadn't. I told him not to worry, things happen, it wasn't his decision and life goes on. Whilst working my notice I found another job, I was offered the job after an interview, which Harsco allowed me to undertake whilst still working for them. One door closes, another one opens !.

The new company I was now working for was Boughey Distribution. They ran out of a huge depot and warehousing complex at premises in Wardle which is near Nantwich in Cheshire. It was a good hour and a quarter drive from my house to get there but I only had to go once there on a Monday morning and back home on a Friday evening or Saturday morning so that didn't worry me.

Bougheys main work was delivering grocery products to RDC's and cash and carry outlets all over the UK. Grocery manufacturers products were collected by Boughey drivers from all over and brought to Wardle for storage and distribution as well. It was and still is a very big operation which is run very well. The pay was above average, the lorries and trailers were all in a top class condition, the units were all fitted with fridges and microwave cookers, making life away from home very comfortable.

Once again, luckily, I had fallen on my feet. I would go to the depot at Wardle on a Monday morning, I've had to be there to start at 04.00 on many occasions which meant me getting up at 02.15 to be there on time. I would be given a load, it may have been multi drop or one straight drop, I never knew 'till I was handed the paperwork. The load could have been for the other end of the country or semi local to the depot, it didn't matter. There was so much work that even if I had a local delivery I'd come back later and be given another load which may have been for a long distance run.

Most of the deliveries were timed, and the customers were pretty strict about adhering to them. I would deliver to the big regional and national distribution centres for Asda, Tesco, Morrisons, Sainsburys, Marks and Spencers, Londis. Lidl, Aldi, Co-op, Iceland, Ocado and Waitrose to name just the bigger brands.

I would also deliver to big and small cash and carry outlets all over the UK. I recall once that I'd unloaded at Tesco's in Weybridge, Surrey. A horrible place to deliver to. If your booking in time was say 10.00 you would not be allowed into the premises yard until fifteen minutes before the time and fifteen minutes after the time. If I was going to be late I'd ring Bougheys who would have to re-book the delivery for either a later time or even another day. There was only enough space in the yard at Weybridge for around eight lorries, if I was booked in at 10.00 and I arrived in the area at around 09.00 then I would have to find a place to park up until the fifteen minutes before the booking. There was nowhere to park up at Weybridge, there were yellow lines everywhere on the industrial estate where their premises were but many was the time when I found a quiet corner and parked up, hoping that a warden wouldn't show up.

That was the situation at most of the delivery points I went to, it was a real pain, but to travel over two hundred miles and arrive at a set point bang on time was almost an impossibility, I just had to manage as best as possible, as did every other driver delivering to them.

I was going to write a completely separate paragraph on the way drivers were treated at some of the delivery points but I will incorporate it into this chapter. Many years before I was at Bougheys I went to a grocery warehouse in Scunthorpe, Lincolnshire one morning. It didn't have the waiting to deliver problem that Weybridge had, as lorries turned up there and parked, usually, in a long queue on the estate road outside the premises. I was queuing there around two hours, moving forward a lorries length every half hour or so until it was my time to go into their yard and park up alongside five or six lorries that were before me waiting in there.

Once in the yard I took my paperwork to the office to book in, I only had half a load as I'd been somewhere the day before with a delivery. On the way over to the office there were steps that led up to the door at the side of the loading bays, there was a toilet which had a "Drivers Toilet" sign on the door. I'd been outside the premises for some time so I felt the need to pee. The vacant sign on the door handle was green so I opened the door to go in. The smell I was greeted with was disgusting, don't get me wrong, I've been in some smelly loos but this was overpowering, there were loads of flies buzzing about and the place was absolutely filthy, a dirty dripping sink, and the toilet itself, well I won't go into detail as you may be eating, but there was no way I was going to use it. I tried to wet my hands in the sink but the tap was solidly stuck, it was just dripping so I wet them for as long as my nose could stand the smell I and made a quick exit.

I carried on up the few stairs and through the door into the driver booking in room which had a two foot square open window in the wall which looked into the office. I handed in my notes and was told brusquely "you should have been here at 09.30" I explained that I was outside at 09.15 and had been waiting for just over two hours to get in. That was greeted with a "humph, right well just go back to your cab and someone will shout you when they're ready for you" This was a somewhat usual request at a lot of delivery points so I was half expecting it. I then asked in a friendly manner "have you a toilet I could use please ?" Again, very brusquely I was told "there's a drivers toilet at the bottom of the steps for drivers, did you not see it on your way in ?" I told him that I had indeed seen it, been in it and due to its condition had no intention whatsoever of going into it, let alone using it. Again, but this time in an more aggravated tone he replied "well that's the drivers toilet, if you lot want to have nice one you should look after them better, we don't want drivers using our toilets, you either use it or don't, that's up to you" he turned his back on me as if to dismiss me and began busying himself.

By this time I had had enough of his attitude, I was going to swear at him in a prelude to something else but I gathered myself together and said very loudly "well if you won't let me use your toilet I'll just have a piss here then !" Everybody in the office looked up towards me, the guy spun round too. I made movements as if I was opening my zip in order to pee. He said "don't you dare do that here ! I've told you, the drivers toilet is outside" I replied still fiddling down below "and I've told you, I'm not using it, I didn't mess it up and I won't be blamed for it, I'll do it here if you don't find me another toilet !"

At this a guy at the back of the office stood up and said "hang on hang on, let's all calm down" he must have been the office manager or something, he walked to the guy I'd been arguing with and told him to get one of the lads from the loading bay to escort me to the staff toilet inside the warehouse. This was good enough for me and I thanked him loudly through the window. I was escorted to their toilet, I did what I had to do and made my way back to my lorry.

A similar thing happened at a place in Bristol, I used the same method I had at Scunthorpe and it worked there too. I am a decent human being, not an animal, and I won't be treated like one, I wouldn't expect anyone to use a loo in such a bad condition and neither should they have. In fact they have a duty of care to provide clean toilets for use, and ensure they are in a clean and tidy condition.

On my travels I have been to many RDC's and NDC's (regional and national distribution centres) They are not all like the ones in Scunthorpe and Bristol, but drivers are, in my opinion, treated shoddily at a lot of them. I did not name the previous two companies to save their embarrassment, I will continue in that manner and please believe me when I tell you that I'm not exaggerating, it's all true.

There's big supermarket companies who have RDC's all over the UK. When you deliver to them it's with a booking time, as with Tesco's. When you finally get onto an unloading bay you have to take your lorry keys to the office and hand them in. You then wait in a pokey ill lit room until the unloading and checking of the load is completed at most of them. This is for safety, it's to stop drivers who think they are unloaded, pulling away from the bay when they are not, which has happened in the past resulting in injuries to staff.

I think that taking your keys off you is a fair thing to do but why are you not allowed to return to your lorry whilst waiting ? Unloading at these places can take from half an hour to... well, I've been on a bay for over four hours at one place. If I was in my cab, I could have a much needed nap if I so wished. I could brew up my own cuppa rather than having a cup of watered down gnats piss from an expensive vending machine, there's a whole host of things I could do in my cab, but no, I'm stuck in a waiting room that's never big enough for all the drivers to find a seat, a seat that's made of steel, with no padding at one of the bigger supermarket chains. The toilets they provide are reasonable and cleaned regularly but the vending machines they have are expensive for what you receive from them.

Some, very few, have a canteen that drivers can use, Weybridge was one of them, most of them sit you, if you're lucky enough to get a seat, like caged animals in an afterthought of what should be a waiting room for hours and hours. Then there's the ban on drivers using the canteens that some firms operate, not all firms mind you, there are some who appreciate a drivers efforts and treat them with decency, but there are also a lot who don't. I may have driven two hundred miles to get their goods to them for a lunch time delivery and they expect me to fend for myself as "drivers are not allowed to use the canteen / restaurant" What is that all about !?, do drivers not deserve to get a hearty meal after getting up early to drive for four and a half hours to get someones goods to them ?

Whenever a lorry delivered carpets to our carpet warehouse I treated them with the utmost respect, gave them a brew, allowed them to use our facilities and spoke to them in a decent manner because I knew what they'd done to get my load there. There's no reason to treat a driver like something you've accidentally stood in. It makes my blood boil. Rant over.

When I was working for Bougheys, if we'd unloaded in the South East of England, London and that area, we were often sent to reload at a rival firms premises in Lenham, Kent.

Bougheys would reciprocate by finding loads for their drivers when they unloaded in the North West. I used to go there, usually in the afternoon, report to the traffic office and they would tell me where to leave my trailer for overnight loading, then they'd tell me what time to come back for it the following morning.

I went there one afternoon at around 15.30. I was told to drop the trailer on a trailer park in their yard, they then told me to come back for it at 01.00. I was a little astounded, I was expecting an early start, but not that early, so I asked where the load would be going to. I was told it was for delivery to a Waitrose store in Sandbach, Cheshire. I was told that it was booked in for delivery at 07.00. Now if I'd finished and was parked up for 15.45 that would mean I could have nine hours off, which was the minimum, and start at 12.45 the next day. However by the time I had dropped the trailer and found somewhere off their premises to park (as was the requirement by them) it was 16.15.

I started exactly nine hours later at 01.15. I drove the mile or so to their depot and went into the office there to collect the paperwork for the load. The clerk behind the desk wasn't too happy with me, he said I should have been there half an hour earlier. I explained my situation and he grudgingly accepted that I had done the best I could have under the circumstances. I collected the trailer, strapped the load inside it and fastened the curtains before leaving at around 01.45.

It was around 07.30 when I got to Sandbach and not a word was said about me being half an hour late, they weren't bothered in the slightest. If I'd have known that I'd have had longer off duty. It made me wonder if people sat in offices making all these early bookings know what loaders and drivers have to go through to get the goods there on time.

As the last story proves, there are a lot of unsociable hours associated with driving lorries, and working for Bougheys I did just that, as did all the other drivers. It was all part of the job, I was away from home so it didn't really matter, each delivery I made brought me closer to the end of the week. I was quite happy there until….. yes here we go again, the company decided it was going to "streamline" the operation, bring it into line with other logistic companies, they were all doing it.

It was decided that we would all start to work a rolling four day week. Each week your starting day would move forward a day so you could work a Monday, Tuesday, Wednesday and Thursday. The following week you'd work Tuesday, Wednesday Thursday and Friday, then it would be Wednesday.... well I think you get the picture.

In essence it meant that you could work from Friday all weekend and finish on Monday night. This would be for the same money, no premium, and if your shift fell on a bank holiday then you had to work those for nothing extra.

It definitely wasn't for me, I had other irons in the fire, so before it came into practice I put in my...... yes you've guessed, my notice and left.

Chapter Eight.

Steel…. I need it with all this health and safety !

My sister Anne had passed away in 1998 followed six months later in 1999 by my Mum, both victims of the dreaded cancer. I was still regularly in touch with my brother in law Dave though, he was and still is a real mate as well as a member of the family.

I'd asked him to keep his ears open for any vacancies that may have arisen at Gwynedd Shipping once I'd heard the whispers of what Boughcys were planning. He told me that one of the local day men was leaving and asked was I interested in doing that work, there would then be a good chance of me getting a tramping job if one came up and I was already working there. So it was there that I went next, to Gwynedd Shipping who had taken over the contract from Harsco.

They had got the lions share of work from the Shotton and Llanwern steelworks which were run by Tata Steel. Shotton had ceased producing steel some years before, it was now used for coating steel, for uses such as roofing, fencing and the like. Coils would come to Shotton by road and rail from Llanwern and Port Talbot to be coated, once done the coils would be distributed to companies to be used however they wanted to. Whilst on days a typical run would be a 05.00 start at Shotton where Gwynedd Shipping (GS) were based, I would collect a loaded trailer, I'd then run to a factory in Sherburn which is about half way between York and Scarborough, where the coils were unloaded. I would then run across country, passing over the Humber suspension bridge, and make my way to Immingham docks near Grimsby. I would load twenty four tons of zinc ingots which had been imported from Europe and then take them back to Shotton.

Once back at Shotton I'd unload the ingots which were used in the processing of the coatings. If all went well, and it usually did, I would finish between 17.00 and 17.30. This run could have been my work for five consecutive days, but there were many other places I took steel to, always returning back to Shotton in the evenings so that the night man could have use of the unit.

I was not on day runs for long, new units had arrived for the trampers and Dave got one, I got Dave's old unit, a Volvo. I became a tramper then, going away from home on a Monday and not returning back to Shotton until Friday night or Saturday morning.

The loading and carrying of steel products requires many different skills. If a very heavy steel coil is not fastened down securely in the correct position on the trailer, the consequences can be fatal. It's not just the securing of the coil that's important, it is the manner in which the vehicle carrying it is driven too. I know of one case where a lorry which having being driven erratically from Port Talbot turned over on a roundabout over a motorway, the coil broke away from the trailer and fell onto a passing car.

Safety in these matters is paramount of course, but some health and safety "practices" can sometimes have the opposite results, I'll explain what I mean, but first, for those that don't know, let me fill you in with a little information regarding the sort of specialist trailers that coils are generally loaded onto.

At GS we had what were known as "sliders" They have timbered floors, in the centre of the trailers length, inside the steel chassis support beams there is a sort of "V" shaped valley which we call the well, it has about a two foot depth to it all along its length. The coils are then lowered down into the well, up tight against timbers at the front edge which are held in place by supporting posts so that they sit firmly in the valley well, which is there initially to help stop the coils moving sideways. This is definitely not enough though, it's just an extra precaution to quell movement, to travel with a coil like that would be extremely dangerous.

Once in position the driver should use at least three ratchet straps, one through each side of the bore (centre) of the coil pulling forwards and the other going over the coil, all are fastened to the vehicle chassis. At one time drivers used chains, which I always preferred to use as they were more secure, but they could cause damage to the outer and inner edges of the coil so they were replaced by the ratchet straps which didn't. In the old days you would then sheet and rope over the coil to keep it dry. The sliders we had made the job so much easier and quicker. There was a waterproof canopy which was stretched and fastened over staple shaped bars around five foot high, each bar had steel runner wheels fitted to it which sat in a track on either side of the trailer bed. There were fastenings fitted to both the front headboard and at two posts at the rear of the trailer. This meant that you could push the canopy backwards and forwards freely on its wheels, concertina style. You'd access the front of the trailer by pulling the canopy to the rear, load maybe just one really heavy coil or several smaller size coils there and then push the canopy back up to the front in order to access the rear end to finish loading. Once the coil(s) were strapped down, the canopy would then be pulled closed and fastened, you were then set to travel with a secure load which would be kept dry.

Here's where problems can arise. Many places where steel coils are loaded and unloaded have, quite rightly, safety protocols and procedures which drivers and their staff must adhere to. At Shotton it was like that, to load you reversed into and onto a steel framed bay which was trailer bed height all around the trailer, it was fitted with outer safety rails, there was a gap of around six inches on either side so your reversing skills had to be pretty good, as most HGV drivers' are.

Before you leave your cab you have to put on a safety helmet which was fitted with ear defenders which were placed over your ears, you can then get out from your cab. You then open the fastenings at the front of your trailer allowing the canopy to move backwards to the rear of it before climbing some steps leading up and onto the bay. Once there you push the canopy all the way to the back, once that was done you prepare the the trailer for the coil, setting up the forward moving restraint timbers and posts.

When all that was done you leave the bay area, going down the stairs, and make your way to a driver waiting area well away from the bay and your lorry. An overhead crane then brings your coil to the lorry, slowly lowering it down into the well and up to the forward movement restraint timbers. Once the coil was fully down and firmly in position the crane would release it and move away, you then go back up the stairs and strap the coil in the way I have described previously.

It worked well at Shotton but at some places the safety procedures were blurred, they were there for a good reason but had not been thought out properly. They were usually concocted by

184

a health and safety rep' belonging to the company who worked in an office nowhere near where the loading/unloading operations that took place, I always maintained that if loading staff and the drivers were involved whilst these procedures were being thought up it would give a broader view of the problems that may have arisen and how to avoid them.

At one place in the Midlands there was a company that did not have raised loading bays, you had to enter the slider from the rear, climbing up a set of really heavy steps which were on wheels, you had to roll these on your own which is a health and safety concern all on its own, I'm sure most people will have pushed a supermarket trolley which had wheels that seemed to go one way whilst you wanted them to go another, well thats how these steps could be, but they aren't light trolleys, they are made of solid steel, eight feet wide, taller than a man, and bloody heavy !

So as I said, once in position, if you haven't given yourself a hernia mauling them to the back of your lorry, you climb them, wearing of course the safety helmet with ear defenders and then enter the trailer, stepping into the darkness underneath the closed canopy, you then had to navigate your way around the trailer, crouching down, in the almost pitch black darkness, and set up the trailer for loading. I got myself a magnetic torch which gave me very limited light whilst moving heavy timbers and posts into position for the loading of the coil.

I, and many other drivers I know have tripped up or stumbled whilst performing those tasks in virtual darkness. It had to be done that way as the company concerned would not let you open the slider and walk about on the open deck as there was the possibility of you falling off. They obviously did not want to be held liable for any injuries that may have been sustained whilst you were on their premises, but underneath that canopy in the darkness it seems was quite acceptable. You then exit the trailer once it's set up, by the steps again, release the front or back fasteners and slide the canopy which ever way was best for the coil(s) you wished to be loaded.

Once open you would move to the driver safety waiting area and stay there until given a green light signal to return to your lorry in order to strap the loaded coil(s) down. You would then have to go back into the darkness of the canopy which you had to close before entering or alternatively, you could attempt to strap you coil(s) down from floor level. This was very difficult to do properly, as straps had to be literally thrown from the floor through the bore of the coil you were strapping.

To work to their maximum capability the strap should run flat against the steel coils surface, twists or kinks in it would reduce efficiency. The company provided a step you could use if you wished, it was around eighteen inches off the ground, which, surprisingly to me, was a health and safety issue, if you fell off that step whilst throwing your strap you could sustain as serious an injury as you could by falling off a trailer. If you tried, because you weren't seven foot tall !, to partly clamber up the side of the trailer to check if your strap was straight and you were seen, you would get a bollocking and a warning off one of the companies staff. I usually went onto the trailer with the canopy closed as I thought, despite the darkness, it was the better option, at least I knew that the coil(s) had been strapped correctly.

Other companies had differing methods, some had rear and side safety platforms which were on wheels too. The side ones were around thirty five feet long and taller than an average man, and they WERE heavy, at some places one of their staff would help you, at others you moved them into position yourself, at both sides of your trailer, on your own. I have suffered sprained wrists mauling those really heavy platforms into position, where's the health and safety protection there ?.

At some you had to wear safety harnesses which were attached to the rails of the platforms, I'm not a big man, I'm not small either, but most of the harnesses I've ever had the displeasure to "wear" didn't fit me, they were usually too big, resulting in them slipping down my body to the floor ! So I'd be trying to move something heavy on the trailer and have to pull the harness back in place around my midriff, again a major safety concern in my opinion.

Some of the things put in place for "safety" were doing quite the opposite. At Llanwern, if you loaded at the steel mill, you would back onto safety platform bays as you do in Shotton. Before you left the cab you would don your safety helmet, put the affixed ear defenders over your ears and then wear a pair of safety goggles or glasses. I wear glasses anyway but I had to wear the safety glasses or goggles over the top of them. You would then go up the steps to set up your trailer, only it wasn't

186

an easy task, in the steel mill it was very very hot, as soon as you stepped out of your vehicle the safety glasses would steam up ! You could hardly see a thing, let alone the steel steps you had to climb up ! If you were caught lifting your goggles up to see a bit more clearly you risked being banned from the bays should a health and safety rep' spot you. It was a joke. Health and safety my backside !

Then the "boffins" got involved in the strapping of goods. If I loaded steel plates at one customer in South Wales, I had to put on twenty six straps ! Ridiculous, I, and most experienced drivers know what is necessary to secure a load so it is fully safe enough to travel with. Someone who had never done it came up with this extremely over the top method which is strictly adhered to by the loading staff, they would not let the lorry move until the farcical strapping system was in place.

A lot of unnecessary practices have been put in place which I find offensive, someone is telling me that I'm stupid, and don't know what I'm doing, I don't need that thank you. Safety is of the utmost priority, and I would never compromise it.

Whilst working at GS, as well as living with the H&S practices, I had to contend with matters that had developed which affected the job. Many roadside transport cafes, where I could park up for the night at, had closed down. They were replaced in some areas by mobile burger type bars in lay-bys. The result of the cafes closing meant that the places I could safely park up were rare. There are some big truck stops and a few of the old established cafes left, but not enough.

Motorway service stations provide parking for HGV's but it is so expensive. Most drivers get paid for expenses later in their wages, but it's still a large cash (or card) outlay. For the money you pay to park the facilities are dreadful, and security of your vehicle, particularly your load is not their priority whilst parked at service stations. Many lorries have their trailer curtains cut to see what you are carrying, which can result in part of your load being stolen, mainly by gangs of organised thieves whilst you sleep. That can and does also happen in lay-bys, industrial estates and almost everywhere else except in secure guarded truck stops.

That's how much the job has changed, when I first began driving, thieving was a rare occurrence, it is commonplace nowadays. It's not just your loads, diesel is stolen from lorries parked up overnight too. It happened to me one night whilst I was sleeping in a lay-by near Scunthorpe, I never felt a thing. I had parked with my diesel tank almost in the bushes and shrubbery of the lay-by thinking that the limited access may have put off potential thieves but it was to no avail. I woke the next morning at 05.00 opened my passenger window in order to inspect the tank, the first thing that greeted me was the strong smell of diesel. It had been robbed. I hadn't felt a thing, I was left with just enough fuel to get me to the nearest garage where I could fill up.

I always maintained that I would feel the lorry move if someone was tampering with it whilst I slept. One night in past times I felt the lorry move slightly when I was parked at an industrial estate, I awoke and made a lot of noise, beeping my horn etc. I saw two lads running away from the rear of the trailer, they had opened one door before I had disturbed them, there wasn't anything to steal though as I was loaded with twenty two one ton bags of fertilizer.

Another time however, I was parked up at an industrial estate sleeping, it was earlier when I worked for HF Owen. I had a trailer which had a moveable hiab grab crane fitted to it. I was loaded up with concrete blocks, but it wasn't the load the thieves were interested in, it was the hiab crane batteries, two of them were stolen that night. They had just cut the cables and taken them away, and I'd not felt a thing. These sort of episodes made me a little warier of where I should park up to stay.

I started to try to go the places where other drivers headed for to park up, it was a kind of comfort knowing there were others keeping an eye out for each other, safety in numbers and all that. It was things like the worries about being robbed, the lack of safe places to eat, rest and stay at that started to take its toll on my love of the job. In the earlier days drivers all looked out for each other in the main, the culture was less regimented and the options for parking up were plentiful, whereas I found that a lot of modern day drivers didn't give a toss about their fellow truckers. There was the "fuck you Jack I'm alright " attitude becoming more and more prevalent.

The lorries and the pay was much better than the olden days but the job was changing, and not for the better in my opinion. It was an episode that happened to me whilst I was working for

GS that eventually brought me to the conclusion that tramping was not what I wanted to do any more.

One Thursday I went down to Cardiff and delivered some coils. I had unloaded fairly late in the afternoon and rang the manager at GS's office at Llanwern steelworks to find out what I would be doing next. He asked me to make my way over to Llanwern and report to him upon arrival. It was around a forty minute drive across from where I was in Cardiff to Llanwern. On the journey there my mobile phone, which was connected to the vehicles hands free system, rang. It was my younger brother Peter. He had been a lorry driver too, I had worked alongside him whilst at Geoffrey Reyner's. He told me that my Dad, who, after separating from my Mum had moved to live near Pete on the Fylde coast, was in hospital. Pete told me that Dad, who was then in his mid eighties, was very ill. He had been plagued by illness many times in the recent past but this time, according to Pete, it was serious, he asked me where I was and advised me to get up there as soon as possible.

Upon arrival at the office at Llanwern I relayed the news to the manager there. Now I'm not blaming him for what happened, all I can say is that he must have heard all sorts of stories from drivers who wanted an early finish on a Friday, so when I relayed my story to him about wanting to get home ASAP he may have thought I was "swinging the lead" shall we say. He told me that he had a job which would involve me picking up a loaded trailer at Llanwern and travelling inland to a works on an industrial estate near Tredegar. I was to unload there first thing the following morning then make my way to Port Talbot, load a coil, which I could then take up to Shotton for delivery there and then finish. Now normally that would have been a nice days work on a Friday but despite my plea for an even earlier finish he told me there was nothing else he could give me, everything else was covered. I reluctantly agreed to do it and after getting my trailer I set off to Abergavenny where I parked up for the night.

I was pulling off the lorry park at 05.05 the next morning and hadn't gone five hundred yards when my phone rang, it was my other even younger brother John, he asked me where I was and did I want to stop whilst he spoke to me. There was nowhere I could sop at that point, I asked him what was up, although I knew it was bad news before he spoke again. He told me that my Dad had passed away around ten minutes before he'd phoned me. The news, although half expected, knocked me side ways. I had thought that maybe he'd recover a little or that he might hang on until I got there. Even if the manager had told me to go up to Shotton straight away when I'd asked, I still wouldn't have made it in my driving hours and would have had to park up somewhere en route. I wouldn't have been back in time to be there when he passed away.

I remember when I hung up the phone after speaking to John how desolate I felt. I didn't break down and cry but I was heart-broken. The manager at Llanwern used to come into the office at about 05.30 so it was about that time when I rang him to tell him, in a cracked and tearful manner that my Dad had gone. There was a moments silence before he spoke, he said he was sorry about my Dad and followed up by saying that when I had unloaded at Tredegar to carry on with the plan and go to Port Talbot, he said he would inform the lads, who worked for a rival firm in the office at Port Talbot about what had happened and ask them to load my trailer for me when I got there. Really, on reflection, I should have told him to shove his plan where the sun doesn't shine, but my head was all over the place, it was like I was in a dream so I just went along with it.

I unloaded at Tredegar, and I recall a bloke looking at me oddly and asking me if I was OK to which I replied "no, not really" before turning my back on him, getting into my lorry and finally breaking down and crying. I got to Port Talbot at about 09.45 still numb. One of the guys in the office there looked at me as I entered and I heard him say to the other one "here's the Gwynedd driver who's Dad has just died" The other bloke looked up and told me to go and wait in my lorry until a shunter came to take me to the loading bay I needed to be in to collect my coil. The first guy said "I thought we were going to load it for him ?" To which the second bloke said "we haven't got anyone spare to do it, he'll have to load himself"

I didn't say a word, I went back to my lorry and waited. Eventually a shunter came to me and asked me to follow him, he took me to a bay door, told me to reverse in and make my lorry ready for loading, which I did. I loaded the coil and went back to the office for my paperwork. The guy who had spoken to me first looked away when I walked into the office, the second bloke eventually got up from his seat and brought me my notes, he didn't say a word to me nor I to him.

I left Port Talbot and drove up to Shotton. They had obviously heard what had happened, one of the clerks there asked me where the trailer was and had I unloaded it. I said "no I haven't, I just want to go home"I did what I had to in the office and told them I would ring them with any news. I then left and went home. That episode was the straw that broke the camels back, It wasn't long after that that I decided that I no longer wished to be away from home, and not long after making that decision that I put in my notice whilst on a holiday and never went back there as a GS driver.

Chapter Nine.

I ease up, the countdown begins.

Whilst I was on holiday I phoned an agency which was based at that time in Conwy. The guy in charge there, Chris, a lovely down to earth man who was an HGV driver himself, invited me in for an interview and within minutes of hearing my experience he offered me some work there and then. I told him I was working my notice but would be free to start for him a week Monday. He asked me to pop into the office on the Saturday before I was due to start with him so he could kit me out with overalls and safety vests, I would also fill out all the paperwork that needed doing. I did this and whilst I was there he asked me would I mind doing night work as he'd found it difficult to find drivers that would, even though the rates of pay were higher. I told him that I had no problem with nights, in fact I had grown to prefer the somewhat quieter situations that nights had brought me in my past.

He was delighted and told me that on the Monday night I was to go to the office and speak to the manager at..... Gwynedd Shipping in Shotton steelworks ! My first job on the agency was for the company I had just left !. On the Monday night I went there I knew exactly where to go, my old gate pass was still allowing me in, I knew where to park my car....... everything.

To say the staff in GS's office were surprised would be an understatement, there had been a little bit of bad blood between GS higher management and I over the way I had quit but I held no grudges with the lads in the office at Shotton.

At first they were a bit reticent, under orders from management, to give me any work, but after a chat with the office manager there I was given three deliveries to do overnight which all went without a hitch. It had been OK for me and I wouldn't have minded going back there for the agency if I was asked but it never happened, I never went there again. Perhaps the powers that be higher up the chain at GS had said they didn't want me there again, I don't know, but one thing I do know is that I would have been a safer option of agency cover driver whenever GS was stuck than a lot of other not so experienced men.

After that I did many jobs for the agency, flitting from firm to firm, days and some nights, nothing permanent. One day Chris phoned me and asked me would I mind going on a contract as a night trunk driver, I'd be hauling a double deck trailer owned by McCarthy Distribution who were based in Wrexham, from a satellite depot in Bangor to a central hub near Bilston, an area in the Black Country of the West Midlands near Wolverhampton. I told him I had no problem with it and was given a time to be at the depot on the Llandygai Industrial Estate near Bangor.

I started at 18.00 there, the job entailed me taking the trailer which had been part loaded with pallets, drums or whatever needed to be delivered somewhere in the UK the following day, it was an overnight freight service. The goods on the trailer had been collected by four lorries who worked days delivering what ever came up from the hub overnight.

On the way to the hub I had to call in at the main depot in Wrexham. Once there the load was re-jigged and I was filled out with whatever they could fit on the trailer. I'd then go down to Bilston along with another McCarthy lorry from Wrexham and join what would be around two hundred other night trunkers who had come to the hub from all over the UK. Each lorry went into a huge warehouse, ten at a time, once inside they were unloaded within five minutes, you then had to pull out of the premises and go to a central parking area that the company there owned. You then took your break and waited to be phoned by a banksman in the hub, he'd tell you to return to the hub where you'd wait in a queue to go back into the warehouse, again ten at a time, and re-load with anything that had been brought there by the other lorries and was for the North Wales area. It was a good system and worked well most of the time.

Once I was loaded there I had to go back to Wrexham again, where my load was re-jigged and then filled out for my return to Bangor. I stayed on that job for three and a half years. In the last year, I reduced my nights from five to three, then later to two. I had wound myself down to where working full time for a living, would be over.

Chapter Ten.

Retirement, the easier life.

I finally retired and hung up the keys to my lorry when I was sixty six years and three moths old. It was in March 2020.

The Covid pandemic was just starting to gain momentum. I recall that during my last week or so going to the hub at Bilston I was carrying full loads of toilet rolls down there, as people seemed to be losing their minds and were filling cupboards with them, how crazy was that !

As well as being about to draw my state pension the pandemic sealed it for me. I worked my notice and finished with driving as a living for good. You may look at my list of jobs and think that I've had a lot compared to some other folk. It's true, I have, but there have been good reasons to finish in the majority of cases. If I'd have stayed at Reyners I may well have stayed in Manchester, who knows. They were eventually taken over by another company and were then closed down.

John H finished with RH Stevens who themselves eventually decided to wind the company up and then closed.

Hotpoint closed the factory in Bodelwydden and moved production out of the country.

City Link amalgamated with another company before going out of business and the company in Cheshire folded too.

Londis closed down the satellite depot at Holywell and ran the operation from South Elmsall and City Transport folded as well.

Hays lost the contract at Trafford Park. HF Owen, LE Jones, McCarthy Distribution Bougheys and Gwynedd Shipping though are still very much afloat.

After retiring, I returned my HGV driver card, saying that I did not wish to renew it within two months of finishing. All I have now is my ordinary driving licence. People, including my brother in law Dave, urged me to renew it and go back on the road as the pay is much higher than it was, mainly due to the fact that there is a driver shortage, which I saw coming years ago. It wasn't just Brexit that caused that shortage, although there were many foreign drivers living and working here before it came into effect. It was because the industry had stopped doing what Geoffrey Reyner Ltd. had done for me when I was a youth, start young lads in their teens and give them a sort of apprenticeship in the road transport industry.

Medium sized transport companies who used to do that sort of thing were either put out of business by huge logistics companies who undercut their rates, or were swallowed up by them to gain their work. It also became a no win situation for would be HGV drivers as it was so expensive to take the courses and lessons to become one. If you could afford to do it and passed your test, you were not given a start at these companies because their insurance stipulated that you had to have at least two years experience.

Most of the ones who were passing HGV tests were doing so on a class two lorry anyway, not class one, as the earnings for class two drivers was almost as good as class one due to the big conglomerates who had cut the wages down.

Whilst all this was going on the number of drivers who were retiring or leaving because they'd had enough of the way the industry was going, were not being replaced. It was because of short sighted university degree managers, people who didn't have a clue about how transport really operates and a government without the foresight to do anything about it. That is my opinion and I stand by it.

I have seen the deterioration in the industry over many years. A computer programme doesn't fully understand transport and how it operates in real time. Geoffrey Reyner and companies like theirs had good knowledgable transport people running the business who did know how it worked.

I have not stopped driving completely though, in fact I still do many miles a year on the road as I have had a motorhome and now a caravan. Myself and Pat, who now has also retired, have travelled all over the UK in it. We did have a trip to France booked for this year (2023) but we had to cancel it due to illness in the near family, Pat and I wish to stay nearer home in case there are any problems and to help out wherever possible.

We have between us got quite a few family members near by creating quite a dynasty. My sister Anne as I have already stated, passed away some time ago but her sons all live not too far away from us.

Pats youngest sister and husband, Julie and Keith are a five minute walk away and their children live in Wales too.

My youngest brother John also moved into the area with his partner Wendy and is now only a five minute drive from us. Dave my bro' in law met and married Viv, an old family friend, and they live a five minute walk away surrounded by most of Viv's grown up children who live in the area.

Pats other younger sister Jacqueline and her husband John also moved close to us, although they've now relocated and live in Eire.

My other younger brother Peter moved away to the Fylde coast with his wife Barbara and daughter before we ever came to North Wales, and although we don't see each other quite as much these days we speak fairly regularly on the phone.

I have plenty to do at home as well. I have found that I'm not too bad at little jobs around the home that at one time I may have side stepped. I have more time now to think about things and do them in a proper way. Between us we have transformed our back garden, completely reshaping it, installing quality false grass and having the pathways relaid by a top stonemason who lives near us.

We now have the time to travel down to London to visit my eldest daughter Andrea who lives there with her fiancee Damien and my grandson Roman. Our younger daughter Joanne lives a five minute walk from our home and we see her and her hubby Steve, and our other grandchildren James and Caitlin regularly.

I still have contact with some of my old mates from Reyners, there's Dave who still lives near us, Graham, John S, Steve, Mark and their wives, who we see at least once a year if not more. My old best mate Dangle passed away suddenly some time ago, it came as a real shock to me and I still miss him dearly. We are still in contact with his wife Janice though, speaking on the phone now and then to her in Manchester.

Life is good at the moment, I'll be seventy years old in a month (at the time of writing this it's Nov. 2023) I'm still in good health, still got my own teeth and hair, although that's... erm...receding ! Pat and I go out to our local club for a few drinks at least once a week and we regularly go and stay with our great friends Eifion and Margaret at their house in Sandbach, where we also usually sample a beer or two !!

I've also had enough time to be able to write this book which has been a labour of love for me. Recalling the old memories, good and bad, has kept my mind occupied and I've enjoyed doing it.

So there it is, a pocket book history of my life so far, most of it spent on the road. I'm getting on but I still feel young. I'm not quite as agile as I used to be but I can still have a dance when I want. I can also get up to some mischief !! Take care all.